LIBERTY

JUSTICE

ORDER

Books by John Morton Blum

LIBERTY
JUSTICE
ORDER

Essays on
Past Politics

JOHN MORTON BLUM

W · W · Norton & Company
New York   London

Copyright © 1993 by John Morton Blum
All rights reserved
Printed in the United States of America
First Edition

The text of this book is composed in 12/14 Garamond
with the display type set in Onyx
Composition and manufacturing by Maple Vail Book Manufacturing Group
Book design by Margaret M. Wagner

Library of Congress Cataloging-in-Publication Data
Blum, John Morton, 1921–
Liberty, justice, order : essays on past politics / John Morton Blum.
p.   cm.
Includes index.
1. United States—Politics and government—20th century.
I. Title.
E743.B6134   1993
320.973—dc20   93-16305

ISBN 0-393-03548-4

W. W. Norton & Company, Inc., 500 Fifth Avenue, New York, N.Y. 10110
W. W. Norton & Company Ltd., 10 Coptic Street, London WC1A 1PU

1 2 3 4 5 6 7 8 9 0

For E. E. M.

CONTENTS

III Poet, Philosopher, Judge

FOREWORD

In compiling the pieces that constitute this book, I selected from essays and reviews that I have written during the past forty-five years. As I reread and reconsidered them, I realized that they had much in common besides a single authorship. All of them dealt largely with the United States during the first seven decades of the twentieth century or with preludes that helped to shape that period. All of them pertained to past politics as I understand that subject. And all of them, directly or indirectly, spoke to the continuing tension between liberty and order, and to political ways to control that tension and preserve social tranquility, especially in an industrial age. The Introduction elaborates on those commonalities.

As the content of this book suggests, I have spent a considerable part of my time as an historian in editing letters and diaries, a task I have always found engaging. It was emphatically so during my first venture as associate editor of the eight volumes of *The Letters of Theodore Roosevelt*. Elting E. Morison, the editor of those volumes, made that project a memorable experience for all of those who worked under his easy direction. He also made it an intellectual adventure of extraordinary gladness. For half a century he has been a special personal and professional friend. So I have dedicated this volume to Elting, a man nobly irreverent, pellucid, and wise.

JOHN MORTON BLUM
Andover, Vermont

L I B E R T Y

J U S T I C E

O R D E R

INTRODUCTION

PAST politics, so most political historians would now agree, involves much more than past elections and legislation. For as in the present, so in the past, politics at once reflected and influenced the society and culture in which political activity and political theorizing took place. It is and was the function of politics to make government possible by reconciling conflicts within society. In the United States those conflicts have arisen from differences of income and wealth; differences of race and religion and national origin; differences of section and occupation. All those subjects, the stuff of politics, mark the terrain of political history, a capacious arena.

Nevertheless, the compilation and publication of a collection of essays about past politics now runs counter to the dominant fashion of the historical profession. Political history focuses on public policy, on the state and the uses of the state. But among academic historians that focus has fallen out of favor. The energy of most of those historians has flowed instead primarily to social history, to the history, in the current phrase, of "race, class and gender," of ethnicity and of the family. The resulting illumination of those matters has much enriched the understanding of the past. Many social historians, however, harbor a guarded hostility to political history. That hostility is in one way curious because the state has continually affected the treatment of questions of race and gender and the family. Indeed for more than a decade politics has resounded with debate over abortion, affirmative action, family values, and ethnic diversity. Sundry racial and ethnic groups, as well as groups of the rich and of the poor and especially of the middle class, have competed to gain control over the uses of the state. That competition and the effects of its outcome continue to provide the agenda of political history and to make political historians indispensable colleagues and potential benefactors of the very social historians who spurn them.

The hostility of some of the latter faction reflects in large degree a generational bias. Within the academy the foremost practitioners of political history belong largely to the generation born about the time of World War I. That generation, John F. Kennedy's generation, was exposed successively to the trauma of the Great Depression, the inspiration of the New Deal, the danger of World War II, the difficulties of the uncertain peace that then ensued. Those experiences built the interest of the historians of that generation in active and creative government, in democratic leadership, and thus in political history and statecraft. That same interest had characterized the eminent historians of the twenty years or so before World War I, for example, Frederick Jackson Turner and Charles Beard, both committed progressives, both long influential in the interpretation of the national past. But after World War I, with American rejection of the Treaty of Versailles and with the retreat from progressivism, the disillusionment that swept over American intellectuals affected the younger generation of historians, who then turned away from the state and made social history their preferred domain. That was the case, for three examples, of Arthur M. Schlesinger, Sr., of Dixon Ryan Fox, and of Merle Curti, all masters of their craft. Then, particularly after 1945, many of the rising generation returned to political history, with C. Vann Woodward, Richard Hofstadter, and Arthur M. Schlesinger, Jr., leading the parade. Their confidence in the capacity of the state to improve the lot of its citizens matched the confidence of their peers who staffed government during the Kennedy and Johnson years.

The New Frontier and the Great Society enhanced the conditions of American life. They did so not the least by assisting the poor and by enlarging opportunity for women and for minorities within American society. But they by no means solved the problems of those constituencies, who became increasingly impatient with the persistence of their troubles. Many of the new generation maturing in the 1960s, Americans in their late teens and twenties then, shared that impatience. They formed the ranks of agitation for civil rights and women's rights and the rights of the impoverished. And they blamed the Kennedy generation for not moving faster and farther in making over American society. Especially they blamed the Kennedy generation for the diversion of American resources, for the waste of life as well as wealth, in the war in Vietnam. That war, the younger generation believed with ample cause, was as unjust as it was unnecessary. And in support of that war and of domestic politics favoring that war, the governments of Lyndon Johnson and Richard Nixon violated the personal rights and privacy of American citizens who disagreed with them. Consequently the children of the Kennedy generation, the baby-boomers, learned to distrust, even to despise the state.

Their conservative peers and elders believed with Ronald Reagan that government was the problem, not the solution.

That attitude, as well as the lassitude of the federal government during the 1980s, helped to shape the culture of the youth of that time. Accordingly many of the children of the boomers had no perceived experience with active and creative government, and consequently little interest in the history of the state.

So, in writing history, the Kennedy generation and its children's generation went their separate ways. The children of the New Deal era, rediscovering the politics of the past, especially explored reform and reformers, and described anew heroic Americans in previous eras of active government. With few exceptions those heroes were Dead White Men. They were just the subjects whom many of the boomers' generation scorned, partly because of their color and gender, partly because they had embroiled the United States in the Cold War, which Marxist historians of the boomers' age wrote off as just another error of American imperialism. Among academic historians of that generation, a generation that had played at revolution in the 1960s, many continued to believe with Marx that redemption was the sure reward of successful revolution. In contrast, most of the Kennedy generation of historians, their consciousness shaped by the rise of fascism and the perversion of the Soviet state, had rejected Marx and had concurrently concluded that life was never free of guilt, that power was always corruptible, that neither revolution nor any uses of the state could alter the essential human condition.

The boomers' generation resolved to write history with minimum attention to Dead White Men, particularly dead Great White Men. Most historians of that generation chose instead to fix their professional attention on the history of the issues that absorbed their youth, on the disadvantaged with whom they had identified, on black Americans and other minority groups, on women, and therefore on ethnicity and labor and the family. Those especially excluded from the past that they reconstructed were dead white politicians.

But the history of dead white politicians speaks to all aspects of the American past. That history examines the processes as well as the substance of politics, the nature of political leadership, the making and interpretation of the Constitution and of the laws of the land, changing party structure, the growth and decline of political coalitions, the creativity possible for the state, and the dangers, too—the corruptibility of power. Those matters, fortunately no longer the exclusive preserves of white men, have important implications for the family, for ethnicity, for social and racial and economic justice in American life and in the American past. Past politics in fact affected and was affected by the very groups that social historians prefer to study. Further, the stage of political history, the drama of power and of its uses and temptations, projects an unmatched historical excitement in which dead white men did not play all the parts, though for years they dominated the action.

With the return to Washington of positive government, the boomers' generation has power in its own hands. As it deals with the state, it will cope with the conditions that concern the social historians among its members. If those social historians do not know others of the craft who focus on the uses of the state, if they do not welcome a young generation of political historians to join the academic enterprise, they will miss the meaning of the drama beginning to unfold. Further, to understand that drama in the context of American history, to identify both the problems and the precedents of the endless adventure of governing, historians of all stripes will have to continue to rediscover past politics and past political thought. That was the intention of the essays collected here.

POLITICS has always served as the process through which ambitious men and women sought office. Their rivalries of course increased the possibility of conflict. Nevertheless American politics, even politics in the turbulent twentieth century, ordinarily succeeded in its mission of reconciliation because of the influence of individuals who devoted themselves to using as well as gaining power. Those individuals, as well as others concerned with political theory, have been at once the recipients and the creators of their ideas, as much so as poets or philosophers, though arguably the ideas of poets and philosophers occupy a higher plane of creativity. For politics that hierarchy is unimportant. John Maynard Keynes, whose essays in biography displayed an artistry no less commanding than his economic theory, put the matter very well: "Practical men, who believe themselves to be quite exempt from any intellectual influences, are usually the slaves of some defunct economist"—or other social or political theorist, he could have added.

For historians of politics in the United States, including historians of the twentieth century, in the beginning was the Constitution. The Founding Fathers wanted it all. The preamble of the Constitution stated the purposes of that instrument of government, among them: "to establish Justice, insure domestic tranquility . . . promote the general welfare, and secure the Blessings of Liberty." A large order. But in the body of the Constitution the founders divided the powers of the government they created, and they limited that government still more by forbidding it to infringe upon the individual rights they stipulated in the first eight amendments. The founders were men of affairs, men who had known war and revolution, who understood politics and understood power. They recognized the variety of interests that would divide men and women into self-seeking political factions.

Though they despised political parties, they soon formed them as necessary means for combining factions into coalitions large and strong enough to gain and use power. Once in power, the parties the founders built expanded the authority of the federal government beyond the range that most of them had anticipated. The resulting system worked. Though not without continual friction, amendment, interpretation and reinterpretation, not without one terrible war, the system endured. Two hundred years and more after the Constitution was drafted, politics and government continued, as the founders had intended, to operate to resolve the tensions between liberty and order, between the rights of individuals and groups of individuals and the needs of the community.

Why and how? Attempts to answer those questions make up the agenda of political history. But for most political historians, generalities about liberty and order gather meaning primarily through the examination of particular instances of past politics and the particular purposes and ideas of past politicians and political theorists. Thus the essays in this volume. They do not raise, much less answer, all the questions worth asking about American politics in the twentieth century. They examine only some of them, those at one time or another most interesting to the author, admittedly an idiosyncratic criterion. But as a whole they address some of the large issues that have occupied politics and government during the first seven decades of this century, and some of the successful, as well as some unsuccessful, ways in which those issues have been resolved. As a group the essays here compiled speak directly or indirectly to the persisting problem of reconciling liberty with order.

They therefore also speak to the need to cultivate social justice so as to preserve domestic tranquility. For particularly in the twentieth century, tranquility has depended on the ability of politics at least periodically and in some measure to promote equity in American society. So these essays contend, for without access to social and economic opportunities, and without a decent minimum of the fruits of the American economy, no individual can enjoy the blessings of liberty which the founders valued. Deprivation in itself, moreover, has always sooner or later bred discontents that threatened order. Consequently American politics has had to take into account the implications of inequality. The Constitution, to be sure, is silent about equality, but the founders listed it first among the truths they held self-evident in the Declaration of Independence.

THE first of the essays gathered here, "The Burden of American Equality," argues the persistent vulnerability of social order to the alienation inherent in inequality, especially inequality arising from race and from poverty. The politics of reform began to attack the latter condition at the start of the twentieth century. The men and women who then embraced reform believed not in automatic progress but in progress conditional upon the success of their objectives. Those "progressives" shared a deep anxiety about the social unrest of the 1890s, the violent clashes between capital and labor, the ominous disaffection of the southern and western countryside. Most of them shared, too, a faith in the essential goodness of humanity. Poverty arose, in their view, not from some evil or inadequacy in the nature of the poor, but from social circumstances the poor could not overcome on their own. The progressive reformers, middle-class men and women by and large, aimed to change those circumstances, to offer opportunities for the poor to escape their lot. The resulting effort to improve society, blending with the determination to forestall insurrection, informed the missionary spirit of progressivism.

The Progressive movement, like later, more secular episodes of American reform—the New Deal, the Great Society—turned to active government as the agent of its purposes and to the federal government where those purposes required national scope. The politics of reform had to mobilize the power of the state. But not too far. American reformers, most labor leaders included, though believing as they usually did that more government was better government, were nevertheless generally comfortable with constitutional protections of individual rights. Further, the agenda of reform, while requiring active government, posited government working gradually to alleviate the injustices that capitalism fostered.

Though periods of reaction succeeded each episode of reform, successive generations of reformers—excepting those on the far left—agreed on approaching social justice in experimental, incremental steps. Nevertheless they rejected mechanistic theory, laissez-faire political economy. The very social conditions they meant to alter indicted unregulated capitalism for its faults. So they could not believe that free markets worked best without governmental intervention, or worked for the best either socially or economically. But the characteristic American reformer in all periods of the twentieth century intended positive government only to remove the injustices and excrescences of capitalism, never to abolish capitalism itself. Historical determinism, Marxist style, appealed to those reformers no more than did laissez faire. They rejected the inevitability of Marxist history just as they doubted the beneficence of free markets. Indeed, as they saw it, Marxism contemplated revolution while laissez-faire capitalism fostered revolutionary discontents, both sedulously to be prevented.

Mainstream American reformers, in other words, were essentially conservative men and women, protective of the American system of government and economics but dissatisfied with the way it was working and resolved therefore to improve it in order to preserve it. In general they agreed that social justice required at least a modest redistribution of income and wealth to be achieved by keying taxation of individuals and corporations according to the ability to pay. Their good society also required sufficient regulation of interstate business to prevent predatory competition, to protect labor and consumers, and to preserve natural resources and a habitable environment. By the 1960s reformers also agreed about the need for federal protection and empowerment of women and of disadvantaged ethnic and economic groups. Yet the conservatory nature of American reform made the immediate goals of the reformers typically piecemeal and practicable. Reform politics, a continuing process, had no explicit ideology or teleology. On that account, "The Burden of American Equality," an essay concerned with the limits of reform, ends on a hortatory rather than a conclusive note.

THE absence of an explicit ideology allowed American reform politicians to bargain with their more conservative opponents in order to move at least part way to their remedial goals. Both groups, after all, though each in its separate way, were eager to preserve capitalism. Further, since reform politics had no orthodoxy, it had no heterodoxy. In the politics of reform, there was ample room for disagreement about emphasis, priorities, and strategies. And in the absence of doctrinal discipline, disappointment or impatience or fatigue often prompted individuals to move from enthusiasm for reform to doubts about it. The typical reformer stood in what Arthur Schlesinger, Jr., has called "the vital center" of American politics, usually slightly left of the midpoint, as Franklin Roosevelt was, often wavering, but never at the extreme right or radical left. It is that center area that these essays explore.

Under the pressure of national crisis or seeming crisis, some erstwhile reformers on regrettable occasions joined for a season in misdirected efforts to preserve order by repressing dissent, as in the aftermath of World War I. Then politics succumbed to biases about race and class always inherent and temporarily renascent in American culture. The politics of reform, for all of its periodic triumphs, shared the sentiments and sometimes the disasters of American politics in general. That is the message of the sixth essay, "The Foreign and the Radical: The Red Scare of 1919–20."

THE foregoing generalizations apply to the first generation of twentieth-century American reformers, the generation of Theodore Roosevelt and Woodrow Wilson. The essays in the first section of this book examine the ideas and experience of some of those progressives. Most of them, like most of the middle class, adhered to a tradition of genteel values that helped to mold their behavior and also indirectly to shape their political orientation. Elements of that tradition provide the subject for "Virtuous Texts," the second essay included here. A study of some typical children's literature of the post–Civil War era, this essay discusses the genteel code that American Victorians imposed upon their offspring. Though in some respects that code came to appear merely quaint, it had a serious social function. In the interest of orderly relationships, it meant to constrain personal behavior. By the 1870s war and industrialization had begun to transform the social conditions that the authors of the children's literature cherished. To preserve the conventions of a more rural past, Victorian preceptors admonished their pupils to cultivate the modest virtues they associated with a fading, golden era. The young folks were to eschew ostentation, a failing of parvenus, to revere both the Gospels and the patriotic symbols of the reunited Union, to practice temperance and charity, to work cheerfully and hard. The code also spelled out a social hier-archy. Women, unequal to men, occupied an inferior sphere of their own. Black Americans and immigrants, especially Irish Catholic immigrants, both lacking character, stood below all native white citizens. And the Victorians intended to keep it so.

It was easy for adults who had absorbed those lessons as children to resent the extravagance and vulgarity of the newly rich, as Theodore Roosevelt did, and to blame them as much as any Populist or labor organizer for the class conflicts of the 1890s. Out of that attitude came some of the stirrings of reform. But it was just as easy for the same adults to associate the foreign with the radical and to make "Americanism" a synonym for conformity, as many—including Roosevelt—did in 1917–20. But most of all the virtuous texts indoctri-nated a profound conservatism about work as the salvation of each individual. And that doctrine persisted in parts of American culture into the 1930s and beyond. "In the past, as is true today," wrote one Andover master who knew George H. W. Bush, ". . . men and boys came to terms with life even if the terms were hard. There was a job to do, and they did it . . . without tears and without loud cries for help to the government, the courts, or the psychiatrists. They had a sense of duty . . . and they passed it down." And imposed it in their politics even on those unable to help themselves. Against that attitude those who served social justice had to struggle for at least three generations.

THE political leaders and their intellectual companions in each season of American reform believed as John F. Kennedy did that "one man can make a difference and every man should try." Most of the remaining essays in this volume are about men or women who did try and who did make a difference.

"Theodore Roosevelt: Power and Order" relates the personal experience of Roosevelt's early life to the pursuit of social and economic stability that characterized his presidency. To promote order, Roosevelt operated both as a champion and a designer of reform. Early in his term in office, his advocacy of his expanding program met the occasional opposition of one of the stalwarts of the Republican Old Guard, Senator Marcus Alonzo Hanna of Ohio. But Hanna also often agreed with Roosevelt. Though perceived as a reactionary, Uncle Mark shared the very penchant for order that characterized Roosevelt. One of Roosevelt's ardent young admirers, Herbert Croly, a leading progressive intellectual and a founder of *The New Republic,* discovered in Hanna a suitable subject for a sympathetic biography. That relationship provides the focus for the fourth essay, "Heroic Values: Herbert Croly and Mark Hanna."

As it had evolved by 1912, the vocabulary of American politics labeled Hanna as "conservative" and Roosevelt and Croly as "progressives." Woodrow Wilson, in spite of his growing progressive identifications, stood somewhat apart from both camps as a "liberal." A Democrat, Wilson had grown up in the South and was also a devout Presbyterian and an admirer of the leaders of the English Liberal Party of the nineteenth century. Those factors helped to account for his doubts about Roosevelt's preferred uses of the presidency and for his advocacy, as he put it in 1912, of "regulated competition" rather than what he called Roosevelt's "regulated monopoly." The fifth essay, "Woodrow Wilson: A Study in Intellect," considers those and other aspects of Wilson's assumptions. Wilson understood the organic nature of the state, so that essay argues, but his recourse in the ultimate crisis he faced was to righteousness. In his unsuccessful struggle to obtain the Senate's approval of the Treaty of Versailles and the League of Nations, he believed in his own righteous-

ness as an individual informed by God in an essentially atom-
istic universe. In that sense Wilson conformed to the principle
of an earlier American liberalism. But righteousness then as
ever could carry few precincts, and liberalism was shedding
its nineteenth-century meaning.

"Liberalism" in the usage of the 1930s and thereafter came
to subsume what had been implied by "progressivism." By
that time it was "conservatism" that implied reliance on a
market economy and preference for minimal government. In
contrast, "liberals," advocates of active and creative government, were committed to social reform and to regulation for
the common good of business behavior. That transformation
of labels was completed while Franklin Roosevelt presided
over the New Deal. But the labels remained fuzzy as always,
as is suggested in the first essay in Part II, " 'That Kind of a
Liberal': Franklin D. Roosevelt."

Like Theodore Roosevelt, the man he most admired,
Franklin Roosevelt believed that only reform could rescue
capitalism from itself, in the 1930s especially from the business cycle and its ravages. In reforming and rescuing capitalism, both Roosevelts, as well as their successors in the 1960s,
were also preserving the corporations which had become
essential engines of capitalism. Critics of capitalism and of
the agenda of American reform in recent years have referred
to "corporate liberalism," which they find basically indistin-
guishable from conservatism. They are thinking about systems—about the difference between socialism and capitalism,
for example—whereas politics in the United States has not
been concerned with systems. In the 1930s the question of
social justice did distinguish conservatives from liberals, as it
continued to do, even though each intended to preserve the
system. Franklin Roosevelt understood that distinction and
welcomed the antagonisms of the most conservative of his
critics.

He also recognized the usefulness of liberals on his left. On occasion they persuaded him to change his mind, as in the case of his Keynesian advisers who in 1938 overcame his conventional views about the federal budget. Among others, his extraordinary wife Eleanor, and his second vice president, Henry Wallace, often pressed for more extensive reform than he as president initially thought politically practicable, but he let them test their ideas in public forums and adopted those that received a favorable response. "First Lady: Eleanor Roosevelt" and "The Price of Vision: Henry A. Wallace" survey the considerable space on the political spectrum with which Roosevelt was comfortable.

As with the progressives, so with the New Dealers, the process of containing conflict over class and race took on special urgency in time of war. So the federal government relied on the sentiments and symbols of unity and also, alas, on some deprivations of liberty to maintain social stability. That is the concern of "Unity and Stability During World War II." The war ended before the nation suffered another red scare, but before the end of the decade the tensions contained during the war burst into the anti-foreign and anti-radical hysteria of McCarthyism.

Even in the midst of war, Henry Wallace drew the fire of some fellow liberals for advocating a more generous peace settlement than they considered compatible with the needs of American postwar defense, especially against the Soviet Union. They contended that the United States had to guard against the expansionist tendencies of the Soviet Union. In 1945–46, Wallace for his part argued that American policy provoked Soviet fears. In 1948, running for president during the developing Cold War, he accepted political support from American Communists. His liberal critics condemned that decision, partly because they resented the fallacious identification it encouraged between liberalism and communism. But the labels of domestic politics, vague as they were, did not fit foreign policy. Indeed Walter Lippmann, essentially a conservative man and often a critic of the New Deal, like Wallace interpreted much of the foreign policy of the Truman years as American adventurism.

THE last section of this book contains essays about two men who represented in their different ways some of the fundamental qualities in the American political dialogue. "Walter Lippmann and the Problem of Order" examines the changing ideas of its subject. Lippmann, precocious, learned, and stylish, even in his youth a major spokesman of progressivism, came by stages to express the essence of responsible American conservatism. "Archibald MacLeish: Art for Action" looks at one of Lippmann's contemporaries who had a passionate democratic faith. From the 1920s through the 1970s Archibald MacLeish struck consistently liberal positions on both domestic and international issues. He did so with his special eloquence as a poet, a dramatist, and an essayist, and with his compassionate and humane timbre. Each man prescribed his own solutions for reconciling liberty with order; each believed in social justice. No less than presidents, then, poets and philosophers fall within the wide terrain of past politics.

Judges belong there, too, for politics includes policy, and law, so the legal realists have preached, is policy. That is also the contention of "The Politics of the Warren Court," the last essay in this book. Theodore Roosevelt considered the federal judiciary on the whole an obstacle to his progressive program. Franklin Roosevelt found the Supreme Court even more so until in 1937 and thereafter he had the opportunity to appoint enough justices to alter the Court's decisions. In the 1960s, the third season of twentieth-century reform, the Supreme Court led the way toward social justice and the protection of individual rights. In that respect the Warren Court compiled a splendid record. But partisan critics of the Court succeeded in blaming its decisions for much of the disorder of the late 1960s that spurred the conservative revival of the ensuing decades. Though the Court as well as the executive had been an agent of liberty and justice, the tension between liberty and order remained, as it had long been, central to American politics. This collection of essays on past politics speaks necessarily to those issues.

I

PROGRESS TO
CONSERVE

1

THE BURDEN OF AMERICAN EQUALITY*

In Jacksonian America, the America in which Alexis de Tocqueville pondered the implications of democracy, Duff Green, a perceptive newspaper editor, regularly travelled long distances by stage coach. "He had always lived in the South," his son later recalled, "and was accustomed to the social equality among the whites there prevailing. In a tour through the Northern States, he rode generally with the stage driver to see the country. At the first meal-stand in Pennsylvania, he was struck with the fact, that the *white* stage-driver was not permitted to take his seat at the same table with the passengers; and, as he progressed northward, he found the rule universal that, in the non-slaveholding States, the driver was required to eat at a separate and inferior table. . . . [Then on returning South] the first day out in Virginia, he reached the meal-stand with a traveller's appetite, and seeing dinner ready, he was about to take his seat, but was stopped and told by

* This essay is adapted from the pamphlet *The Burden of American Equality* (Oxford: Clarendon Press, 1973).

the waiter that the passengers must wait until the driver—a white man—who was washing his hands, was ready to take his seat with them."

As the younger Green went on to write about the South, "the ownership of Negro slaves carried with it the necessity of making color and good conduct (not wealth and poverty) the only basis for distinction. In the presence of their black slaves and of . . . poor white men . . . the slave-owners found themselves compelled to treat the poor white man as an equal because he was white, and the Negro slave as an inferior, because he was black." In contrast, in the North, as Tocqueville noted, there was "no real bond between . . . the rich and the poor." The sectional difference, long part of American practice, had earlier struck the British Minister to Washington during Thomas Jefferson's administration. Sir Augustus John Foster was surprised, he wrote, to see in the North a greater attention to social distinctions than in the South. Southerners, he decided, "can profess an unbounded love of liberty and democracy in consequence of the mass of people, who in other countries might become mobs, being there [in the South] nearly altogether composed of . . . Negro slaves."

Foster there identified one of the truths that Jefferson had not held as self-evident, though Jefferson understood it, as did most of his peers. The social control of the poor, in the American South a control through black slavery, precluded a class uprising. That preventitive in its turn permitted the rest of men to contemplate republican government characterized by egalitarian behavior and dedicated, in theory at least, to those liberties Jefferson celebrated. Further, the South was not peculiar, though the institution of slavery was. On both sides of the Atlantic, the prosperous worried about preventing violence and vagabondery among the poor. Paupers, those who owned no property, were perceived as a threat to society. In that view, for one example, yeomen could safely bear firearms and serve in a militia, but the propertyless poor could not, for they might turn their arms against wealth.

Similarly the poor, distinctive from others because of their color and servitude in the South and because of their lack of property in the North, had to be held to their work. Accordingly John Locke, to whom so many American political theorists repaired, had proposed special schools for the children of paupers so that they would learn labor—in his phrase "and nothing but labor"—from the age of three. Little short of enslavement, that prescription was intended to dispose of "idle and disorderly persons." It defined the poor in a sense as an alien race that had to be held to close discipline.

In the American South that race had a visible stamp and visible bonds. In the North, other bonds, because they were invisible, were less confining but no less a brand of inequality. In the first great industrial complex in the United States, management imposed a severe discipline upon the propertyless labor it hired. The magnificent textile mills in Lowell, Massachusetts, recruited young New England women to tend their machines. Those female operatives, temporary fugitives from the poverty of a harsh countryside, were subjected at Lowell to the regulation of their hours of work, their place and condition of residence, their menus at table and their time to consume their food, even their ambulations to and from dormitory and loom. Against that regime, not the level of their wages, the operatives came first to protest. As women, they had never been accepted as equals, but now as operatives rather than farm girls, they were treated almost like serfs. So in various ways were the immigrants who succeeded them in the employment of the young industries of the nation. Work gangs, company towns, indentures for destitute children, those and other social institutions severely restricted the individual behavior of the poor.

Fear of paupers in the North reached hysterical proportions

with the flush of immigration of the 1850's. Now differences in speech and ordinarily in religion set the new working force apart, and northern men indulged in their first modern saturnalia of nativism. The propertyless immigrants, able to find only the meanest work, drifted into neighborhoods of their own. Everywhere they were ridiculed and reviled, often turned on by mobs. Like color in the South, Catholicism in the North came to constitute a basis for social discrimination, one form of discipline of the poor.

For their part the proscribed Irish preserved, as did others among the impoverished, a sense of superiority of their own by despising black slaves and freedmen. The growing agitation for the abolition or the geographical containment of slavery attracted few paupers. Indeed by the mid-nineteenth century the American poor were divided into several mutually antagonistic groups: old-stock Americans, immigrants, and blacks. The resulting disunity precluded any general protest based upon class and thus enhanced the effectiveness of existing social controls, legal, institutional, or informal.

Thomas Jefferson had hoped to prevent those developments and the obvious tensions they created between the ideal creed embodied in the Declaration of Independence and the actual conditions of American society. To escape from the perils of urban poverty and urban mobs, and thus from the need to control them, he had proposed the distribution of large agricultural holdings to all propertyless men. To that end, among others, he was moved to the purchase of the Louisiana Territory, where the availability of free land might help to promote a society of free men, as he saw it, free yeomen. But the land was never really free, as Jefferson knew. It was unavailable to blacks. It was also out of reach for all others who lacked a modest capital to finance their removal to a new home and the development of its site, out of reach, too, for those who lacked the will to face the trials unavoidable in that venture. The vast expanse of Louisiana, as of other spectacular American territories, promised only a limited possibility for equality of opportunity, the most that Jefferson could have expected. Patently the land assured no actual equality of condition, a circumstance which the founding fathers and their Jacksonian successors in any case never considered practicable, much less self-evident.

Indeed Jefferson's friend, James Madison, had doubted that there would ever be enough land or wealth to go around. Madison foresaw continual conflict arising from the uneven distribution of property among men. In an effort to check the resulting factional contest, the Constitution, besides protecting slavery, had included, as Madison intended, a variety of devices to temper the voice of the people before it could become the voice of the government. To the same purpose, the American states at the brink of nationhood had limited the franchise effectively to those men who owned property or at least paid taxes.

Even during the Jacksonian years, the decades of "freedom's ferment," indeed with special fervor then, men of property gave eloquent, if also frenetic, expression to their continuing fear of permitting slaves in the South a freedom of person or paupers in the North a freedom to vote, or at least to vote for all public offices. The presumed need for social control provided the rationale for the foremost intellectual advocate of slavery, George Fitzhugh. His *Sociology for the South* (Richmond, 1854) described the dangers he attributed to the changing status of the villeins of Medieval Europe. "Pauperism and beggary," Fitzhugh wrote, ". . . were unknown till the villeins began to escape . . . and attempted to practice a predatory and nomadic liberty . . . very much like that of domestic animals that have gone wild. . . . The new freemen were bands of thieves and beggars, infesting the country and disturbing its peace. . . . It was necessary to restrain them in slavery . . . about the wharves . . . of cities." It fell then to their masters, their employers, to require and enforce "ordinary morality and industry," exactly the task, as Fitzhugh saw it, of Northern employers of his own time. In contrast, the South had wisely preserved slavery and with it the discipline essential for the prevention of predatory liberty.

However distasteful Fitzhugh's thesis, it reflected anxieties common also among Northern men. Chancellor Kent, opposing universal manhood suffrage at the New York constitutional convention of 1821, had warned that "the extreme democratic principle" invariably resulted in "corruption, injustice, violence and tyranny." "The men of no property," he went on, "together with the crowds of dependents connected with great manufacturing and commercial establishments, and the motley and undefinable population of crowded ports" constituted a majority which, as in every age, would, when given the chance, "tyrannize over the minority." "There was," he maintained, "a tendency in the indolent and the profligate to cast the whole burthens of society upon the industrious and the virtuous; and there is a tendency in ambitious and wicked men to inflame those combustible materials."

Kent's words, like Fitzhugh's, revealed attitudes on which Foster, Tocqueville and Green successively remarked. And like the democratic reformers whom he opposed, Kent linked property and the franchise, though he also tied the privilege of the latter to the practice of self-restraint which he considered an uncommon virtue. The reformers, for their part, believed that property, the franchise and virtue itself could and should become universal among Americans.

No antebellum democrats had a surer sense of the fundamental significance of property, and of the relationship of property to the vote, then did the leaders of the first movement for women's rights. In demanding the franchise, those women indicted men for denying them not property only but all opportunities to gain access to property, all opportunities for potential equality. Man had taken from woman, so read the Seneca Falls Declaration of 1848, "all right in property . . . he had monopolized nearly all the profitable employments. . . . He closes against her all the avenues to wealth and distinction which he considers most honorable to himself. . . . He has denied her the facilities for obtaining a thorough education. . . . He has endeavored . . . to destroy her confidence . . . to lessen her self-respect and to make her willing to lead a dependent . . . life." As those women realized, the right to vote provided one sure route to the right to property and with it to self-fulfillment and self-esteem. Yet they did not demand, indeed among themselves they did not contemplate, an equality of condition. Rather, they looked upon the Declaration of Independence, which they adapted as a preamble to their charter, as assuring to women as well as to men an openness of careers to talent, an equality under the law as well as in the eyes of God, an equality of opportunity.

So, too, Horace Mann and other antebellum proponents of free, public education harnessed their cause to the issues of property and of the vote. Speaking directly to those who shared the fears of Chancellor Kent, Mann in his 1848 report as secretary of the Massachusetts Bureau of Education marked the utility of education as one means for instilling a respect for property among the propertyless who were, by the time he wrote, entitled to the franchise with adulthood. Simultaneously he noted the importance of education for providing those skills with which the propertyless might themselves acquire property and with it, their own stake in a stable society. "To what extent," Mann inquired, "can competence displace pauperism? How nearly can we free ourselves from the

low-minded and the vicious . . . by their elevation? . . .
Cannot the classes of crimes be lessened, and the number of
criminals in each class be diminished? . . . Massachusetts
. . . is exposed . . . to the fatal extremes of overgrown wealth
and desperate poverty. . . . Now surely nothing but universal education can counterwork this tendency of the domination of capital and the servility of labor. . . . If education be
equally diffused, it will draw property after it. . . . Education . . . is the great equalizer of the conditions of men. . . .
It gives each man the independence and the means by which
he can resist the selfishness of other men. It does better than
to disarm the poor of their hostility toward the rich: it pre-
vents being poor."

That was a telling, if optimistic, formula. It allayed the
anxieties of the comfortable and awakened the aspirations of
those paupers eager to place their children on the ladder to
success. Yet the case Mann made for education had little to
do with the life of the mind. Rather, like the feminists, he
spoke to the need for an open society. So, of course, did the
abolitionists, and because there could exist no open society
where the institution of slavery obtained, the movements for
women's rights and for free education, like abolition itself,
had insignificant currency in the South.

Yet even for Andrew Jackson, the symbol and spokesman
of democratic possibilities in his age, as for Abraham Lincoln
who succeeded him in those roles, equality had a limited
definition. The rich and the powerful, Jackson held in his
veto of the recharter of the Bank of the United States, had no
right to "bend the acts of Government to their selfish purposes." Rather, "the humble members of society—the farmers, mechanics, and laborers—who have neither the time nor
the means of securing . . . favors to themselves, have a right
to complain of the injustice of their Government." They had
a right, various Jacksonians asserted, to the vote and to edu-

cation, a right also to free land. Those were the conditions of an open society, conditions that applied also for women and for blacks. Those conditions would relieve the burden of inequality of the poor, but they would not erase the differences among men. "Distinctions in society," Jackson wrote, and Lincoln agreed, "will always exist under every just government. Equality of talents . . . or of wealth cannot be produced by human institutions." Every man, he continued, was equally justified to protection by law "in the full enjoyment of the gifts of Heaven and the fruits of superior industry . . . and virtue," but no laws could alter "natural and just advantages," natural human distinctions.

Even so, there remained a wide range of necessary change in order to establish a genuine equality of opportunity, a release of the poor, black or white, from the burdens of partial equality which the metaphor of the coach had illumined. The Northern victory in the Civil War and the sequential end of slavery did not affect that change. In the South, patterns of social discipline, altered though they were from their antebellum form, persisted in their incidence. The black codes, until the Supreme Court disallowed them, attempted to prevent the black freedmen from becoming Fitzhugh's predatory and nomadic villeins. Those codes held the freed blacks to a lawful home and employment, to their contracts for work, and to the support of their children. After the codes were declared illegal, the evolution of the sharecropping and crop lien systems nailed Southern paupers, now blacks and whites alike, to the land where most of them still lived. In the circumstances, the tradition of social egalitarianism among Southern white property owners persisted.

Indeed that tradition and the emotional bulwarks sustaining it survived the challenge of late nineteenth century Populism. That movement in the South temporarily brought together the destitute of both races in a wave of protest against their more privileged neighbors, as well as against the wretchedness of their own lives. Like their predecessors of the age of Jackson, the Populists, western as well as southern, demanded a democratization of electoral processes and governmental intervention to accomplish a broader distribution of property in land. They railled, to be sure, against the build up of "colossal fortunes" born of special privilege, but they were less levellers than aspirant political and agricultural entrepreneurs. They sought not a quick equality of wealth but a guaranteed opportunity to make their votes count, to earn the true fruits of their labor, and to use that competence to acquire land of their own. If they were nostalgic for a yeoman's garden of Eden that had never really existed, they were also quintessentially American in their definition of the means for their escape from the burdens they carried, the burdens that sustained the partial equality that their propertied contemporaries enjoyed. Yet to men of property the Populists seemed radical, just as the democratizers had to Chancellor Kent.

With the defeat of Populism in the 1890's, the crop lien system remained in the South. Further, the white South strengthened its ancient social controls with a resurgence of the rhetoric of racism, a successful recourse for again separating the white poor from the black. The accompanying emergence of modern Jim Crow kept Southern blacks in a separate place, separate and unequal, and excluded them, as well as most poor whites, alike from the ownership of property and from the franchise.

The South, as before, had its peculiar institutions, but its essential problems were common to the nation and becoming more so. Still primarily agricultural when the twentieth century turned, the South thereafter surrendered increasing percentages of its population to its own growing mill towns and later to northern cities. The migration of blacks to the North swelled during each of six successive decades so that issues of race by 1940 had become national rather than regional. Southern migrants, white and black, like immigrants from Europe and Asia, provided the unskilled labor on which northern industrialization depended. But in northern society in the forty years after 1865, as in Tocqueville's time, there was no "real bond between . . . the rich and poor." On the contrary, a persisting fear of violence and vagabondry still informed the tough resistance with which the propertied met intermittent outbursts of discontent.

Yet like Populism, those expressions protested only against inequalities of privilege. The Knights of Labor, for one example, called in their constitution for unionization and an eight hour day not in order to level all incomes but in order to prevent pauperization in the face of aggression by "aggregated wealth." The indictment was valid, but aggressive retaliation destroyed the Knights. So, too, Henry George and the Single Taxers demanded the abolition of special advantages and advocated levies on monopoly in land so that "the advantages of social growth and improvement" could accrue to "society at large." They did not suggest that each man would acquire an equal share, but so deeply did they rattle the dovecotes of New York that patricians there made league with Tammany Hall to keep George from becoming mayor. Similarly management opposition to the trade unions of the American Federation of Labor obscured the degree to which those unions were themselves agencies of inequality. They organized primarily the skilled. They excluded for the most part blacks, Asians, women and children. They fought for the right of their members to bargain collectively, but they opposed social legislation designed to assist the preponderant majority of workers, whom they disdained. The benefits that the trade unionists gradually gained for themselves, as well as their basically middle class aspirations, made them as hostile as were merchants, professional men, and enterprisers to the occasional militancy of the deprived and the despised.

Just before and after the turn of the century that militancy emerged because of the continuing destitution of the bottom fifth of the working force— blacks and recent immigrants especially, because of the indifference of organized labor and moderate reformers to their plight, because of the intransigence of the wealthy and the managers of their property, and because of the impact first of depression and then of inflation on the lives of those who labored in mills and mines. The alienation born of those frustrations assumed a genuinely radical cast in the socialism of Eugene V. Debs and in the syndicalism of Bill Haywood and his Industrial Workers of the World. The avowed watchword of the IWW was "abolition of the wage system" and of capitalism itself. In practice those doctrines had little bearing on industrial actions that became violent only in response to fierce retaliation, but doctrine and action alike seemed to the comfortable to forbode revolution. Speaking the mind of the middle class, Theodore Roosevelt identified Debs and Haywood with Marat and Robespierre and mustered federal authority against them. He also championed, as Jackson had, the elimination of special privileges that impeded the functioning of an open society and thereby encouraged recourse to the radicalisms he detested. In the absence of meliorative reform, in the absence of moderate unionism, as Roosevelt realized, the nation would not only have a revolution but, in his words, would deserve a revolution.

Roosevelt, though never an original thinker, had a special genius for phrasing and for galvanizing the progressive temper, and progressivism, for all its internal contradictions and doctrinal vagaries, gave a twentieth century thrust and cadence to the tradition of American reform. It translated Jacksonian precepts into a language relevant to an industrial nation, and it provided a primer from which later reformers, the New Dealers and the New Frontiersmen particularly, would learn their elementary lessons. So Roosevelt had a continuing importance not for what he said or did, but for what he represented.

Like Madison, Roosevelt discovered the source of social conflict in the unequal distribution of property. Further, like many of his broad constituency, he held the spoiled and irresponsible rich to be as culpable as the radicals he feared. On that account, while President he proposed to police big business, its labor policies not the least, to tax the transmission of swollen fortunes, to relieve the poverty of the countryside, and to advance urban reform through social work. A few years later, he also advocated a federal minimum wage law and old age and unemployment insurance.

Concurrently Roosevelt gave a steady emphasis to didactic and proscriptive remedies for social unrest. At times a Jeffersonian in spite of himself, he prized the tradition of the independent yeoman. The personal values he associated with the yeomen, the habits of hard work and of patriotic duty, shaped his definition of Americanism. As he saw it, though all of his countrymen might learn those habits, the newcomers among them, the immigrants from southern and eastern Europe and Asia (and by implication blacks from the South), had first to be instructed in the traditions of their adopted land. American culture, in that interpretation, allowed small room for pluralism. Indeed the divisive risks of pluralism persuaded Roosevelt that there remained little space for further immigration, and that only selective.

So it was also among his like-minded contemporaries. Jacob Riis, for one, exposed the evils of New York's slums, agitated for tenement legislation, and yet also blamed immigrants— the Chinese and the Jews especially—for their presumably inherent tendency to accept the conditions of life in which they found themselves. A Southern reformer might have said as much about black laborers in Birmingham, Alabama. In a similar vein, Robert Hunter, in his influential study of poverty, separated the worthy poor from the tramps and vagabonds who, he believed, lacked the character to improve their lot. In those readings, so persuasive among Americans of the early century and its aftermath, persisting anxiety about pauperism and its dangerous volatility, and a persisting association of that danger with disadvantaged ethnic groups, weighed just about equally with humanitarian good will.

Overall, the separate but related sets of Roosevelt's proposals carried the dual attractiveness of the earlier arguments of Horace Mann. The near exclusion of further paupers from Europe and Asia, and the indoctrination of those already arrived, relieved the worries of the propertied about radical violence. A modest redistribution of property, sufficient to reduce the wealth of the very rich, combined with a further democratization of election procedures, appealed to those among the working force who were organized enough to use politics to their own social advantage. Indeed Roosevelt expected them and others through vigorous application and prudential bearing to earn a decent standard of personal comfort.

Again in the manner of Jackson, Roosevelt considered "the farmers, small businessmen and . . . mechanics" his natural allies. As the immigrant poor achieved a similar status, they too would become "fundamentally sound, morally, mentally and physically." That fundamental soundness, existing or potential, of the people gave Roosevelt confidence that the devices of direct democracy, the direct primary for one, would safely result in the election of able governors, men like himself. In contrast to Jackson, he believed that the management of public, as of private, affairs required an elite of talent, but his sense of identity with the people allowed him to reconcile majoritarianism and elitism, and supported his faith in an open society.

The hopeful presumptions of progressives about American prospects for social mobility rested upon those data that seemed to confirm the glad folklore of deserved advances from rags to riches. In their day the harder data had yet to be accumulated that showed the profile of the distribution of American wealth as substantially unaltered for a century after 1860. Other, more impressionistic perceptions argued to the contrary. In fact the growth of the national economy, especially after 1870, gradually provided such a bounty of goods and services that some overflowed into the earnings of workers whose real incomes continually rose above that of most of their counterparts in other countries, particularly those from which immigration was heaviest. The children of many, if not of most immigrants felt better off than their parents and especially their grandparents had been. So, too, remigrants, characteristically those from Italy and Greece, returned to their homelands with the means to acquire land or a shop or later just a taxi that gave them a new distinction in the region of their birth.

Roosevelt and his generation had yet to learn about a growth dividend, but Roosevelt for one sensed its continual application to American conditions just as he sensed that wealth had to be created before it could be shared. Partly on that account, he welcomed industrialization and admired its agents, whom he proposed to discipline only if they offended his standards of business conduct. The consolidators, the enterprisers, the American modernizers had made the nation rich as well as strong. Accordingly he intended that they should be accountable to the government for their behavior but not subject to destructive harassment. The business executive, like the farmer, the mechanic, or the warrior, deserved his just reward, but justice did not require that those rewards be equal in property, though Roosevelt believed they would be equal in satisfactions, the satisfactions of engagement and vitality.

In several respects, the progressive analysis was wanting. Wholly apart from the growth dividend, the American sense of continuing social mobility depended upon immigration itself. Each tide of immigration brought to industry and the cities a new source of cheap labor for the meanest available jobs. Upon the backs of newcomers their predecessors climbed to callings more remunerative and more dignified. Just as the Italians and Greeks, Poles and Bohemians succeeded the Irish around the wharves and in the coal pits, so later, with the cessation of extensive European immigration, blacks from the South and Spanish-speaking peoples from neighboring American states in their turn picked up the burden of equality. With each stage, those who won parole not only detested the prisons of poverty they had left but also scorned the new prisoners. The captured unfortunates were the guarantors of the enhanced status and prospects of those who now lived and worked above the abject level to which the dividends of growth did not descend. Yet the ethnocentrism of most Americans, reformers included, ascribed personal blame, in the manner of Riis and Hunter, to the victims of social and economic constraints as yet to be eliminated.

Just as the pattern of immigration provided an illusion of greater mobility than the data disclosed, so exceptional experience also fostered that illusion. Within every immigrant group, over at least three generations, admission to superior education, to professional training, and to managerial responsibility—access to elite status—was strikingly uneven. The minority of each group to enjoy that access gained the prestige and patronage to assist increasing proportions of their fellows to similar success, and the growing incidence of that success often sustained the myth of a fully open society, as did the erosion of particular prejudices during each episode of national reform. Yet poverty and discrimination closed the way to countless deserving but unidentified aspirants, especially those who were stigmatized because of their pigmentation. The progressives and their heirs recognized the indispensability of an elite of talent in a modern society, but they failed adequately to comprehend that American society was open disproportionately to the children of the elite.

During the progressive era itself, Walter Lippmann, that most astute of American journalists, set the issues in their proper context in his precocious *Drift and Mastery* (New York, 1914). Unlike Roosevelt, he had no fear of socialism. The divorce of management from ownership, Lippmann realized, had made socialism as irrelevant as capitalism. What was relevant was continuing experimentalism and efficiency in the management of every kind of enterprise. So, equally, was an industrial democracy that would give workers a larger voice—a franchise as it were—in the control of business and the equitable distribution of its profits. That kind of democracy, by no means literally egalitarian, would exist only "when every adult has enough education not only to do a job, but to know why he is doing the job." Or as he put it in an alternative phrasing: "Sufficient education and a sufficient stake in the community are necessary to what in a modern sense we may call a free man." That freedom, in Lippmann's compelling sense, entailed the lifting of the burden of bourgeoise equality that the destitute continued to carry, the opening of the avenues to satisfaction that circumstance and sentiment continued to block.

Franklin Roosevelt and the New Deal moved the nation toward those objectives. Though the depression of the 1930's resisted their remedies, their reform programs created devices for a partial redistribution of income once prosperity returned with the Second World War. Operating at last in a time of full employment, New Deal revenue measures affected that redistribution more markedly than during any other quinquennium in American history. The innovative promotion of industrial unions, which temporarily enlisted an increasing fraction of the unskilled, and the establishment of federal social insurance, militated to the same end. Beyond all that, the Roosevelt Democrats, admittedly seeking votes for reelection, drew into visible and prestigious public offices unprecedented numbers of able Irish, Jewish and Italian Americans, and undertook a symbolic, though only a symbolic, recruitment also of women and blacks. Further, as Lippmann had prescribed, New Deal relief programs aimed to preserve and to cultivate the skills, mechanical, artistic and professional, that brought a sense of purpose to work and stocked a national reservoir with significant talents.

Those policies, projections of the best of the progressive agenda, yielded important social dividends during the postwar decades. In company with the largess of economic growth, now deliberately pursued by federal initiatives, they provided enough workers with the emblems of middle class status, with private homes, automobiles and electrical appliances, to diminish the number of propertyless and the intensity of alienation of the marginal beneficiaries of prosperity.

Nevertheless the apparent affluence of postwar America neither erased poverty nor dispelled the drudgery of the millions of men and women who labored only for the satisfaction of income. The expanding elite that fostered and guided economic growth excelled in the skills of law, engineering, science, investment and management. Those so gifted and so trained made up an American meritocracy whose adroitness never hid its exclusiveness or its privileges. As ever, industrial, clerical and commercial laborers recognized their own relative inequality, envied as well as emulated the more prominent, and gained what compensation they could in their hopes for their children and their hostility toward the indigent, the foreign and the black.

For their part, marginal workers, perhaps a tenth of the nation, found no dignity or satisfaction in digging and lifting, loading and carrying, once the chores of slaves. They and the unemployed, close to another tenth, lived as late as 1970 with ignorance, disease and ennui. By that date the most important achievement of the civil rights movement, federal guarantees of the right to vote, had given the depressed minorities the political strength to influence the enactment of stringent affirmative action laws that bore upon employment and admission to higher education, legitimate goals also of American feminists. But the impoverished minorities in particular still awaited an adequate and equitable delivery of compensatory public services like housing, training and medical care. In a country where social status had always correlated with occupation, the inequality of access to salient education made chimerical either an equality of opportunity or one of easy social intercourse. In the metaphor of the coach, still applicable, the driver was not invited to table either because he was poor or because he was black.

In contrast, among those whose occupations made them peers—in professional associations, in executive suites, within labor unions, among college students—a rough equality of station reflected an anterior equality of opportunity. There prevailed, too, a freedom in transitory exchanges between yeoman and patrician, mechanic and executive, who met in queues for the cinema, at football games, in shopping plazas and airline terminals. But that equality excluded the propertyless majority of blacks and Spanish-speaking Americans, along with other paupers. There was no pretence of equality between those on welfare and those who paid their bills, and those on welfare knew modern social controls designed to keep them in their place.

Yet the burden of American equality had shifted. The poor villeins of the American cities, though they bore the weight of their station, had become more and more sullen and sometimes rebellious. Autoworker and engineer, stenographer and executive , dental assistant and attorney, all came to fear the slums in the dark. Most schools in those slums functioned only as bastions of discipline, closed buildings where policed corridors confined angry youths until three in the afternoon, where the black poor and the white poor plotted reciprocal warfare, where incantations of middle class expectations evoked derision, and where the visible record of the culture of poverty proclaimed the futility of learning conventional lessons. That culture, as it always had, bred crime, disease and anomie, while the last recommended to its victims recourse to alcohol, insanity, drugs or death. The drugs leaped beyond the ghettoes to the suburbs, isolated from the poor but not from their mood and their temptations. In all those ways, the cost of inequality, the expense of control of the poor had fallen gravely upon those who feared the dark.

The burden of American equality shifted to those best able to bear it at just the time when they could no longer expect to discharge it by relying primarily on the dividends of economic growth. By the 1970s the "people of plenty" had so exhausted the resources of which they had constructed their wealth that further sustained growth was bound to tax available supplies of energy. Accordingly Americans whose personal security, whatever their consciences, depended on a steady progress toward a society open for all of its members, had now, as never before, to make an unqualified effort significantly to reduce inequalities of condition and of reward. They had to undertake a redistribution of income and wealth sufficient to bring the least privileged an honest equality of opportunity. But the comfortable, as the 1980's demonstrated, were loath to do so.

Though the burden had shifted, the problem was two hundred years old. The safety and tranquillity of the republic, so Jefferson believed, depended on the broad distribution of land, the property he most valued. That was also his precondition for the equality his famous declaration asserted. Even after two centuries some Americans cherished his propositions, at once so just and so distant. Those so minded put forth venturesome possibilities for their attainment. With the costs of welfare and of poverty so high, even an expansive guaranteed annual income could effect economies while promoting equity. A compensatory delivery of public services to the poor, of education especially, could start the process that would ultimately leave machines with most unskilled jobs. A redistribution of wealth far short of equality of reward could ease access to technical and managerial positions for those of courage and assiduity, including those who in their destitution had yet to learn to hope.

Yet in more than two hundred years, the burden of American inequality had reached beyond the tolerance of prevailing national purpose. As the 1990's began, it remained for Americans to return to their ancient goals, to fit the realities of their society to the ideals Jefferson had proclaimed.

2

VIRTUOUS TEXTS*

THOSE of us who edited the letters of Theodore Roosevelt devoted a leisurely consideration to the literature which the Rough Rider read as a child. The references in the letters he wrote as an adult made it abundantly clear that he was saturated in Bunyan's *Pilgrim's Progress,* Emerson's *Brahma,* and the other standard items in the literary diet of an American boy of good family who grew up during the 1860's and 1870's. But there was clearly more to it than that. The similarities in style between Roosevelt and Kipling suggested that the eminent Edwardians on both sides of the Atlantic had been exposed to some common models of English prose. Like others in England and America, Roosevelt was by no means always a crisp or skillful writer. Some of his letters seemed extraordinarily gushy, especially those he wrote to his own and other children, and in these he frequently included rough line drawings—similar in purpose to Kipling's sketches for the

---

* This essay is adapted from the Introduction to *Yesterday's Children* (Boston: Houghton Mifflin, 1959) pp. xi–xxviii, an anthology compiled from the children's magazine *Our Young Folks.*

Just So Stories—calculated to amuse his readers as much as to depict his text.

Roosevelt and his contemporaries could have derived inspiration for the products of their pens from an enormous range of literature, good or bad, classic or ephemeral, didactic or effusive. As it happened, however, Roosevelt left a record of his continuing pleasure in the pages of *Our Young Folks,* a children's monthly published from 1865 through 1873 by the Boston house of Ticknor and Fields. And *Our Young Folks,* a quick investigation showed, printed line drawings that Roosevelt's were to resemble. So also with less graphic concepts, it developed on further investigation, and so also with other readers who, like Roosevelt, took the magazine for many months.

Our Young Folks was not substantially different from some of its competitors, of which the most celebrated were surely the *Youth's Companion* and *St. Nicholas.* (The latter purchased the subscription list and other assests of *Our Young Folks* in 1873.) Like its more famous rivals and like other children's magazines—*Oliver Optic* was one—which had only a brief life in the jungle of mass media, *Our Young Folks* brought to American children the incidental work of some leading British and American authors, and the major work of some incidental writers of Victorian prose and poetry.

But more than its competitors, *Our Young Folks* was a New England magazine, even a Boston magazine. It rounded out Ticknor and Fields's rather impressive list, providing a special outlet for the work of authors who contributed also to three other Ticknor and Fields journals. These, the publishers advertised, were the weekly *Every Saturday,* which included "papers on subjects of present interest and general importance, themes of social life, unpartisan aspects of political affairs, literary topics, and . . . excellent stories . . . essays, sketches, narratives on travel and adventure . . . and a full and carefully prepared summary of home and foreign news"; *The Atlantic Monthly* "conducted on the same general plan which has hitherto proved so acceptable to intelligent American readers . . . the medium through which the most original thinkers and most popular writers of every part of the country reach the public . . . the organ of no clique, section, or party"; and the quarterly *The North American Review,* which "maintained and advanced the standard of American letters and scholarship . . . elucidated and defended the principles on which American institutions rest . . . and . . . addressed itself to those who were not averse to serious thought on the most important topics of the time."

Ticknor and Fields, later Fields, Osgood and Company, much later Houghton Mifflin Company, claimed no less for *Our Young Folks* than for its illustrious companions. It was "the best juvenile magazine ever published in any land or language." Its editors rejected "dull and trashy articles as alike worthless" and took "all possible care to procure reading that shall furnish healthy entertainment and attractive instruction. They endeavor to make the Magazine so fresh and valuable that young people will greet its monthly appearance with eagerness, and parents welcome it as an indispensable ally in the education and amusement of their children."

The chief editor, John T. Trowbridge, anticipating by almost a century the commercial insight which has given rise to adult westerns on television, designed his product for older readers as well as young. Like the children, the oldsters were to be instructed and entertained. For themselves or their offspring, they brought *Our Young Folks* into homes all over the United States. The subscription lists are lost, but other records of the publisher contain correspondence from readers who welcomed Boston's words in communities throughout New England and the middle states of course, but also in Denver and Knoxville, Carthage and Cleveland, on the West Coast, and in Florida and Alabama.

Before it became a commercial liability (partly because Trowbridge and a fellow editor, Mary A. Dodge, "fell out"), *Our Young Folks* had the opportunity, at least, to impress its precepts and its prose on the growing minds of large numbers of boys and girls. Some of them, like Roosevelt, must have greeted the magazine's monthly arrival with joy. Many, in any case, wrote its editors for advice or contributed essays and stories to special columns set aside for those who in their early teens aspired to the career of a Harriet Beecher Stowe or a Thomas Bailey Aldrich.

Our Young Folks, then, was a vehicle for the transmission of the culture of New England to the generation that reached prominence about the time the twentieth century began. New England, moreover, had special things to say, and what is more important, young people in middle-class homes throughout the United States apparently absorbed a good deal of New England's message. From a literary point of view, some of *Our Young Folks* was wheat and more was chaff, but doubtless few readers could always discriminate, and even the chaff, after it was boiled enough, provided obvious sustenance. The pages of the magazine, artistic and inartistic, gave direction and possibly also courage to children, whatever their place of residence, who did their reading in New England's lingering twilight.

SPURNED by Azalia, the young lady of his heart, Phillip walked home alone, out of sorts with himself and boiling over with wrath toward Paul, his successful rival. He thought about his losses of the evening until his steps, falling on the frozen ground, seemed to say "Character!—Character!—Character!—something Paul had and he had not." Years later Paul, a wounded hero of Chickamauga, was removed to a Rebel prison where he recognized Phillip Funk, the youngster from whom he had won Azalia's hand, now a Confederate lieutenant, a thief who had skulked in battle, his face bloated, his eyes bloodshot. Character told. Even the Rebels court-martialed Phillip, while Paul preserved his patriotism and devotion through the gloom and darkness of Andersonville to return to Azalia. Their pure and true love deepened through the years.

"Character" was of "more consequence than clothes." "Be good," the hero knew, "and let who will be clever; do noble things, not dream them all day long." Character, said J. P. Morgan, who as a child read aphorisms like these, was the only basis for a business loan. Character was what Woodrow Wilson's Princeton meant to teach. Character, wrote Theodore Roosevelt at least a hundred times, was to intellect as two is to one. Throughout the land the Edwardians of America concurred. Their leaders had character; they had character; and if need be, they would teach the parvenus and immigrants, the Mexicans and Germans, too, the indispensability of character in the life of men and nations.

What the Victorian proposed, the Edwardian disposed. The culture New England encapsulated for its young made its way throughout America, and the children who read New England's literature apparently put a high premium, as children often do, on what they saw in print. In any case, when near the turn of the century they sat in the seats of the mighty, they made their parents' teachings a common creed that bathed and sustained and rationalized the national spirit.

Almost as soon as the Civil War ended, the perceptive New Englander began to realize that he, too, had lost his cause. "We hoped," Emerson wrote, "that in the peace . . . a great expansion would follow in the mind of the country;

grand views in every direction. . . . But the energy of the nation seems to have expended itself in the war." From the point of view of Concord and Cambridge, there was abroad in the land something crass and turgid and fetid, something alien to the whole purpose that New England had expected would suffuse the nation. Even the veteran was a kind of Ichabod, a "very disorganized member of society, and hard to deal with," as Rebecca Davis put it. "You cannot take a man away from his work and life . . . and send him to fight for five years, without turning his ideas and himself topsy-turvy." Annie Howells centered this inversion in the "frightened eyes" of a little Michigan boy whose father during the war, "tempted beyond his strength to resist," had taken a first drink to throw off the weariness and cold of a long, hard march, a drink that became "his bane" and sent him at last teetering over the edge of a rowboat to his death.

Some of the disenchanted fled the twilight in New England, the somberness of disillusionment. Others, like Mrs. Stowe, sought to reconstruct the spirit as well as the scene they valued "before the hot suns of modern progress" should bleach beyond recognition the high colors of the past. This kind of effort produced such works as *Oldtown Folks* and Bailey Aldrich's accounts of his boyish escapades in prewar Portsmouth. It also produced a monitory literature, sometimes humorous, more often maudlin, that John T. Trowbridge selected for publication in *Our Young Folks,* by design an *Atlantic Monthly* for teen-age readers. Here Trowbridge, Aldrich, Lowell, Whittier and Longfellow, Edgar Fawcett, Rose Terry, Louisa Alcott, Lucy Larcom and lesser kin in mind and mien aired their faith that New England was the "Dorian hive" of the United States, the seed bed, as Mrs. Stowe called it, "of this great American Republic, and of all that is likely to come of it."

But this was a faith rooted in anguish, for the past seemed

at times more remote than usable, challenged as it was not
only by the war and the postwar climate, but also by the
machines and the cities and their inhabitants then working a
metamorphosis in the country and its people. Precisely because
the times challenged what New England held dear, New
England told itself and told the country that the true American, past or future, was a New Englander or his mirror image.
New England gave its localism the sanction of nationality,
disallowing every counterclaim. An occasional Southerner, to
be sure, like little Missy in Helen Wall Pierson's "Under the
Flag," had "heroic stuff in her," and on that account helped
a slave to run away, earning for her deed cutting strokes from
a leather strap with which her mother beat her until great
scarlet welts were raised upon her skin. No question but that
this mother expressed the spirit of the South. As Trowbridge
put it, "God permitted the war in order that slavery might
be destroyed. . . . Slave holders and slave-hunters became so
violent, unreasonable, and wicked . . . that it was right to
resist force with force."

The normative Rebel, as *Our Young Folks* saw him, was the
embodiment of evil, a tall, ragged ruffian who ran his bayo-
net through the body of the wounded before taking their
jewelry and their money. With excited countenance, lip curved,
and eye in fine frenzy rolling, the men of the South directed
their un-American loyalties to narrow state boundaries and
to corrupting caste. Even the rare gentleman Confederate was
damned, like General Lee—"the man who neither smokes,
drinks, nor chews tobacco; who has, in short, none of the
smaller vices, but all of the larger ones; for he deliberately,
basely, and under circumstances of unparalleled meanness,
betrayed his country, and, long after all hope of success was
lost, carried on a murderous war against his own race and
kindred." All that was worth saving from the South was "the
venerable figure" of Washington to whom Trowbridge con-

fidently attributed a Yankee soul: "There was one great danger he feared—the separation of the States. But well for him,
oh, well for the great-hearted and wise chieftain, that the
appalling blackness of the storm . . . was hidden from his
eyes. . . . Saved from the sordid hands of a degenerate pos-
terity, saved from the desolation of unsparing civil war, Mount
Vernon still remains to us."

The western American was merely the New Englander
transplanted. The son of Indiana like the son of Vermont
hated caste and loved the Union. That Paul whose character
undid young Phillip Funk was Ohio born but of a Connecticut father. And his father had the best stock in him, the
blood of Anglo-Saxons.

As Mrs. Stowe found qualities of character and manner in
various "races" of dogs, so did her friends find qualities they
cherished in special human bloods. With condescending tolerance the Yankee attributed to the colored freedmen a "love
of gaiety" like children's, "a propensity to brag, and a disposition to magnify everything." Much worse were the mean
and grasping Irishmen, characteristically itinerant peddlers
who bullied innocent Yankee girls. But like the spaniel, the
Anglo-Saxon was gentle; like the mastiff, strong and coura-
geous; like the terrier, smart and active. And of the Anglo-
Saxons, the best, the elect, had emigrated to New England.
The Pilgrims, first true Americans, left "a bad king" who
would not "let them be Christians" and "but for those brave
men and women, we should have had no quiet homes, no
peaceful villages, no blessed New England."

The English settler and the Scotch-Irish made the American nation, differentiating it in every essential way from the
civilization left behind. One T.M.B. took issue with Charles
Darwin for the naturalist's assertion that the American cuckoo
built too rude a nest and ill attended to its young. Darwin's
American critic could not see "any resemblance between the

selfish, unconjugal, unparental European, and the self-sacri-
ficing . . . American bird. If the latter builds a rude, inartistic nest, so does also that most devoted of all the families of
birds, the Dove. . . . In their relations with one another our
Cuckoos are exemplary and tender." So, too, with art. Bailey
Aldrich, the American critic speaking to American themes,
sang the praise of Winslow Homer for the artist's "high order
of excellence in the treatment of purely American subjects."
Homer won Aldrich not for his virtuosity as a painter but for
his pictorial representations "of the most desperate struggle
that the good knight Freedom ever had with the Prince of
Darkness."

Besides section and race, industrialism and urbanism seemed
agents of the Prince of Darkness. For the spiritual daughters
of Emerson, technology symbolized disaster. "Huge monsters
of engines" could do the work of 150 men and 75 horses, but
they brought with them foreign ways. "When I was a little
girl," one lady remembered, there were no gaslights, no fur-
naces, no buses, but ways of living then were better as well
as different. Only five widths of cloth went into silk dresses,
and "very nice people were contented to have haircloth-cov-
ered chairs and sofas." More significantly, "the sweet country
roads wound still and green out from the paved thorough-
fares, crossing no iron tracks, and bestridden by no warning
signs forbidding 'Beware of the engine!' "

The locomotive was for 1870 almost what the atom bomb
became for 1945. Walt Whitman could see the engine as
"type of the modern—emblem of motion and power—pulse
of the continent," but "Gail Hamilton," speaking through
one small girl, "in the depths of her quaking heart . . . saw
. . . herself and all the family forced to rove homeless over
the world" when the railroad came. "The dear old trees had
to come down, and their dear old roots to come up. The dear
old pinks that had bloomed for unremembered years left their

last sweetness in the soil. All the robins' nests were rifled, and the robins did not know what to make of it." Nor, indeed, did the authoress, who took her meager solace in commending a stubborn mother goose for sitting undisturbed between the tracks while the locomotive passed her over. Even Trowbridge, delighted though he was by the wonders of the spectroscope and steel furnace, brought the flying machine of Darius Green to abrupt catastrophe in the barnyard.

Machine was mammon; God, as Thoreau had instructed, lived in nature. So said Lucy Larcom, alumna plenipotentiary of the *Lowell Offering,* whose favored heroine "danced with joy to the music that went echoing through the wide world, from the roots of the sprouting grass to the great golden blossom of the sun." Aldrich agreed, for "what fairy in all your romances / is such an enchantress as she / who blushes in roses and pansies / and sings in the birds on the tree?" Building castles high and fair, Longfellow kept his simple faith in mysteries that also enchanted Elizabeth Agassiz, who found the chapters of geological evolution linked from first to last by a transcendent intelligence. And Mrs. Stowe, setting precedents for Thornton Burgess and Walt Disney, made Mother Magpie and her friends among the frogs and squirrels anthropomorphic exemplars of the behavior dear to nature and to nature's God.

Children were not only to observe nature but to live in it. Dio Lewis found one young Suzy with pale face and shadowed eyes. He dressed her favorite rosebush in a suit of clothes, leaving it to become, like its mistress, pale and sickly. The lesson was clear: Suzy and the rosebush were to live out in the broad, genial sunshine together. She did, as did her siblings, and all became black as Indians, improved in health, for "the good Lord has so made children that they are as dependent upon the sun for their life and health as plants are." Miss Larcom gave the cult of fresh air a metric phrasing:

"White little housed-up things / why don't you run / out in the sun / Beauty that blossoms and sings / never was made / strong in the shade."

Important as it was, fresh air was not enough. To remain close to the soil, boys were to farm and girls to garden. For both sexes, exercise was also imperative. Addressing his "young fellow countrymen," Dio Lewis complimented them on the "great size" and "ceaseless activity" of their brains, on their "organizations for the spread of the Gospel, for temperance, for relief of the sick and wounded." But, he added, the "complete man" needed also a "healthy body. . . . Your weakness is in your bodies. Here lies your danger. I see nothing which distresses me so much as the physique of our children. . . . Great heads, beautiful faces, brilliant eyes; but with that attenuated neck, thin, flat chests, and languid gait." There was a proper way to stand, to lie, to sit and study, and especially to walk with "shoulders, head, and hips drawn well back, and the chest thrown forward. . . . I have seen the queens of the stage walk. I have seen a few girls and women of queenly bearing walk in the street and drawing-room. They move their arms in a free and graceful manner. . . . If I were asked what exercise I thought most effective for developing the chests of American girls, I should reply at once, *swinging the arms while walking.*" There is ample evidence that this admonition seared the minds of future Gibson girls.

The future Gibson boys were directed to athletics. "If you will show me what games, and with what vigor and resolution, the boys play," Charles J. Foster wrote, "I will tell you what energetic disposition the men bring to their business pursuits, and what degree of freedom and prosperity their nation enjoys." Exertion and exposure not only increased the muscles and expanded "the internal organs" but also fortified resolution and strengthened the will. Even in 1867 there was a model institution whose fame was long undiminished, for as one observer wrote, "the popularity of baseball" was immense, and "when two crack clubs play at Brooklyn . . . the multitude is so great that it is well into the night before the ferryboats have brought them all back to . . . New York."

Life out of doors was best of all when it tested the valor of a man. Afloat on a tropical stream, hunting big game in Africa, exploring the Arctic, climbing mountains, braving glaciers—these were the ultimate challenges of unspoiled nature, demanding nerve and sinew, building moral fiber while they tried the body. If the locomotive was a malign industrial symbol, the grizzly bear was the symbol of nature's ferity, the ideal opponent for the benign atavism of man. He who would most prove himself by his physical endeavor would stalk a grizzly with bow and arrow or, better yet, confront one with bare hands and unsheathed knife. The ablest and most daring were invited, now that the needs of war were gone, to transmute the simple cult of fresh air and swinging arms into the life of strenuosity. Here again the children listened, and from Victorian parlors there marched out the Edwardian conquerors of such wilds as remained, the Percivals whose grails became the beasts in any jungle save that of Henry James.

Nature and fresh air and strenuosity at once nurtured and revealed the virtues with which New England gave chase to the Prince of Darkness. In the interminable struggle against the temptations of the flesh and of the world, it was principle that counted. Assigning to the martyred Lincoln a Puritan soul and pedigree, New England found him "great because he was good." His silent lips instructed thus: "Do good, and love to do it, not for pleasure or reward, but because it is right before the eternal God; avoid all evil, and love to avoid it, not for fear or on account of punishment, but because it is sinful before the Lord and fit only for the devil and his angels."

There was good and there was bad; there was bravery and cowardice, love and force, liberty and tyranny. The child could be a Paul or be a Phillip, and fortunately the ingredients of character could be defined. Tip Top, one of Mrs. Stowe's anthropomorphic birds, succumbed to the guiles of a fawning feline. "So, Jamie," Mrs. Stowe warned, "remember, and don't try to be a man before your time, and let your parents judge for you while you are young; and never believe in any soft white pussy, with golden eyes, that comes and wants to tempt you to come down and play with her. If a big boy offers to teach you to smoke a cigar, that is Pussy. If a boy wants you to go into a billiard-saloon, that is Pussy. If a boy wants you to learn to drink anything with spirit in it, however sweetened and disguised, remember, Pussy is there; and Pussy's claws are long, and Pussy's teeth are strong; and if she gives you one shake in your youth, you will be like a broken-winged robin all your days."

The fragile virtue of Mrs. Stowe's world was best protected, as one Auntie put it to her Ethel, by "the armor Daniel wore in the lion's den." This kept grown-up women from wasting time altering the shape of a bonnet, leaving them instead the opportunity for "doing good to someone." If a young lady was gentle, soft-speaking, generous, truthful and obedient—Mary A. Dodge counseled—it made no difference how she dressed. Besides envy and worldliness, girls of character would abjure flirting, a "selfish and dangerous" habit— as Miss Dodge had perhaps learned sadly from John G. Whittier, and guard their honor, taking care always to be "ashamed to do that which you would be ashamed to confess having done."

Similarly, if a boy were brave, honest, manly, and polite, it made no difference if he had no pony. Indeed poverty seemed to "Gail Hamilton," Miss Dodge's pseudonym, "to be favorable to the best mental and moral training of the vast majority of persons." Through work man achieved contentment, even joy. William Allen Butler divided the field between "I Can" and "I Can't." "I Can't" was a dwarf, a poor, pale, puny imp, a sluggard, a coward, half fainting with fright. "I Can" was a giant, strong, skillful, the first in the field, seeking always a share "where labor is honest and wages are fair." Whittier warned in verse against self-love and in story against bragging of any fish until it was landed, for "it's no use to boast of anything until it's done, nor then either, for it speaks for itself."

The editors of *Our Young Folks* expressed total confidence in the uplifting quality of their journal and its message. According to one story, a bright lad altered the character of his community simply by subscribing to the magic periodical: "On Sundays especially they changed their style. Sunday had been a very bad day. . . . The men, not going to their regular work . . . and never going to church, got drunk, or played cards for money, or swapped horses. . . . These poor men were led to spending their time in this manner chiefly from having nothing else to do—which want is at the bottom of a world of mischief. . . . The children, too, were in danger of being drawn into these ill habits . . . through the vague weariness and sense of dull monotony which weighed upon them. . . . But when, instead of looking on at the Sunday rowdyism of the place, they improved their leisure time to sit down in any corner, where they could pore over the old numbers of their beloved magazine, or gather in an eager circle, where the last number was read aloud,—when they had this great resource, they kept away from the coarse noise which profaned the gracious day, and some influence stole from these quiet little groups even to shame and correct the elders."

In the world of *Our Young Folks* work and virtue made their own reward. There were families that starved on fifty acres, while others lived comfortably on one or two. Even in panning gold, only those who labored steadily and wasted not could husband what they mined. "We can do almost anything we keep trying to do," J. H. Browne maintained, pointing to his own success in traveling across Ohio in an aerial balloon.

The classic statement of the argument was by Horatio Alger, Jr., who in 1866 published his "How Johnny Bought a Sewing Machine." Johnny was the son of the Widow Cooper, who had lost her husband at Fredericksburg. Though the boy wanted to go to work, she insisted he remain at school while she sewed to supplement her pension. Determined to ease her lot by buying a sewing machine, Johnny labored after school and during weekends, picking cranberries at two cents a quart, running errands, turning the grindstone. He accumulated only $50 in a year, but he persevered. One morning, crossing the fields near a small pond, he heard a gentleman in a boat call out that his daughter was drowning. Unhesitatingly Johnny plunged in and seized the child as she sank for the third time. The grateful father pressed upon the boy a $100 bill. "Now," Johnny cried, "I can buy Mother a sewing machine." Then the whole story spilled out. The girl's father arranged to purchase the machine and have it sent to Johnny's mother in time for her birthday. When it arrived, "her eyes glistened with pride and joy as she heard, for the first time, how [Johnny] . . . had worked for months." He did not know it, but the machine had cost lots more than $100. More marvelous still, he received a letter from his benefactor containing $100 for himself. "Continue to love and help your mother," it read, "and when you are old enough to go into a store I will receive you into mine." There was, Alger concluded, great joy in the little cottage that evening. Doubtless Alger felt the joy himself, for in ensuing years he altered his plot only to extend it far enough to permit his Johnnies to wed the girls they saved from death.

It paid those who won the boss's daughter to be generous. The gospel of wealth grew alongside of the cult of success, and the stories in *Our Young Folks* assured little readers that when Willy and Suzy gave up their Christmas presents in order to buy a tree and turkey for the poor, their father was bound by New Year's to produce the cap and drum, the doll and candy they thought they had relinquished. In the same vein, plucky Charlie unselfishly spent his Fourth of July money to buy shoes for an impoverished but deserving girl in his class at school, and shortly thereafter, on the sixth of that very July, the child's father returned from Australia "with the fortune he had been seeking, and on learning of Charlie's kindness he went out . . . and bought a wonderful brass cannon, and a box of marvelous soldiers with . . . all the . . . accessories for a grand army."

Though one did good for the sake of God, then, and not for the sake of reward, reward tended to follow good. There were even a few tricks for self-help. Edward Everett Hale published a series of how-to-do-it articles on talking and writing and entering society. "Right and wrong depend much more on the spirit than on the manner in which the thing is done," he wrote, but "we shall not make many blunders if we live by the four rules they painted on the four walls" of a club house in Detroit (rules redolent with the spirit of Chambers of Commerce to come): "1. Look up, and not down. 2. Look forward, and not backward. 3. Look out, and not in. 4. Lend a hand."

The lesson was writ so plain that one fifteen-year-old reader from Davenport, Iowa, while dutifully noting that the brightest scholars came often from the families of the poor and uneducated, added rather plaintively that the "tendency to drive ahead" was so strong that boys no longer had much "time to be boys." Perhaps they had never had, but certainly the incipient Edwardians were heavily put upon. Santayana, who lived with them, summed it up well: "Irreligion, dissoluteness, and pessimism—supposed naturally to go together—could never prosper; they were incompatible with efficiency. That was the supreme test. 'Be Christians,' I once heard a president of Yale College cry to his assembled pupils, 'be Christians and you will be successful.' "

So also preached the Titaness and her brothers. In a world they no longer really understood or really liked, their incantations soothed anxiety and nostalgia. New England dared not let the war and the changes that attended it register their awful tremors in the conscience of New England's children. The Puritans and their seed had made America, *Our Young Folks* testified: possess the Puritan virtues and struggle on, out of the Slough of modern Despond to success and further glory.

What the children learned they carried with them through their lives. Much of social Darwinism confirmed the lesson. More often than not, as the century moved on, the habits and manners of the newly powerful in industry and of their associates in politics seemed by contrast to enforce the definition Mrs. Stowe had given character. There was a good deal of *Our Young Folks* in the Social Gospel, a good deal of it in progressivism and in the psyches of the voters who accepted Roosevelt and Wilson, consummate moralists, as their spokesman. Continuity in history lies in some measure between the generations, and what the Victorians taught their children, those children retained.

3

THEODORE ROOSEVELT: POWER AND ORDER*

1. The Man

THEODORE ROOSEVELT was born in 1858, the second child of parents who provided him and his siblings with the advantages of their station and the support of their love. Younger than his sister Anna, he was older than his constant childhood playmates, his brother Elliott and his sister Corinne.

Their mother, Martha Bullock Roosevelt, with her dark hair and "moonlight-white" complexion, her melodious southern voice and her vivacious southern charm, adored her family as they adored her. Corinne recalled her mother's devotion "which wrapped us round as with a mantle"; Elliott thought of her as his "sweet little China Dresden" mother; Anna spoke of her "darling little mother's exquisite beauty"; Theodore referred to her as his "sweet Motherling." That she was, but she was also incapable of discharging even the limited duties expected of ladies of her breeding. "I never exactly

*From *The Republican Roosevelt,* 2nd ed. (Cambridge, MA: Harvard University Press, 1977), pp. xii–xix, 106–24.

keep my appointments," she wrote in a coy understatement of her constant tardiness. She could neither manage her household nor keep its accounts, tasks that her husband turned over to Anna when she was only fourteen. Martha Roosevelt was compulsively clean, given to taking two baths—one for washing and one for rinsing, eager to shield her person from dirt, even her knees while she prayed. Her health, in the phrase of her children and their day, was "delicate," but she was sufficiently robust to enjoy travel and parties and riding. If she was neurotic, her family never said so. Except as a loving wife and mother, no small role, she was simply ineffective.

"Don't be too hard on me," Martha Roosevelt once wrote her husband. Her older son was not. He never criticized his mother, and like the rest of her children, even before his father's death, he felt protective toward her. Obviously he recognized her inadequacies. Throughout his life he kept his appointments, managed his affairs, and let neither sweat nor dirt stay in the least his exuberant adventures. He may also have felt subconsciously about her, as he came to conclude openly about so many others, that her failures—at best her idiosyncrasies—stemmed from the want of strength and the will to expunge them. In that event hers was a flawed character, a possibility he would have been loathe to admit even to himself.

Roosevelt's father, in contrast, provided the example of character and purpose that his son strove always and ardently to emulate. Theodore Roosevelt Sr., a patrician and sophisticate, was gregarious, at home with nature, a devout Christian who witnessed through his good works, a "fine disciplinarian," and a steady support for his children. His young son Theodore, "sickly, delicate," asthmatic, found relief in the arms of his father who often walked him for hours at night until the boy's breathing became regular again. Whether or not the asthma was psychogenic, the method of relief was effective. So was the sympathetic discipline. "You have the mind," the father told his frail and precocious eleven-year-old, "but you have not the body. . . . You must *make* your body." And the boy, as the story was later told, set his jaw and answered: *"I'll make my body";* and he did. His father, Theodore Roosevelt recalled in his autobiography, "was the best man I ever knew," and "the only man of whom I was ever really afraid."

"I never knew anyone who got greater joy out of living than did my father," Roosevelt also wrote, "or anyone who more wholeheartedly performed every duty; and no one whom I ever met approached his combination of enjoyment of life and performance of duty." (Roosevelt's own children were to say much the same of him.) He was not gilding his recollections. While he was at Harvard he wrote his father that "I am *sure* that there is no one who has a father who is also his best and most intimate friend, as you are mine." When the elder Roosevelt died of cancer less than two years later, his son recorded in his diary his "dull, inert sorrow." In a letter to a friend, he described the few days after his father's death as "a hideous dream. Father has always been so much with me that it seems as if a part of my life had been taken away." He would still *"feel* his presence," he told his sister. He always felt it, because of his love and, as he suggested, perhaps because of his fear. That presence instructed him to go on, in spite of his sorrow, with his studies. It instructed him to control his feelings and to control himself as he had taken control of his body.

The descent from love and joy to loss and grief must rend the human heart. When his father died, Roosevelt responded with an act of the will that blocked the enervation that he, like his father, would have called weak and maudlin, the anger that he had learned to restrain. That response must have cost him more than he was conditioned to recognize or to confess. Because it was for him the right response, he would not count the cost, even when life dealt him another, more shocking blow.

Roosevelt was beginning his junior year at Harvard when he "first saw her . . . and loved her as soon as I saw her sweet, young face." She was Alice Lee, the seventeen year old daughter of a prominent Boston family, a young woman in Roosevelt's eyes "beautiful in face and form, and lovelier still in spirit." Her many beaus agreed but fell away as Roosevelt pressed his courtship until Alice agreed to be his bride. "I am so happy that I dare not trust my own happiness," he then wrote. ". . . It was nearly eight months since I had first proposed to her, and I had been nearly crazy during the past year. . . . How she, so pure and sweet and beautiful, can think of marrying me I cannot understand, but I praise and thank God it is so."

They were married on October 27, 1880, in the autumn following his graduation, on his twenty-second birthday. She was just nineteen. After a delayed honeymoon, they set up housekeeping in New York City. Her gracefulness won the affection not only of their friends but also of his less polished new companions in the New York State Assembly. In 1884, expecting her first child, Alice moved in with her mother-in-law, and since the assembly was in session, awaited the week-end visits of her doting husband. On February 12, 1884, her child was born, a girl, also Alice, and at first the mother seemed well. But when Roosevelt, who left Albany in high spirits upon receiving the news, arrived at his home, Alice, a victim of Bright's disease, could barely recognize him. She died that night. Earlier within the day, by an awful coincidence, so had Roosevelt's mother.

"We spent three years of happiness," Roosevelt wrote in his memorial to Alice, "such as rarely comes to man or woman. . . . As a flower she grew, and as a fair young flower she died.

Her life had been always in the sunshine. . . . None ever knew her who did not love and revere her for her bright, sunny temper and her saintly unselfishness. Fair, pure, and joyous as a maiden; loving, tender and happy as a young wife; when she had first become a mother, when her life seemed to be but just begun . . . by a strange and terrible fate, death came to her. And when my heart's dearest died, the light went from my life forever."

But not, in spite of his great hurt, the will, the control. Two days after Alice's funeral he decided to "come back to my work at once." A day later he returned to his seat in the assembly. Three weeks after Alice's death he replied to a note of condolence from a friend: "It was a grim and evil fate, but I have never believed it did any good to flinch or yield for any blow, nor does it lighten the blow to cease from working." And then an unbroken silence about Alice. He did not speak about her again, even to her daughter. He did not mention her in his autobiography. Years later, in a letter to a sister whose daughter's fiancé had died, Roosevelt delivered the advice he had clearly given himself: "The one and only thing for her to do now is to treat the past as past, the event as finished and out of her life; to dwell on it . . . would be both weak and morbid. Let her try not to think of it; this she cannot wholly avoid; but she can wholly avoid speaking of it . . . let her never speak one word of the matter . . . to you or to anyone else."

That counsel, like his own behavior, reached beyond mere self-control to obsessive self-denial. In the face of the unpredictable, the chaos that could visit life with pain, Roosevelt's love had not protected Alice. Yet he retained his zest for living, he even came to love again, for first he denied that pain by driving it out of mind. He denied that chaos by willing an artificial but an orderly control. Few others could have done so; perhaps fewer still have wanted so to do.

Years before Alice died, Roosevelt had had to begin to observe his younger brother surrender self-control. Elliott Roosevelt had been a strong, agile, beguiling child, afflicted by none of Theodore's physical frailties. When both boys were small, Elliott served sometimes as Theodore's protector. They remained companions in their youth. When Elliott visited Theodore at Harvard, he could, Theodore wrote, beat his older brother at rowing, swimming, and sailing. He may also, so one friend surmised, have been overwhelmed by an older brother who "thought he could do things a little better than anyone else." Yet Elliott, Theodore wrote at that time, was "a noble fellow, wonderfully grown-up in every way." That fond assessment was disingenuous, for Elliott was already behaving in ways Theodore at first joked about but never approved. In the summer of 1880 the two went hunting in the west. "Elliott," Theodore reported to Corinne from Chicago, "revels in . . . epicurean pleasures. As soon as we got here he took some ale to get the dust out of his throat; then a milk punch because he was thirsty; a mint julep because it was hot; a brandy smash 'to keep the cold out of his stomach'; and then sherry and bitters to give him an appetite."

Elliott was an alcoholic. He had earlier begun to escape life in other ways. At St. Paul's School in 1875, he was studying, he said, "as hard as I can," but he suffered "a bad rush of blood to my head" that left him "rather nervous and therefore homesick and unhappy," and Theodore had to come up "to take him home." Sent to regain his health at a frontier post in Texas, Elliott found that roughing it left him still unable to apply himself systematically: "I feel," he admitted, "like a general fraud." After his father's death he drifted, repentant but unreliable in spite of his marriage to Anna Hall, a wealthy New York beauty. He foundered in an effort at banking, but he frolicked at the hunt on Long Island and there lived extravagantly and rode recklessly and to exhaustion. "Poor, dear old Nell," Theodore wrote Corinne in 1889; "I suppose it is useless to wish that he would put himself completely under a competent physician; I did my best to get him to." "I wonder," he asked on another occasion, "if it would do any good to talk to him about his imprudence! I suppose not."

Elliott now drank excessively and when necessary surreptitiously, became violent, frightening to his family. His wife, assisted by Anna Roosevelt, confined him to an asylum for six months of treatment in 1891. The family, hoping to protect the balance of his estate, applied to the courts to have him judged insane and incapable of managing his property. Theodore in his affidavit attested that since 1889 he had observed Elliott's loss of memory and irrational behavior. Elliott had even threatened three times to commit suicide. When Elliott fought the suit, Theodore went to meet him in Paris. Elliott then reluctantly agreed, in return for termination of the proceedings, to put his estate in trust for his wife and children, and to return to the United States to undertake another "cure."

Elliott's deterioration quickened after his return. In Paris he had taken up with a woman, a liaison Theodore never discussed but surely despised. Separated from his wife, Elliott wrote her now conciliatory, now threatening letters. He was not allowed to be with her when she died in December 1892. Her will made her mother, not Elliott, guardian of her children, a decision Theodore endorsed, for Elliott, he had concluded, was irremediably irresponsible. Elliott's continuing erratic behavior, his affair with a woman in New York not the least, served to confirm that judgment. "He can't be helped," Theodore wrote Anna in July 1894, "and he simply must be let go his own gait. He is now laid up from a serious fall; while drunk he drove into a lamp post and went out on his head." A month later a further letter reported, "Elliott is up and about again: and I hear is drinking heavily; if so he must break down soon. It has been as hideous a tragedy all through as one often sees." Two years later Elliott fell again, was knocked unconscious, and died. Theodore, as he wrote Corinne, felt a great relief: "There is one great comfort I already feel; I only need to have pleasant thoughts of Elliott now. He is just the gallant, generous, manly boy and young man whom everyone loved. I can think of him . . . the time we were first in Europe . . . and then in the days of the dancing class . . . or when . . . he first hunted; and when he visited me at Harvard."

Roosevelt had observed Elliott as a drunkard, as an unfaithful husband, as a feckless father. Their mother had been harmlessly ineffective because of her idiosyncrasies, her small weaknesses of the will. Elliott had become a disgrace because of his total failure of the will. He had let himself go entirely out of control. No one could explain why. His daughter Eleanor and his Paris mistress believed, probably correctly, that more sympathy from his family would have helped him. But Theodore Roosevelt never sympathized with weakness, not weakness in his brother any more than weakness in himself.

As much as Alice's death, Elliott's disintegration also underscored the uncertainties of life. As love had not protected Alice, so good blood and good breeding had not saved Elliott. By permitting his standards to decay, Elliott had abandoned his duty to order the vagaries of experience. So, at least, Theodore seemed to believe. The terror of private excesses, he also seemed to suggest, resembled the terror of social excesses. Elliott's life, writ large, recalled the chaos of the French revolution. Its leaders, in Roosevelt's view destructive renegades, had lost control of themselves just as Elliott had lost control. Those fit to govern, those fit to hold the power that checked the potential chaos of social experience, had first to govern themselves, to check the potential chaos of private experience.

"Buck-fever," Roosevelt wrote in his autobiographical discussion of hunting, meant "a state of intense nervous excitement which may be entirely divorced from timidity. It may affect a man the first time he has to speak to a large audience just as it affects him the first time he sees a buck or goes into battle. What such a man needs is not courage but nerve-control, cool-headedness . . . this is largely a matter . . . of repeated effort and repeated exercise of will-power. If a man has the right stuff in him, his will grows stronger and stronger with each exercise of it." Roosevelt's did.

2. The President

"THE word happiness," Lionel Trilling has proposed, "stands at the very center" of liberal thought. It is a word which Theodore Roosevelt used rarely when speaking of himself and almost never when referring to other people. This was not an accident. Roosevelt concerned himself not with happiness but with hard work, duty, power, order. These conditions he valued not as prerequisites for some ultimate happiness but as ends in themselves. All interrelated, they blanketed myriad specifics. Hard work involved, among other things, an identity with task, whether the mining of coal or the writing of history; it was a part of duty and a preliminary of order. Duty demanded alike service to the nation, productive labor, and devoted attention to family. It demanded also physical and intellectual courage, honesty, and constancy. These qualities can produce frightening obstacles to personal happiness. There is a story that Roosevelt, more than two years after the death of his first wife, while contemplating his second marriage, for three days paced in a small guest room of a friend's home, pounding one fist into the other palm, expostulating the while to himself: "I have no constancy. I have no constancy." Not even in love was Roosevelt a liberal.

Roosevelt's politics, certainly, pertained not at all to happiness. There was none of Bentham, none of Mill in his public pronouncements or his private letters. Like those more reflective men, Roosevelt had a good deal of difficulty in defining his beliefs, but manifestly he believed in power and in order. With power he sought to impose order; only with order, he contended, could there be morality.

Because after his fortieth year Roosevelt experienced no major change of thought, all this, inherent in his early thinking, contained the substance of his behavior as President. But during his Presidency he came better to understand himself, and with this new understanding he formalized, candidly and rather consistently, the principles that underlay his purpose. Distinct long before Herbert Croly wrote his *Promise of American Life,* these principles in 1912 provided Roosevelt with a rationalization, indeed with some motivation, for his devastating departure from the Republican party. Consequently they merit analysis not only in themselves but also as a measure of the conduct of the man.

Roosevelt began with power. Attaining it, he appreciated the chase and the reward. "There inheres in the Presidency," he observed, "more power than in any other office in any great republic or constitutional monarchy of modern times. . . ." "I believe," he added, "in a strong executive; I believe in power. . . ." This conclusion Roosevelt fortified with Hegelian conviction. The animal energy of that "bore as big as a buffalo" that so distressed Henry Adams provided the very force on which Roosevelt unerringly relied. Heroes, he knew, were not made by epigrams. His audiences of "townspeople, . . . of rough-coated, hard-headed, gaunt, sinewy

farmers . . . their wives and daughters and . . . children.
. . ," he sensed, "for all the superficial differences between
us, down at bottom" had "the same ideals. . . ." "I am always
sure of reaching them," he confided to John Hay, "in speeches
which many of my Harvard friends would think not only
homely, but commonplace." "The people who believed in me
and trusted me and followed me. . . ," Roosevelt asserted,
felt that "I was the man of all others whom they wished to
see President." Such confidence sustained heroic moods.

Every executive officer, in particular the President, Roosevelt maintained, "was a steward of the people bound actively
and affirmatively to do all he could for the people. . . ." He
held therefore that, unless specifically forbidden by the Constitution or by law, the President had "to do anything that
the needs of the nation demanded. . . ." "Under this interpretation of executive power," he recalled, "I did and caused
to be done many things not previously done . . . I did not
usurp power, but I did greatly broaden the use of executive
power." To this interpretation, Roosevelt confessed, his temperament compelled him. So, of course, did his profession;
elected or appointed, the bureaucrat would exalt his valleys.
Realizing this, the second Charles Francis Adams feared a
regulatory bureaucracy as much as he despised the competitive confusion it was intended to stabilize. Not so Roosevelt.
He broadened power precisely for the purpose of establishing
order.

Throughout his life, Roosevelt displayed a morbid fear of
social violence which, he seemed to feel, lay ominously on
the margin of normal political life. He convinced himself
that William Jennings Bryan, Eugene V. Debs, the Socialist
leader, and Wild Bill Haywood of the Industrial Workers of
the World had inherited the mission of Marat and Robespierre. This was not just campaign hyperbole. In season and
out, with wearing repetition he discovered the Jacobin in

each dissenter of his time. To their evil he apposed a twin, the evil of those "malefactors of great wealth" who on lower Broadway held their court of Louis XVI. Unleashed, the energies of these extremes could in conflict wreck society. They had therefore to be curtailed.

To modulate the threatening conflict Roosevelt in part relied upon that indefinite composite which he called national character. He meant by this not only personal morality but also the conglutinations that history prepared, the accepted traditions of political and social behavior by which people imposed order on themselves. Yet these traditions, he recognized, depended heavily upon material conditions which in the twentieth century were changing rapidly. The change Roosevelt welcomed; he foresaw more strength than danger in the new industrialism. But it demanded, he realized, concomitant political changes whose contours tradition could not draw.

If self-imposed order was in his time no longer to be anticipated, it had to be provided from above. This called for strong, disinterested government equipped to define, particularly for a powerful executive prepared to enforce, the revised rules under which the America of immense corporations, of enormous cities, of large associations of labor and farmers could in orderly manner resolve its conflicts. Definition and enforcement were needed at once, for within the lifetime of Roosevelt's older contemporaries social relations had changed "far more rapidly than in the preceding two centuries." The ensuing weaknesses in traditional political behavior strained the fabric of personal morality. In the United States of 1908, the President remarked in his perceptive last annual message to Congress, "the chief breakdown is in dealing with the new relations that arise from the mutualism, the interdependence of our time. Every new social relation begets a new type of wrong-doing—of sin, to use an old-fashioned word—and many years always elapse before society is able to turn this sin into crime which can be effectively punished at law."

Through mutualism itself Roosevelt hoped to stabilize social arrangements. His recommendations were designed first to create a political environment favorable to social and economic combinations which, he believed, the nation needed, and second, ordinarily through responsible administrative agencies, to prescribe the rules for the operation of those combinations. American industry afforded a salubrious example of "the far-reaching, beneficent work" which combination had already accomplished. In steel alone a Spencerian progression from the simple heterogeneous to the complex homogeneous suggested the almost limitless possibilities of power and productivity. Such a progression, Roosevelt believed, neither should nor could be arrested. But it had to be disciplined. Combinations in industry, susceptible as they were to the temptations of unbridled power, had to be made responsible through government to the whole people. They had, furthermore, to be balanced by other, also responsible combinations, voluntarily formed to promote the efficiency of less well organized parts of society. "This is an era," Roosevelt preached, "of federation and combination. . . ."

"A simple and poor society," he later postulated, "can exist as a democracy on a basis of sheer individualism. But a rich and complex industrial society cannot so exist; for some individuals, and especially those artificial individuals called corporations, become so very big that the ordinary individual . . . cannot deal with them on terms of equality. It therefore becomes necessary for these ordinary individuals to combine in their turn, first in order to act in their collective capacity through that biggest of all combinations called the government, and second, to act, also in their own self-defense, through private combinations, such as farmers' associations and trade-unions."

Attempting as he did to apply this doctrine to agriculture, labor and industry, Roosevelt envisioned an equilibrium of consolidated interests over which government would preside. To the farmer his purpose appealed least. Roosevelt was, after all, primarily an eastern, urban man. He had never fully understood the dreadful anxieties that underlay the agrarian movements of the 1890s or the deficiencies in national banking and credit arrangements that aggravated farm finance. He developed his program, furthermore, at a time when agricultural prosperity tended to obscure even for farmers the continuing weaknesses of their situation. Nevertheless, much of his advice was sound.

"Farmers must learn," Roosevelt proposed, "the vital need of co-operation with one another. Next to this comes co-operation with the government, and the government can best give its aid through associations of farmers rather than through the individual farmer. . . . It is greatly to be wished . . . that associations of farmers could be organized, primarily for business purposes, but also with social ends in view. . . . The people of our farming regions must be able to combine among themselves, as the most efficient means of protecting their industry from the highly organized interests which now surround them on every side. A vast field is open for work by co-operative associations of farmers in dealing with the relation of the farm to transportation and to the distribution and manufacture of raw materials. It is only through such combination that American farmers can develop to the full their economic and social power."

Through the Department of Agriculture, within the restrictive limits of its budget and authority, Roosevelt promoted farm co-operatives. To the recommendations of farm associations about changes in national transportation policy he gave a sympathetic hearing. "To ascertain what are the general, economic, social, educational, and sanitary conditions of the open country, and what, if anything, the farmers themselves can do to help themselves, and how the Government can help them," he appointed in 1908 the Country Life Commission. The report of this commission, although ignored by a Congress which refused even to appropriate funds for its printing, was a landmark in national thinking about the melioration of almost every aspect of rural life. To it, as to Roosevelt's own counsel, federal administrations later profitably returned.

Roosevelt intended that farm life should become increasingly institutionalized. While he urged this, he expected the farmers voluntarily to form their own organizations. Still the most individualistic-minded of Americans, they proceeded slowly. He could not command them, as he advised them, to exploit more fully the bicycle and the telephone; he could not force them to emulate the marketing co-operatives of Denmark. Consequently the immediate results of his advice were negligible. When he acted himself, however, instead of simply urging them to act, he accomplished more. His employment of the strength of the government, especially of his office, imposed upon the country a conservation policy from which the farmers, however much they disliked it at the time, ultimately benefited.

Roosevelt sponsored conservation not so much to preserve a domain for agriculture as to preserve and enhance the strength of the whole nation. He was inspired not by farmers and ranchers but by intellectuals and interested commercial groups. Nevertheless, in effect his policy organized an essential element of prosperous rural existence. This it did directly through the irrigation act which compelled its beneficiaries to mutualism. Indirectly, Roosevelt's public power policy, resisting uncontrolled exploitation of water power sites, began to reserve control of power for the federal government. Through government agencies, interests of agriculture could be con-

solidated and advanced. By "planned and orderly development"—"essential to the best use of every natural resource"—
these agencies could define and attain objectives which farmers' organizations, even if they had had the perspicacity to
define, lacked the authority to attain. The varied purposes of
his power policy, the need to restrain the haphazard and selfish methods of private direction, and the inadequacies of voluntary associations alike persuaded the President that for orderly
development order had to be established from above.

Much more favorably than did the farmers, American labor
responded to Roosevelt's doctrine of federation and combination. Agrarian spokesmen at the turn of the century, still
anti-monopolists in their orientation, proposed to solve the
trust problem by disintegrating industrial combinations. The
representatives of organized labor, on the contrary, intended
to live with big business by bargaining with it. The general
secretary of the United Garment Workers, the head of the
United Mine Workers, and the president of the American
Federation of Labor, among others, accepting the consolidation of industry as inevitable and salutary, sought to lead
labor to comparable consolidations and to persuade government to protect the processes of combination and negotiation. Roosevelt spoke, therefore, to a receptive audience when
he maintained that labor should reap "the benefits of organization," that wageworkers had "an entire right to organize"
and "a legal right . . . to refuse to work in company with
men who decline to join their organizations."

Repeatedly Roosevelt acted upon this principle. He drew
upon the advice of the leaders of the railroad brotherhoods
and the American Federation of Labor in fashioning his recommendations to Congress for legislation to govern the hours
and working conditions of women and children, to extend
the eight-hour day, to provide for comprehensive employers'
liability, and to improve railroad safety precautions. During

the most celebrated strike of his term in office, his intercession defended the right of the anthracite miners to bargain
collectively. Continually he endeavored to restrict the use of
injunctions, the most formidable weapon against labor. The
court's order prohibiting boycotting in the Buck's Case he
criticized severely; he ordered the Justice Department to assist
an iron molders' local whose strike had been enjoined. There
must, Roosevelt insisted, "be no . . . abuse of the injunctive
power as is implied in forbidding laboring men to strive for
their own betterment in peaceful and lawful ways; nor must
the injunction be used merely to aid some big corporation
. . . a preliminary injunction in a labor case, if granted without adequate proof . . . may often settle the dispute . . . and
therefore if improperly granted may do irreparable wrong . . .
I earnestly commend . . . that some way may be devised
which will limit the abuse of injunctions and protect those
rights which from time to time it unwarrantably invades."

Encouraged to bargain, allowed to strike, the union was
to consolidate the interests of labor. This had value for Roosevelt insofar as it promoted efficiency and order. But some
unions, like the syndicalist Industrial Workers of the World,
cultivated violence; some labor leaders, like the socialist Debs,
defending these unions, seemed to Roosevelt to court revolution. To handle such cases, he believed it "wrong altogether to prohibit the use of injunctions," for "there must be
no hesitation in dealing with disorder."

The measure of order, difficult at best, Roosevelt would
not leave to the judiciary. During and immediately after his
tenure, the courts granted injunctions indiscriminately and
nullified much of the labor legislation he considered necessary
and just. Underwriting as they did the status quo, they prevented the very changes upon which, he felt, a new social
equilibrium depended. It was judicial interpretation of labor
law that motivated Roosevelt finally to propose the recall of

judicial decisions, a system which referred the interpretation of the needs of society to a momentary majority of the people. Conversely, Roosevelt was impatient with the legal impediments to silencing a Debs or a Haywood. Order for him was order. If a man incited violence, if he only endeavored to incite violence, indeed if he merely defended the prerogative of another man to incite violence, Roosevelt yearned at once to stamp him underfoot.

In dealing with radical newspapers and with the syndicalist Western Federation of Miners, Roosevelt, assuming the prerogatives of a steward of the people, decreed from his high office dicta of order with which many peaceable men could not conscientiously agree. By the same standard, while President he initiated a criminal libel suit—a suit presuming an offense against the United States—against a publisher who had criticized him, and he kept in prison without legal sanction a petty criminal who had violated not a law but his concept of the right. Such lawless uses of power, however meritorious or moral their intent, undermined the traditional principles of restraint upon which American order had been built. This created a danger that labor leaders recognized. They had too often been the victims of arbitrary power— ordinarily industrial rather than political—to trust completely any man who proposed himself to decide when their contests were safe and when they were not.

Labor had other reservations about Roosevelt. Just short of the full meaning of his preachments he stopped. On the issue of injunctions, he retreated in 1908 when the Republican National Convention did. William Jennings Bryan, Louis D. Brandeis and for a while Woodrow Wilson made no such forced marches. Furthermore, Roosevelt's doctrine of consolidation did not quite possess him. He would consolidate for order and also to establish the prescriptions for morality. But in the end he measured morality by the individual. "The chief factor in the success of each man—," he asserted, "wageworker, farmer, and capitalist alike—must ever be the sum total of his own individual qualities and abilities. Second only to this comes the power of acting in combination or association with others." He judged on this basis that the "legal right" of wageworkers "to refuse to work in company with men who decline to join their organizations" might or might not, "according to circumstances," be a "moral right." There fell the union shop. Roosevelt reserved to himself definition of the moral right. He sustained the open shop in the Government Printing Office because he did not consider the circumstances a proper legal or moral basis for unionization. Where could he or his successor be expected next to draw the line?

The farmer could at once agree with Roosevelt about the primacy of individual qualities. The industrialist, protected by the legal fiction that a corporation—whatever its size—was an individual, could accept this dictum. Not so the labor leader. If the union did not contain every interested individual, its position relative to management suffered, and its victories benefited neutral noncontributors. This for labor leaders was a question not of morality but of money and of power. The President's ambivalence confused their issue.

In Roosevelt's program the farm community found discomforting unfamiliarity; about it union labor entertained anxious doubts. Businessmen were more enthusiastic, for from industry and transportation Roosevelt took his model. With accelerating tempo for two generations men of business had made consolidation their instrument not only of profits but also, more significantly, of order. Abandoning the insecurity and debilitation of competition, the enterprising in rails, steel, oil, copper, tobacco, sugar, salt—the list seems endless— had, after strife, in each industry organized stable structures. Their own achievement they admired. It was, they testified at symposiums on trusts, to congressional committees, in essays, memoirs and commencement addresses, the necessary and efficient way of business life, perhaps the only way of any life. With few exceptions they wished to have their institutions left alone. Here only did Roosevelt disagree. Because the consolidations were capable of doing much that was bad as well as much that was good, they had to be supervised. But they were not to be destroyed. "In curbing and regulating the combinations of capital which are . . . injurious. . . . ," he instructed Congress in his second annual message, "we must be careful not to stop the great enterprises which have legitimately reduced the cost of production, not to abandon the place which our country has won in the leadership of the international industrial world. . . ."

Again and again during his Presidency Roosevelt made the distinction between size and behavior that characterized his speeches of 1912 on the regulation of industry. For the orderly system of control in which he believed he first shaped his railroad policy. In developing that policy, he announced his preference for supervised pooling as an efficient regulatory device. Enlarging his thesis, he asserted late in 1911 that "nothing of importance is gained by breaking up a huge inter-State and international industrial organization *which has not offended otherwise than by its size*. . . . Those who would seek to restore the days of unlimited and uncontrolled competition . . . are attempting not only the impossible, but what, if possible, would be undesirable." "Business cannot be successfully conducted," he wrote in the same article, "in accordance with the practices and theories of sixty years ago unless we abolish steam, electricity, big cities, and, in short, not only all modern business and modern industrial conditions, but all the modern conditions of our civilization." This statement recognized associationalism as being as much a part of modern life as were the physical conditions that compelled it. Roosevelt also realized that, just as government could best supply a "planned and orderly development" of natural resources, so was oligopoly distinguished by its ability to provide experts to plan and to allocate from profits adequate resources to implement their plans—by its ability, therefore, to keep order without stultification.

But business had "to be controlled in the interest of the general public" and this could be accomplished in only one way—"by giving adequate power of control to the one sovereignty capable of exercising such power—the National Government." As an initial means for this control Roosevelt led Congress to establish the Bureau of Corporations. In his long struggle for the Hepburn Act he went considerably further. He next concluded and soon specifically proposed that "what is needed is the creation of a Federal administrative body with full power to do for ordinary inter-State industrial business carried on on a large scale what the Inter-State Commerce Commission now does for inter-State transportation business."

After leaving the Presidency, in the columns of *The Outlook* Roosevelt elaborated his plan. He would "regulate big corporations in thoroughgoing and effective fashion, so as to help legitimate business as an incident to thoroughly and completely safeguarding the interests of the people as a whole." The antitrust law, designed and interpreted "to restore business to the competitive conditions of the middle of the last century," could not "meet the whole situation." Size did indeed "make a corporation fraught with potential menace to the community," but the community could "exercise through its administrative . . . officers a strict supervision . . . to see that it does not go wrong," "to insure . . . business skill being exercised in the interest of the public. . . ."

Criticizing the suit initiated by the Taft Administration against the United States Steel Corporation, and deploring the vagueness of the Supreme Court's "rule of reason" in the Standard Oil and tobacco cases, Roosevelt explained how "continuous administrative action" might operate. The commission to regulate corporations was to have the power to regulate the issue of securities, thereby to prevent overcapitalization; to compel publicity of accounts, thereby to reveal the detailed techniques of business procedures; and to investigate any business activity. If investigation disclosed the existence of monopoly—of a consolidation that could control the prices and productivity of an industry—the commission was to have two alternatives. If unethical practices had produced monopoly—Roosevelt cited the oil and tobacco industries as examples of this—the monopoly should be dissolved under the Sherman Act. If, however, the monopoly resulted from natural growth—Roosevelt had in mind the United States Steel Corporation and the International Harvester Company—the commission was to control it by setting maximum prices for its products, just as the Interstate Commerce Commission set maximum freight rates. This was not all. Believing that administrative control should "indirectly or directly extend to . . . all questions connected with . . . [the] treatment of . . . employees," he proposed that the commission should have authority over hours, wages, and other conditions of labor.

Within each industry, then, consolidation was to establish order; acting in the public interest, the federal executive was to insure equity in this order. This fitted the grand scheme. It also offered to farm and labor groups, through the presumed disinterestedness of government, a countervailing force against the most advanced and, at that time, least controlled social group. By consolidation and administration Roosevelt would punish sin and achieve stability. To discipline consolidation, to make possible administration, his first requisite was power. The cycle was complete.

The question remains of how well this arrangement could be expected to function. Even a sampling of evidence suggests that it raised problems as large as those it presumed to solve. There was, for one, the problem of the natural growth of industrial combinations. Roosevelt considered it, in general terms, desirable. He believed, clearly, that an administrative agency could better judge what was natural growth than could the courts. Furthermore, as his relations with his Attorneys General and his directions to the chairman of the Interstate Commerce Commission indicate, he had considerable confidence in his own capacity to make administrative decisions pertinent to transportation and industry. How then explain the suit against the Northern Securities Company? The defendants in that case had by forming a holding company combined into a potentially efficient regional system the basic units of railway transportation in the Northwest. Railways had for decades been consolidating, naturally enough in the logic of railroad economics. The Northern Securities combination restored financial order among the rivals it merged and seemed capable of becoming a useful part of an orderly, integrated transportation network. Yet in 1902 Roosevelt proceeded against it. One suspects that he would have done so even if the I.C.C. at that time had had the authority to set maximum rates.

Two major considerations apparently motivated Roosevelt. First, the farmers of the Northwest and their local political representatives wanted the holding company dissolved. It was good politics for Roosevelt to attack it. Second, as Roosevelt recalled in his autobiography, "the absolutely vital question" of "whether the government had power to control [corporations] . . . at all . . . had not yet been decided. . . . A decision of the Supreme Court [in the E. C. Knight case] had, with seeming definiteness, settled that the National Government had not the power." "This decision," Roosevelt continued, alluding to his prosecution of the Northern Securities Company, "I caused to be annulled. . . ." He attacked to establish the government's power, for the while his power; he selected a corporation indisputably engaged in interstate commerce; he deliberately chose to charge a hill made vulnerable by popular opinion. Particularly when used by a man who has and loves power, such criteria may become terrifying.

This possibility Roosevelt intended partially to avoid by his reliance upon experts. Presumably the specialists who were to staff a regulatory commission would be restrained by the data they commanded. Unhappily this need not be the case. Emanating in large degree from the organizations to be controlled, the data explored by administrative commissions can often capture them. In such a pass, regulation may approach consent, and stability become stultification. Nor do experts, any more than other men, live by data alone. Besides common colds and ulcers, they develop loyalties and habits. In government, as in business or in education, administrators become to some extent the victims of their institutions. For many of them, lines of authority and procedure come to have an attraction of their own, an attraction that frequently induces a soporific insistence on inert routine, a fatal disinclination to innovation, sometimes to formalized action beyond the shuffling of bureaucratic dust.

Furthermore, even meaningful, objective data and personal energy and imagination do not necessarily make regulation by administration what Roosevelt thought it might be. He seemed to presume that politics would stop at the commission's water line. In a sense this is true. Railroads petitioning the I.C.C. may in that process be at once all Federalists, all Republicans. But in another sense it is not true. The conflicting interests whose reconciliation politics must effect continue to conflict before the tribunals of administration. In a contest behind closed doors among spokesmen of management, labor and government, the adroit politician will ordinarily prevail.

The possibility remains that the problems of competition, consolidation and control can be resolved more equitably— though perhaps with more waste—in the open environments provided by the legislative or the adversary process. If it is hard to find good congressmen and judges, so is it hard to find good commissioners. And whatever the deficiencies of parliaments and courts, they concern themselves with concrete rules of conduct, written for all to see, by which behavior can be measured. These rules pertain, moreover, not only to citizens and corporations, but also to their public servants.

The conclusion imperiously suggests itself that Roosevelt did not want to be controlled, that he did not want to be inhibited by a body of law, whether or not it was properly interpreted, nor delayed by the impedance of legislatures. He proposed to govern. Basically this was also the desire of the leaders of American industry and finance. Relentless agents of consolidation, they imposed and administered orders of their own. Many of them were willing in the interest of industrial peace to go a long way in condoning combinations formed by union labor. With the leaders of these newer orders they were then prepared, man to man, to bargain. Some of them foresaw that in the society they molded, big government might have to provide balance. Most of them, however, as was the case with J. P. Morgan when Roosevelt moved against the Northern Securities Company, thought that they could bargain, man to man, with government. Here they miscalculated. Their rule began to fade when Roosevelt began to make of government a superior rather than a negotiating power.

Yet intellectually and emotionally he was always more one of them than was he an agrarian reformer or a partner of little business and of labor—a Bryan or a Robert La Follette or a Brandeis. Perhaps with a sense of this affinity to men of business, Roosevelt called himself a conservative; and with reference to his difference—to his insistence that the governing was the government's—he added that a true conservative was a progressive. This was the position also of George W. Perkins, who for a time personified articulate finance; of Frank Munsey, consolidator of journalism, like Perkins a Bull Mooser; of Herbert Croly, who promised to American life little that Roosevelt had not already offered; of Brooks Adams, who would have arrested the disintegration of a democracy he never understood by consolidation, conservation, and administration—the very trinity of Roosevelt. To champion consolidation as a means to order, to believe in administration and to practice it well, this was the creed of a business elite in the early century and of that conservative intelligentsia they helped to inspire.

It rested upon a feeling about power that J. Pierpont Morgan, prodded by a congressional committee, disclosed, a feeling to which Roosevelt thoroughly subscribed. Morgan saw nothing wrong about the scope of his power, for he maintained that his morality controlled it. He also arranged that the specialists in his house helped exercise it. Roosevelt made a like claim and like arrangements. Yet Morgan was neither virtuous nor successful in his ventures with the New Haven railroad, and Roosevelt was just as vulnerable to failures of the soul and errors of the flesh. In a nation democratic by intent, Morgan's responsibility to a limited number of investors made his power less acceptable than did Roosevelt's responsibility to the whole electorate, but if their power was relatively responsible, it was in both cases absolutely corruptible.

To his great credit and doubtless greater pain, Roosevelt, understanding this, surrendered his power. Explaining his decision not to be a candidate in 1908, Roosevelt wrote: "I don't think that any harm comes from the concentration of power in one man's hands, provided the holder does not keep it for more than a certain, definite time, and then returns to the people from whom he sprang." This decision was a large achievement of restraint. Roosevelt could certainly have had the Republican nomination and would probably have won the election. The temptations to continue were enormous. Nevertheless he declined. This strength of character supported strongly the claims he made to the use of power; yet it was not enough.

Suppose only that Roosevelt was human and fallible—he need not have been paranoid or depraved, fallibility is here enough—and he claimed too much. Four years or eight years or twelve years, the number of terms is unimportant, may be in the history of this nation a brief and placid time or a tempestuous eternity. Roosevelt, it happened, ruled in a time of relative quiet. Even then he made mistakes. He made perhaps his worst mistakes, though he endeavored to be moral and informed, when his power was least restrained—mistakes possibly more of principle than of policy, but mistakes about which Americans since have often been ashamed: the episode in Panama for one, or the criminal libel suit against Joseph Pulitzer for his misinterpretation of that episode. During the last years of his life, after his power was gone, Roosevelt exhibited the characteristics that least became him, prejudices of mind and traits of personality that he had subdued while he felt the responsibilities of office. In office in time of turmoil he might not have conquered them. So too with any man. But Roosevelt especially may have benefited from the limits on Presidential power which men who understood the problem in 1788 created. When he had to proceed with sensitivity for the constitutional balances to his power, the will of Congress and of the courts—or, indeed, for the institutional balances within his party—Roosevelt's performance was noteworthy. Then he demonstrated perception, knowledge, principle of a kind, energy tempered with restraint.

Consolidation, administration, stability—for these he used his power, but they turned on power itself, and power, while it must be, must not be all. . . . Perhaps power particularly must not be all when it promises hard work, duty, order, morality—even welfare—but never mentions happiness. There was strength in Roosevelt's structure and potential for contentment, but in chancing very little, his order risked too much. The wonder is, intrepid though he was, that he never really knew this.

4

HEROIC VALUES:
HERBERT CROLY AND
MARK HANNA*

To a young man who had said he remembered nothing of his childhood, Thornton Wilder once remarked: "What a pity, for then you had no childhood." Mark Hanna had a childhood, which he did remember as he remembered almost everything that happened to him, but he left so little written record of his past that had it not been for Herbert Croly, he would have had more a mythic than a real life. For his part, Croly, his biography of Hanna done, either lost, mislaid, or inadvertently destroyed both the "scarcity of documentary material" on which he had relied for some of his account, and the supplementary notes and records he had compiled in his research. There are no longer any Hanna Papers, not in some library or archive or even in some private attic. Hanna's life, as history knows it, is essentially the life about which Croly wrote.

In part an early venture in oral history, Croly's biography

*This essay is adapted from *The New Republic,* no. 168:28–32, June 16, 1973—a latter-day review of Herbert Croly, *Marcus Alonzo Hanna: His Life and Times* (New York: Macmillan, 1912).

benefited from the fresh memories of those living who had known Hanna well, or at least as well as anybody ever had. The book was published in 1912, only eight years after Hanna died, only sixteen years after the Republican victory of 1896, Hanna's most shiny hour. Had he lived, Hanna would have been seventy-five in 1912; Croly was forty-three and had sure adult memories of his own about the campaign of 1896, during which he opposed, as did Hanna, William Jennings Bryan and all he represented.

Croly's judgment about Mark Hanna was also that of Hanna's later and lesser biographer, Thomas Beer. Hanna "had played in a dream of advancing industry, of men and wealth in one blend." In its time that was the American dream, especially in the culture of the Middle West which Hanna personified. As Beer put it, meaning only to praise: "He was not much different from any well-paid clerk or lawyer. . . . His tastes were plain. . . . He doted on stewed corn and rice puddings . . . and detested the eloquence of Henry Ward Beecher and Robert Ingersoll. . . . Except that he was a daring pioneer of industrialism . . . he was the mental cousin of any prosperous midlander." "He was chock full of energy," Croly observed, and it was his achievements as an organizer and promoter in business and politics that made him important. But as Hanna once asked about a certain rich man said to be worth two hundred million dollars, "Yes, and what the hell else is he worth?"

In the scale of wealth of the community into which he was born, Hanna was one of the privileged. His family, "local capitalists of unimpeachable standing," as Croly described them, were "unusually refined." Unlike Andrew Carnegie, who exemplified the folklore of the era, Hanna had no need to go from rags to riches. Rather, when young Marcus Alonzo moved from New Lisbon to Cleveland, he went to school with John D. and William Rockefeller. When they turned to oil, they had access to family money for investment, just as Hanna did for his early ventures in wholesale groceries, the lake trade and shipping, and later, after his marriage into the Rhodes family, for his further undertakings in coal and iron.

Hanna resembled the Rockefellers, too, in the way he organized his industrial domain. His "very complicated and diversified business," Croly noted, rested upon alliances he had made "covering every aspect of the production, the handling and transportation of . . . coal, iron-ore and pig-iron." One ally was the Pennsylvania Railroad; one strength lay in the sales organization which Hanna had built, another in the firm's ability to consume as well as to sell to others much of the raw material it extracted. A characteristic industrial capitalist, Hanna moved sensibly to verticalization with its attendant efficiencies. Through his "corporate and . . . individual properties, and personal and corporate alliances," he also moved away from unrestricted competition with its wasteful debilitations. But Hanna's company, unlike Standard Oil, retained a "personal character," served its customers "fairly and efficiently," and treated its employees with paternalistic justice. Because it was natural, efficient, and beneficent by the standards of the time, because it was more than just a vehicle for the accumulation of wealth, the company stood as a model of a "good trust,"as Theodore Roosevelt used that phrase in 1912 and as Croly by implication agreed. In contrast, Croly took Hanna to task for those operations in urban transport that depended upon quasi-monopoly control, established in part by bribery, over an indispensable public service. However typical of its time, Hanna's traction company was a "bad trust."

At his best or his worst, Hanna displayed in impressive measure the qualities of the great consolidators of his generation. He had initiative, the ability to organize and to manage, enthusiasm—even passion, fearlessness, assiduity, flair—

even a touch of theater, which he loved. Those attributes marked his quests for wealth and, beyond wealth, for "the power which only wealth can give." It was the desire for power that drove Hanna to politics, as did his belief in the identity of interests between business, including his own business, and the community at large, whether the city of Cleveland, the state of Ohio, or the whole nation. His sense of the primacy and universality of business interests informed his political program. It was, with no significant variation, the program of American business in the late nineteenth century and for decades to come: a protective tariff; a sound currency based on gold; public subsidies for lagging private enterprise (Hanna in the Senate concentrated on the merchant marine); and governmental restraint from interference with the policies of private management.

From those tenets, which construed business confidence and prosperity as the highest good, the distance to imperialism was not long. New, overseas markets for the products of American industry, Hanna concluded, would serve that interest. It followed, though he disliked war, that he saw positive assets in the fall-out from the war with Spain, especially in the acquisition of the Philippines. Since, in his creed, the nation profited thereby, his conscience was easy. The very easiness of his conscience, as well as the special logic that undergirded it, suggested motivations on his part and on the part of businessmen of like mind that coincided with the motivations which Marxist critics attributed to finance capitalism everywhere. Historians who have argued that a quest for economic advantage has determined American foreign policy could properly point to Hanna for confirmatory evidence. "Naturally," Hanna would probably have commented. "Inevitably," Croly as much as admitted, without any pejorative implication.

The Republican Party had counted upon its money raising

and spending in several national campaigns before Hanna enlarged and enhanced the management and the scope of the operation in 1896. The party had also made special appeals to sundry ethnic groups, but Hanna made those appeals broader and more systematic. So, too, the party had had its spiritual seat in the Middle West, and Hanna shrewdly placed one major headquarters office in Chicago, which outstripped New York in 1896 as the center for Republican strategy. Those tactics supported the unprecedented outpouring of propaganda that Hanna organized in behalf of William McKinley and of gold. As Croly's description of that huge effort suggested, it was the first major public relations campaign in modern American politics. Theodore Roosevelt, an emerging master of public relations in his own right, saw precisely what Hanna had done. "He has advertised McKinley," Roosevelt said, "as if he were a patent medicine."

The dominant Republican politicians in their states, men like Thomas C. Platt in New York and Matthew Quay in Pennsylvania, had built alliances among their own kind, equals or inferiors, alliances that bound town and city machines to state organizations and wove the latter into an unstable national confederation. While sufficiently adroit in the mean politics of tradition, Hanna recruited a newer breed of man to take over control of Republican state organizations, particularly in the Middle West, the region of his largest influence. These were men originally trained, as he had been, in industry. He did not abandon the old reciprocal relationships of favor and loyalty, but the alliances he forged resembled in the aggregate the business structures familiar to the men who managed their separate parts, whether in Colorado or in Wisconsin or in Illinois. The Republican leadership, as a result, was not only more genteel than it had been, it was also richer, more efficient, and more energetic in advancing the broad purposes it proudly served. That leadership, while no less selfish than before, became more sensitive to the desirability of accommodating to change by surrendering the appearance of the *status quo* in order to preserve its essence. Hanna's new Old Guard were conservative, but also effective, adaptive, and agile.

The caricature of Mark Hanna, "Dollar Mark," a bloated capitalist with one foot on the throat of the people, expressed the fear and loathing of the Hearst press and the Bryan Democrats who felt, better than they knew, that Hanna symbolized and mobilized the forces in American society against which the radicals of the 1890s protested so bitterly. The caricature was unfair, though Hanna rather enjoyed the cartoons. As a symbol of predatory wealth, Hanna was far less appropriate than were his schoolmates, the Rockefellers, or the Platts and Quays whom the robber barons cultivated. But as an organizer of the politics of conservatism, Hanna had no visible peer. He had an ideal agent in McKinley, whose intellectual vacuity was usually covered by a blanket of soft conventionality and contented religiosity. And both men had a common touch.

A banker once asked Hanna about the "lower classes." "You mean working men?" Hanna replied. "Or do you mean criminals and that kind of people? Those are the lower classes." For the people Hanna liked were working people, whether men working on a railway or in a mill, or in a manager's or stateman's office. He was not by temperament or conviction a generous judge of humanity. He did not suffer in his heart for the deprived. But neither was he greedy or pompous or vain; so by and large, the people Hanna liked, liked him. Herbert Croly admired him.

Energy—physical, social, and personal—fascinated Herbert Croly. So did geniality. Shy though he was, Croly enjoyed cards, tennis, good talk, and good company. Attracted by Hanna's easy companionability, he was absorbed by what he felt Hanna represented. Because of that absorption and because of Croly's own stature as an intellectual, Hanna brought less to his biographer than his biographer gave to him. Croly's *Hanna,* like his more celebrated *The Promise of American Life,* reveals the influence of Auguste Comte's positivism in Croly's "technocratic conception" of society, in his pervasive assumption of "an organic social system with ideas and institutions interconnected and mutually dependent," in his historicism, and in his implicit faith in Comte's religion of brotherhood. From Santayana as well as from Comte, Croly derived an elitist doctrine, including his belief in the "sort of natural aristocracy" that he found among "the boys who played and fought with Mark Hanna," an aristocracy confirmed by its excellence of performance. And from William James, as well as from his own adult predilections, Croly learned that no set of beliefs was fixed and final, but rather a transitory system to be tested and adjusted through experience. There lay his rationale for insisting upon the relevance of Hanna's creed to its times. The social and political ideas of Hanna's America stood for Croly as an inevitable stage in the transition from an earlier, agrarian country to the industrial nation whose necessary reform was implied in the last chapter of the biography.

From first to last in *Hanna,* Croly also expressed various presumptions about man and society that he shared with other middle-class Americans, presumptions that characterized the culture of the early twentieth century. His "natural aristocracy," for one example, depended partly upon the accidents of national origin. Hanna's ancestry, he wrote, included "a compound of the best strains entering into the American racial stock"—Scotch-Irish, Welsh, English, Dutch, French Huguenot (all of them, incidentally, Protestant in religion). "If a thorough mixture," he went on, "of many good racial ingredients constitutes, as is now usually supposed, an heredity favorable to individual energy and distinction, Mark Hanna started life with that basic advantage." By implication, men descended from the new immigrants or from black or brown or yellow parents suffered a natural disadvantage. They were lesser men, and Croly had no argument with Hanna's vote for a bill imposing educational qualifications on immigrants, a bill designed to reduce the flow of lesser men from central and southern Europe to the United States.

Yet for Croly, as for Hanna, Theodore Roosevelt, and others of similar mind, lesser men could win redemption by working hard, while the natural aristocrat surrendered his distinction if he failed to engage in productive work. Croly considered it vital, as he put it, that Hanna "earned by personal economic services his private fortune." The moral distinction between earning money by producing goods or services and earning by lending or speculation had persisted as an article of American faith from the colonial period into the twentieth century. Simple people, good people, whether at work on a farm or in a shop or in the office of a local business like Hanna's, disliked and distrusted Wall Street. So did Croly. So did other sophisticated eastern progressives, among them Louis D. Brandeis, who attacked the manipulation of "other people's money," and Theodore Roosevelt, who denounced the "malefactors of great wealth."

Croly identified the industrial producer with the American pioneer and both with an active and efficient life. Efficiency in this definition existed when "the action adopted is determined by the economic environment." It followed that the industrial capitalist in the United States in the late nineteenth century built for the nation while he worked for himself. "The American democratic state," Croly maintained, "had promised its citizens prosperity and comfort and had recognized the responsibility by doing its best to stimulate economic activity." Accordingly Croly respected private, capitalistic interests which he wanted to preserve, while to protect the superior public interest, he prescribed an agenda of reform that would restore balance "to the whole system." No revolutionist, Croly spoke the language of preservation through reform, and spoke in and to the progressive temper of his time.

Indeed Croly had no sympathy for the indigenous radicalism of the rural West and South, just as he had small interest in farmers or their concerns. His biography neglected even to mention Hanna's involvement in promoting a federal program for irrigation in the arid West. Croly wrote about the 1890s without explicit notice of the severe depression of the decade, or of the suffering and despair of American farmers, or of the genesis and direction of Populism, their spirited movement for substantial economic and political reform. Consequently he revealed an eastern and conservative bias, especially in his disdain for Bryan.

Progressives like Croly, Walter Lippmann, and Theodore Roosevelt put their faith for the future in expert management, including the management of a positive and penetrating federal government. They believed in advancing democratic objectives by promoting and supervising modern industrialism. But Croly exorcised the ambiguity of his elitist doctrine by democratizing those whose course in public life he applauded. He continually called McKinley and Hanna "representative" men. In defense of that assertion, he discerned majorities without recourse to statistical proof. Most Republicans, he claimed, wanted McKinley nominated in 1896. Perhaps they did, but the delegates to the national convention had not been chosen by popular election and the votes of some of them, as Croly admitted, had been bought for McKinley. Representativeness for Croly was not simply a function of majorities. The people were sovereign only if they provided majorities for the discerning elite, which in Croly's reading they had done in 1896. He seemed to believe in Rousseau's general will, suitably Americanized.

Mark Hanna's Uncle Kersey, Croly noted, lived until 1909 and could remember his grandfather, a Scotch-Irish immigrant of 1763. Croly understood, even though he rejected them, the attachments to the soil and to the assumptions of a bucolic culture that beguiled so many of his generation. To reach that audience he had to take those attachments into account. So did Roosevelt, the "natural aristocrat" from whom Croly drew his greatest inspiration. Both men suggested a resolution of agrarian and industrial values through a single, encompassing, and fusing process. For Roosevelt the resolving agency was strenuosity, the vigorous life whether lived in the saddle, at the workbench, or on the hustings. Croly gave identical emphasis to vigor, work, and energy. He identified the spirit of enterprise with the spirit of pioneering; he endowed the creative businessman—Mark Hanna—with the attributes of the pioneer. In the continuous process of national development, though at different stages, the frontiersman and the industrialist had been as one in virtue. In the stage to come, the progressive statesman, vigorously engaged in government, would perpetuate the process and preserve the type. For Croly, as for those Americans to whom he spoke, there was no ambiguity. There was no need to reconcile the agrarian past and the industrial present, for the best values of the two, the values inherent in striving to fulfill the opportunities of the environment, were identical. They were also heroic values, as Croly saw it, that made Hanna a fit subject for his attention and Hanna's career an efficient object for his theorizing.

Yet in the end Hanna's greatest attractions for Croly were energy and success. "He was bound," Croly wrote, "to run until he dropped." Croly attributed to Hanna a greatness he did not deserve. But Croly did have a shrewd sense of the importance of Hanna in history, and in explaining that importance he disclosed much of interest about himself and his fellow progressives. They were engaged in promoting democratic values less for the sake of democracy itself than for the need to facilitate an orderly social adaptation to continuing industrial change.

WOODROW WILSON:
A STUDY IN INTELLECT[*]

AN American Victorian, the child of a time now more remote
than the actual span of the intervening hundred years,
Woodrow Wilson absorbed, and stored away against his future
needs, attitudes of mind and articles of faith common a century ago among the comfortable and polite in the United
States. His was a learning at once inspiring and truncating;
his an intelligence habituated early to seeking moral truths
through faith and intuition, to expecting peaceful progress,
to identifying this with existing British ways. Even in his
own day he was something of a period piece, resisting alike
the harshness of accelerating industrialism and the rigor of
the kind of thinking upon which science and critical realism
depended.

Wilson's deep religious feelings and romantic view of
knowledge set patterns of thought he felt always obliged to
confirm. Inheritance and indoctrination made him a Presbyterian, temperament made him an especially devout one. The

[*] From *Confluence,* Vol. V, no. 8 (Winter 1957), pp. 357–75.

Presbyterians, he learned, were a special people, chosen by God to know His purpose and do His will. They were an elect, an aristocracy of souls, predestined to achieve salvation in the next world, who manifested that graceful state in this world. If God's chosen people were to be the instruments of His just intent, so also were they "sinful and selfish" men, responsible to the Lord and ultimately to be judged by His exacting standards. Yet Wilson's God was accessible, both through prayer which afforded guidance and in His revealed word. The Bible, Wilson once remarked, "reveals every man to himself as a distinct moral agent, responsible not to man . . . but responsible through his own conscience to his Lord and Maker." So persuaded, Wilson habitually found occasion to interpret as God's will convictions other men attributed to less remote sources, occasion to hallow and moralize issues other men considered secular and casual.

In interpreting the will of God, Wilson ordinarily relied less upon data than upon intuition. As his academic colleagues observed, there was in him a great deal of Ralph Waldo Emerson. A confident, individualistic, sentimental romanticism leavened the sternness of his religion. He considered man's own spirit the first, best source of ideas. He described himself as "an idealist, with the heart of a poet," and he concluded from his study of history that great statesmen had the souls of poets. As he believed they had, he sought inspiration in a "long view of human nature" derived more from literature than from empirical data.

Wilson's literature was English literature; Wilson's valued heritage, the English heritage. It was history as he felt it that formed his remembrances of things past. He found a favorite text in Edmund Burke whose glorious prose endowed prescriptive institutions with flexible qualities that could protect and control the naked and shivering nature of man. Wilson especially felt in sympathy with the growth of English liberalism. In it he saw an example of progress effected within the confines of parliamentary practice, of progress accomplished without breaking faith with tradition. This was the kind of evolution that made him comfortable—not a bestial and sanguinary struggle like that which had sent France staggering through fields of blood, but a pacific development controlled by gentlemen whose forays were forensic and restrained. So he found another favorite text in Walter Bagehot: he looked upon himself as a leader of men, and considered that leadership demanded powers of persuasion which depended not so much on information as on a force that crept into the confidence of those to be led, a moral force shaping the future in the ongoing patterns of the past.

In his sixteenth year Wilson hung above his desk a portrait of his model statesman, William Gladstone, that incomparable public exponent of middle-class morality and of Manchesterian political economy. Gladstone represented for him a full flowering of England, of the progress that conserved. Gladstone's life, he judged, had been "one continuous advance, not towards power only . . . but towards truth also." Part of this truth was laissez-faire political economy, the belief that self-adjusting economic forces provided the best of all possible economic worlds; that the best government, therefore, was the government that interfered least with these forces. Part of this truth was a faith that virtue made its own reward, that the individual's ability and industry insured his prosperity—a faith both generated by and assimilated into the Calvinist ethic of Wilson's religion. Part of this truth was a mystic conviction in the superiority of Anglo-Saxons, in their righteous duty to make the world over in their image. This confirmed the special virtue Wilson attributed to his ancestors, the confidence he felt in the destiny of a reunited America, the theory he absorbed in his native South where Negroes were thought inferior beings.

As the nineteenth century drew to a close, Wilson brooded over what he took to be the bankruptcy of American leadership. But he had as yet little new to offer. He worried about the growth of large combinations in industry and transportation, but he opposed proposals for extensive federal control of corporations or their activities. Such schemes, he believed, would infringe upon the domain of the states, violate the liberty of the individual, threaten both the constitutional system and the economic growth of the country. Dismayed though he was by agrarian and labor disturbances in the 1890's, he was unwilling for the government to mitigate the causes of unrest, and he argued that labor unions impaired the worker's freedom of contract. In place of a program he substituted a beguiling jargon. What the country needed was a "sincere body of thought in politics . . . boldly uttered." Public opinion, he allowed, had to be truckled to, but it had also to be educated by a leader who could perceive the inchoate desires of the community and formulate them in broad, obvious, convincing arguments. Such a man would possess poetic insights and poetic talents, would reveal to the masses the wisdom of tradition, would "master multitudes."

This was the role to which Wilson had always aspired. As he came to it during the first decade of this century, his intention was to "hold liberal and reforming programmes to conservative . . . lines of action." "Excess of government," he asserted, was "the very antithesis of liberty." Therefore he would not increase the regulatory power of the federal executive, but he would pass laws against business sin and punish the transgressors. As in life, so in law, guilt was for Wilson a personal thing. To preserve a Manchesterian polity he also preached a new morality. Capital, he warned, "must give over its too great preoccupation with . . . making those who control it individually rich and must . . . serve the interests of the people as a whole." Even banking, he averred, was "founded on a moral basis."

Individualism rooted in morality inspired Wilson's New Freedom, the doctrine of his campaign of 1912. Defining and enforcing the rules of economic behavior would, he believed, eliminate both the dangers of big business and the need for big government or for the welfare state. "In our day," Wilson lamented, "the individual has been submerged . . . swallowed up in the . . . great organization." There had come about "an extraordinary and very sinister concentration in the control of business," a concentration made intolerable because "the masters of the government . . . are the combined capitalists of the United States." He proposed to restore and to preserve a minimized national authority, a society self-adjusted by the competition of determined but decent men, a free economy and a free government. Above all else, the country needed "a body of laws which will look after the men who are on the make," those "sweating blood to get their foothold on the world of endeavor." "Freemen," he postulated, "need no guardians." Indeed they could not submit to guardians and remain free, for there were two kinds of corruption, "the crude and obvious sort, which consists in direct bribery, and the much subtler, more dangerous sort, which consists in a corruption of the will."

If this was, as one opponent put it, "rural Toryism," if Wilson implied the existence of a conspiracy that did not exist, if indeed he proposed a social order no longer entirely feasible, he nonetheless shared and understood the longings of men on the make. The New Freedom, moreover, was more than a paean to social mobility. In it Wilson distilled the principles he had treasured all his life and tempered them with a growing awareness of national needs and popular sentiments. He struck notes at once nostalgic and progressive, affirming, as he did, the accumulated hopes of the farm, of the small town, of middle-class America; as well as those accumulated in the folklore of the nation's history. "There has been," he said in his first inaugural address, "something crude and heartless and unfeeling in our haste to succeed and be great." It was now our duty "to serve the humblest as well as the most powerful," "to cleanse, to reconsider, to restore."

During the next eight years the exigencies of public life and party politics, especially the needs of mobilization for world war, drove Wilson to adopt policies that deviated from his basic creed. But though he found it necessary to design ever larger clusters of national authority, once the war was over he moved rapidly to abolish them. He retained his apprehensions about power; he developed no real sympathy for industrialists or industrialism; he abandoned no part of his suspicion of "great organizations," no part of his faith in the "pristine strength" of the old, individualistic America.

In foreign policy also Wilson remained true to his basic presumptions. "The force of America," he asserted during one crisis, "is the force of moral principle . . . there is nothing else that she loves, and . . . there is nothing else for which she will contend." Moral principle entailed the duty to work for peace, but it involved much more. Anglo-American constitutional arrangements, Wilson believed, like much of the rest of Anglo-Saxon culture, had somehow a special moral as well as historical basis. The United States had a predestined obligation to bring constitutionalism to the people of semideveloped countries. As he saw it, constitutionalism had an international equivalent in the body of law which defined and governed the relations among nations, and moral principle required every nation not only to obey this law itself but also to insist upon obedience by others.

Unhappily these attitudes sometimes conflicted on occasions of moment with Wilson's sincere abomination of imperialism and war. In the name of progress or of friendship he took up at times a white man's burden scarcely distinguishable from that of less altruistic statesmen. This was especially true in the case of Mexico where he intervened to depose a counterrevolutionary scoundrel who had made murder his instrument for political power. Wilson intended, he explained, to "teach the South American republics to elect good men," to develop "constitutional liberty," and thereby to advance the world toward "those great heights where there shines unobstructed the light of the justice of God." He failed not only in the basic purpose of this venture but also in his later effort to contain revolution in Mexico by making American recognition of the government conditional upon its restraint. Mexicans almost universally resented his intercessions, as did other Latin Americans, both because they were understandably jealous of their own sovereignty and because they had legitimate reservations about the relevance of American political habits to their societies. Wilson successfully resisted the demands of jingoes at home for war, but his own insensitive moralism alienated potential friends abroad and brought him perilously close to the war he wanted to avoid.

A comparable insensitivity to new conditions led him to believe that the United States could remain neutral during World War I and at the same time uphold traditional neutral rights to trade and the use of the ocean. He not only neglected to calculate the real interests of the United States in a war in Europe and neglected to ask whether any great power could detach itself from the ordering of international society, he also gave to his interpretations of international law a brittle, moral cast. Because he could not recognize that the submarine was an indispensable though nasty device of barbarous modern war, he had to conclude that the German use of submarines was "of necessity . . . incompatible with the principles of humanity, the long established and incontrovertible rights of neutrals . . . the sacred immunities of non-combatants." "Once accept a single abatement of right," he also maintained, "and . . . the whole fine fabric of international law might crumble."

Wilson's legal and moral arguments confused his countrymen about the reasons for their involvement in a war they had hoped to escape. As the President painfully reached the decision that war was necessary, he knew in his heart that it would unleash the bestial in men and endanger the principles he held most dear. But as a human being he could not afford to believe this, and as a leader he could not afford to say it. With genuine conviction, therefore, he reasserted publicly that absolute identity of law and justice which had always sustained him. Characteristically, he personalized guilt, attributing it not to the German people but to their rulers. Characteristically, he moralized, identifying the submarine and all other issues with an ultimate and absolute right, defining the object of the war as "a universal dominion of right by such a concert of free peoples as shall bring peace and safety to all nations." The Christian optimism of his message gave men the courage, during the awful months of war, to confront their tribulations, and the promise, after the trial was over, of new freedom. But it also misled a groping people about the genesis of the war and the nature of the problems to be solved in creating a lasting peace. Arousing expectations that could not be satisfied, it rendered Americans susceptible to a profound disillusionment.

In fashioning a peace, Wilson did his best to fulfill the hopes he had nourished. Almost alone among the statesmen of the world, he had the vision to understand the need for peace without victory. This was one essential purpose of his Fourteen Points, which were themselves a symbol of what he called "the moral climax of this . . . final war for human liberty." Much of his program reflected his standard tenets. Self-determination was a kind of international individualism;

the League of Nations, a kind of world parliament to make the rules by which its members should live. Wilson never expected the specific items of the settlement to be "altogether satisfactory," but he did expect the League continually to improve the initial specifications of the peace, and to further also his largest purpose—as expressed by Article X of the Covenant, the heart of collective security: the prompt organization not of nations only but of "the moral force of the world."

Now fully aware that the United States could not abdicate the role its power commanded it to play in world affairs, he argued that the country could not "refuse the moral leadership . . . of the world." His theme, he felt, went "directly to the conscience of the Nation." There was, he believed, one thing "the American people always rise to . . . and that is the truth of justice and of liberty and of peace."

In this Wilson was mistaken, but his failure was more than political. Just as he had drawn his country into a troubled relationship with Mexico, so he obscured for himself and for his countrymen certain issues that even organized good will could not dispel. Ready and real force was indispensable for protecting or advancing liberty anywhere. The resolutions of international parliaments left undismayed the furtive toughness of a brutal enemy. But the unbending certitude of Wilson's faith encouraged him to speak too little of unyielding circumstances and to expect too much of justice. And those who followed, less astute and far less convinced than he, substituted homiletics for foreign policy.

This was an unintended legacy of Wilson's moralism. His lifelong faith was in the individual as a distinct moral agent, inspired by and accountable to God; in the individual as the special object of a Christian education; in the individual, so accountable and so educated, as the judicious artificer of his own political and economic life. In the face of what was sometimes overwhelming evidence to the contrary, he believed that man had a transcendent capacity to discover the rational arrangements within which his kind could wend in antiseptic harmony their several ways. He presumed that normative man was a kind of William Gladstone, that a normative nation consisted of a mass of separate human particles, each like him. Because giving these particles a chance to compete was in the twentieth century no longer enough, for they needed help and cohesion; because especially in this century liberal constitutionalism was not everywhere a possible or an attractive prospect, the products of Wilson's faith engendered some unwholesome, unintended consequences.

But the healthy heritage he left overbalanced this. Though moralizing confuses, morals do not, nor does ascetic dedication to the task of governing. Though Wilson trusted the invisible hand that he presumed gave guidance to men on the make, he never let its revelations become his scriptures. His confidence in the individual as the proper repository of responsibility and opportunity, moreover, made him suspicious both of special privilege and of concentrated power. The former he helped in many ways to reduce; the latter he resisted with a spirit that helped preserve a skepticism such as his at a time when public or private pyramids of power seemed to provide an absolute cathartic for the modern state. In office and in memory he served not just the people who had elected him, but also decency, the dignity of the individual, and therefore democracy.

Nor was this all. In the largest sense the end of his efforts did not come with the American rejection of his treaty. He had few friends then; indeed, men had seldom loved him. But as they ordinarily had respected him, so would they again. When he died, men wept for peace. After he died, they gave substance to his objectives in the United Nations. . . . The United States, his countrymen discovered, had continuously to play a leading part in world affairs, had to do so responsibly and morally and in company with other nations. Even more than Wilson realized, discussion had to be a substitute for war. Perhaps even more than he hoped, his triumph was as a teacher, and his lesson was written in the copybooks of generations still unborn. He lived in a world made up in part of his illusions, but for that very reason his statements about it transcended the apparent limits of reality, and therefore constituted a symbol of man's most precious dreams and grandest faiths.

6

THE FOREIGN AND THE RADICAL: THE RED SCARE OF 1919-1920*

IN the United States there was little peace. The guns on the western front were still, but impatient patriots recognized no armistice at home. Federal agents discovered plots against the nation, corralled the plotters, and packed them off to Russia. American courts enjoined the unions. Veterans smashed presses, killed "Wobblies," tarred and feathered Negroes. In many states legislatures defined dissent as sedition. While few Americans were so frenetic, fewer still protested. The country seemed to have met Theodore Roosevelt's wartime demands on the spirit of nationalism:

> There is no room for the hyphen in our citizenship. . . . He who is not with us, absolutely and without reserve of any kind, is against us, and should be treated as an alien enemy. . . . We have room in this country for but one flag. . . . We have room for but one language. . . . The German-American Alliance . . . the Sinn Feiners, the East Side Russian revolutionary organiza-

*First published as "Nativism, Anti-Radicalism and the Foreign Scare, 1917–1920," in *The Midwest Journal,* Vol. 2, no. 1 (Winter 1950–51), pp. 46–53.

tions . . . and most of the leaders of Mr. Townley's Non-Partisan League and the IWW are anti-American to the core. . . . Our bitter experience should teach us for a generation . . . to crush under our heel every movement that smacks in the smallest degree of playing the German game.

Roosevelt appealed to two persistent hostilities. Americans often had demonstrated, at times with fearful intensity, an antipathy for the foreign and the radical. Their confident pride in the achievements of their economic system, their continuing familiarity with a Protestant, Anglo-Saxon culture produced loyalties that provided a useful, conservative social cement. In times of crisis, however, real or imagined challenges to economic and cultural institutions had molded loyalty into intolerance. Exploiting latent prejudices against the radical and the foreign, and identifying these two, organizers of public opinion had translated passive dislike into truculent hysteria.

The lower middle class on farms and in small cities, insecure and badly educated, consequently tenacious of what it had and suspicious of the unfamiliar, had formed the core of earlier nativist movements. In the first decades of this century, this class was again susceptible to such appeals. In the South, where the presence of the Negro created great reluctance to change, Populism had fanned prejudices which had scarcely subsided. Elsewhere, the acceleration of large-scale industrial organization reduced the economic security and the sense of achievement of the wageworker. Such frustrations as occurred in the farmer's life were still unrelieved by the radio, automobile, and motion picture. The felt need of these people for a sense of belonging and recognition could be supplied again by organized nativism.

Early century conditions also prepared their potential leaders. The upper middle class was for a decade the object of continuing political attack. Although progressivism was basically a conservative phenomenon, intent on reforming in order to preserve, it seemed dangerously experimental to many men of large wealth. The progressives themselves saw danger in the labor syndicalism they fought. Fear of socialism and resentment born of constant public reproach fostered an upper-middle-class insecurity. The businessmen who campaigned successively for clean government, preparedness, and sedition laws have usually been pictured as calculating reactionaries consciously creating diversions. The unconscious motive of at least some of them, however, may have been a desire for the approval of their increasing critics.

By 1914, the targets for a foreign scare were also present. Immigrants, largely from southern and eastern Europe, areas previously little represented in the United States, had been arriving at an unprecedented rate. For the most part they found employment only in the cities where, received coldly, they clustered in national groups. Few older Americans welcomed the new. Influenced by a pseudoscientific racism, intellectuals, speaking for each other and for the readers of Sunday supplements, questioned the capacity of the recent arrivals to reach the Anglo-American level of civilization. Native Protestants frowned at the large increment of Catholics and Jews. Craft-conscious spokesmen of organized labor, reluctant to organize the new labor force, considered it a competitive threat. Perhaps the warmest welcome came from political machines that offered a club house, picnics, and naturalization in return for loyalty at the polls; but when the immigrant showed his appreciation, he was blamed for the shame of the cities. Drawing on such attitudes, the Immigration Restriction League perpetuated a genteel Know-Nothingism which Congress endorsed with the literacy test and the Dillingham investigation.

In the same period there were signs of economic radicalism

frequently associated with immigrants. The stereotype of the foreign radical gained strength from the assassination of McKinley by a man with an unfamiliar name. Industrial Workers of the World, recruiting the labor force spurned by the American Federation of Labor, had substantial success among immigrant miners, textile workers, and itinerant farm laborers. Its avowed revolutionary purpose, its method of organization, and its violent tactics provoked widespread fear and counter-violence. The average American considered peaceful socialists, of whom many were aliens, little more tolerable than Wobblies.

By 1914, politicians had begun to increase latent prejudices by exploiting them. In their campaigns in New York and Ohio in that year the Republicans made sectarianism an effective issue. Attacking Wilson's Mexican policy, Theodore Roosevelt appealed to American Catholics, drawing attention to a Catholic bloc which, politically at least, was as much imagined as real. Both parties emphasized the nation's hyphen-consciousness, a product of the European War. The Germans and Irish, particularly in areas where they had long been unwanted, were accused en masse of sharing the views of their unrepresentative spokesmen who condemned Wilson's policies. Defying such critics, the President wished to make Americanism the keynote for the Democratic Convention of 1916. Democratic and Republican campaigners alike invited the opposition of un-American, by which they clearly meant anti-Allied, groups.

The preparedness movement reidentified hyphenism and radicalism. Its leaders, without exception partial to the Allies, were, for the most part, men of substantial property. Their opponents were not only German and Irish-Americans, but also, for different reasons, pacifists, socialists, and labor unionists. Treating these groups as one common enemy, many preparedness advocates, unfriendly to labor, made Americanism a label for the open shop. . . With the coming of war, cohesive national attitudes assumed a new value. Hatred of the enemy was a natural and important adjunct to belligerency. Fortunately there were few dissenters, fewer saboteurs. But the impact of war magnified sensitivity to dissent. Nativist and anti-radical prejudices, already growing, reached pathological proportions.

Through the Committee on Public Information (CPI), a necessary agency in total war, the federal government fed those prejudices. The CPI's spy-hunt posters indulged the popular notion that espionage and sabotage pervaded the country, a misapprehension encouraged also by sensationalist journalism. The dissemination by the CPI of the Sisson documents gave official sanction to the popular illusion that the Bolshevik government was not a Russian government at all, but the creature of Germany acting only in German interests. The cultivated hatred of Germans, which tended to extend to all foreigners, was thus channeled directly toward the already suspect radicals of the new Soviets.

The pressing need for copious, uninterrupted production made wartime strikes intolerable. Even the *New Republic* applauded the government's prosecutions of the IWW. But less radical labor unions, cooperating in the war effort, also suffered. While federal agencies made some adjustments in wages and hours, the CPI gave at least temporary approval to conditions of labor that its chief realized were inequitable. The National Association of Manufacturers, the National Civic Federation, and the National Security League, admitting no such injustice, repeated the arguments of the preparedness campaign that made patriotism their shield for the economic status quo.

Censorship was the effective handmaiden of propaganda. The government, insisting that the war was a people's war, disallowed Marxist dissent and discouraged pacifism. Under the authority of the Espionage and Trading with the Enemy Acts, the Post Office Department banned socialist and foreign language publications on flimsy pretexts and without explanation. One issue of the *Nation* was excluded from the mails for printing an article criticizing Samuel Gompers for his cooperation in government labor policies. Investigating another decision of the Postmaster General, the President's secretary discovered that Burleson's standards of censorship were more severe than those of the Army.

The Justice Department, also overzealous, initiated almost a thousand prosecutions in the first six months of 1918 alone. Frequently it failed to differentiate between harmless, albeit caustic, critics and dangerous incendiaries. Attorney-General Gregory gave official recognition to the American Protective League, an organization of hysterical amateur detectives, pressed for harsher sedition legislation, and criticized Judge Learned Hand for refusing to accept the Department's views on civil liberties.

As in peacetime, politicians utilized the temper of the people. To buttress their campaigns, they exaggerated the scope and influence of dissent. A minority of German and Irish-Americans continued to be unreconciled to American policy. Marxist organizations also opposed the war. In Wisconsin and in New York City, where their party included a large number of Germans, Irish, and Eastern Europeans, the Socialists, declaring for immediate peace, conducted important political campaigns. Both major parties responded with patriotic appeals that equated opposition to the war with hyphenism and radicalism. In the Northwest, the fact that the overwhelming majority of immigrants and their children were loyal Americans, good soldiers, and conscientious purchasers of war bonds was deliberately obscured. Threatened by the success of the Non-Partisan League, the banking and marketing interests and the older political parties capitalized on the national origin of many of the League's members. The farmers of the Dakotas and Minnesota had emigrated from areas culturally close to the Central Powers. Many of them had opposed intervention. But once the war began, they were, with few exceptions, scrupulously cooperative. Their program was remedial, not revolutionary. Yet the opponents of the League convinced most of Congress and most of the press that it was radical, seditious, and dangerously un-American.

The wartime regime fostered increasing hostility to collectivism. The government took over the railroads and the telephone and telegraph systems, requested voluntary rationing, and attempted limited price fixing. Accepting this regimentation as a wartime necessity, the American people nevertheless disliked it. Owners of the utilities were determined to regain control of their properties. Western farmers resented the rigid wheat prices. The inefficient Fuel Administration caused general dissatisfaction with government management. Sympathizing with these attitudes, the Republicans in 1918 asked a mandate to assure "the resumption of normal operations when, after the war, legislation must supersede the many revolutionary measures now on our statute books." A number of Democrats who had hoped to use the war as a laboratory of permanent collectivism realized the effectiveness of the Republican appeal and abandoned their plans.

Solidified by the existence of war, mobilized by the government, excited by agitators, public opinion exhibited morbid sensitivity to any deviation from the usual. Private citizens imposed a personal censorship less tolerant than the government's. In a society that made sauerkraut "liberty cabbage," the press, with few exceptions, applauded the horse-whipping of Herbert Bigelow, a pacifist, in Kentucky. At Bisbee, Arizona, a local posse, exhorted by management, ran the "Wobblies" out of town while the officials of Anaconda, taking over the telegraph, censored news of the affair. While such episodes multiplied, war-born hatreds were assimilated to older prejudices. Rumors had the Germans inciting Negro rebellions in the South, the Irish Catholics cooperating with the Sinn Fein to help Germany, the Socialists planting bombs to prevent the draft. Anti-feminists suggested that suffragettes aided the enemy by pressing their just but divisive reform. The immigration restriction movement gained adherents; the states emulated and exceeded the example of the federal government in passing sedition laws.

The armistice came while emotions were at their peak. Capitalizing on the hatred of Germany, the Republicans had just won an election partly by opposing a Wilsonian peace. They were quick to make similar prejudices weapons against Wilson's treaty. The old-world statesmen at Paris, they insisted, merited no trust. Even Wilson, making French imperialism his favored argument for Article X, encouraged a distrust of foreigners. Both sides in the treaty fight warned against the radical. Proponents of the League declared that it would stem the tide of Bolshevism. Nicholas Murray Butler, speaking for the opposition, held that internationalism was tainted with red, the treaty "sinister," "unpatriotic and un-American," "subtle, half-conscious" socialism.

These invocations of the red menace reflected the hysteria of postwar America. There were, in fact, real dangers which the American people intuitively felt. Communism, already established in Russia, was winning adherents in eastern and central Europe. This intellectual pestilence . . . flourished in societies already economically sick and threatened to infect also those of a stronger constitution. To guard against Bolshevism, Frank A. Vanderlip proposed that the United States initiate a prototype of the Marshall Plan, designed to immunize Europe by strengthening its economy. Reformers like Joseph P. Tumulty and George L. Record urged a domestic program comprehending federal social insurance, federal aid for housing, and compulsory collective bargaining to remove the legitimate domestic discontent on which Communism could feed. But these enlightened schemes received no hearing from people whose hyperemotionalism led them, Quixotic like, to fight Communism by tilting at windmills.

During the great red scare the unspent emotions of wartime followed the paths already delineated. Turning from remedy to repression, public agencies and private organizations, spurred by agitators, attacked the classic objects of national prejudices. The identification of the foreign and the radical was clear: the deportees were largely Russian immigrants whose Bolshevism was too often suspected rather than proved; big steel spokesmen pointed out that many steel strikers were of foreign origin, of the Catholic religion, and of Socialist views—a combination that seemed natural to Judge Gary; Oregon excused its ban on foreign language newspapers on the grounds that the Japanese and the Finns, long unpopular on the coast, were dangerously radical; a learned scientist, opposing Einstein, suggested that the theory of relativity had alien, Bolshevik origins; the *New York Times* implied that the Greeks, Italians, and Syrians of Boston were the brothers-in-arms of the largely Irish police strikers; and James F. Byrnes asked federal intervention to prevent a red-inspired Negro uprising in the South.

Again politicians, sharing and employing the public's fears, increased them. Red baiting ensured publicity, and publicity promised votes. The Republican Lusk Committee in New York by its raids and investigations diverted attention from the reform program of Democratic Governor Smith. On a national scale the red scare served two presidential hopefuls well. Both A. Mitchell Palmer and Leonard Wood were ambitious beyond their immediate political strength. Of Palmer's rivals in the Democratic Party, McAdoo was the favorite of the liberals; Cox of the city machines. Palmer's potential strength lay with non-machine Northern conservatives and with Southern Democrats. His policies as Attorney General, surely by his intention, appealed to those groups. Until 1919 Palmer had been a moderate liberal. Identified with Wilson since 1912, strong in immigrant areas of Pennsylvania, the party's contact man to unions in 1916, he received his appointment as Attorney General partly because of his popularity with labor and with the foreign-born. In 1919 and 1920, however, his recourse to injunctions, his provocative agents, his early morning raids, while alienating his old friends, won the plaudits of those who were capable of procuring a presidential nomination. Leonard Wood pursued a like course. Unlike Governor Lowden of Illinois, he had no state machine; unlike Warren Harding, he was weak with the Old Guard; unlike Herbert Hoover, he could not hope for support from Republican internationalists. Directing his campaign to please those who wanted a strong-man, he called for deportation of Bolshevists on ships of stone with sails of lead, the wrath of God for a gale, and Hell for the nearest port.

Palmer and Wood retreated from those extreme positions in the weeks before the nominating conventions. At those gatherings, they knew, the excesses of a candidate embarrassed his managers in their search for new adherents. The Attorney General, after his highly publicized petition for an injunction against the striking United Mine Workers (UMW), had earlier helped behind the scenes to initiate a settlement on Lewis' terms. In the late winter of 1920 . . . he modified his stand on sedition legislation and declared that it was not, after all, "radicals," but "red radicals" whom he really feared. Wood allowed that certain of labor's grievances were legitimate. If elected, he would give them his attention when things were calmer. He had not, he suggested, really favored drowning deportees. Significantly, these concessions to moderation were made about the time that hysteria began to subside. Whether or not the candidates sensed this change, their reversals none the less facilitated it.

Editors, like politicians, contributed first to the flowering and then to the decline of hysteria. The foreign scare supplied the headlines that replaced the news of battle at a time when headline news was scarce. The negotiations at Versailles and the treaty fight did not provide the stuff of circulation. Bombs, strikes, and Bolsheviks; red hunts, deportations, and injunctions did. But these matters began to receive back-page treatment as they became too routine to be news and as other news became available. The primary and general election campaigns took over increasing front-page space after April, 1920. Later . . . the Black Sox Scandal stole headlines even from Lenin.

Readjustment to peace also dispelled fear and hate. In 1919, the radical fringe in the United States earned its . . . reputation. At the same time, labor, attempting to gain what had been forbidden it during the war, called a record number of strikes. The railroad brotherhoods and the UMW endorsed nationalization in their industries. In propagandizing against the labor movement, management identified those endorsements with violent radicalism. The suppression of such violence, the failure of the major strikes, and the new problems created by the short depression of 1920 made such propaganda less common and less effective. In the same period, Bolshevism was checked in central and eastern Europe. In Russia the complete Bolshevik triumph hastened the recall of the American troops from Siberia. As Europe quieted down, so did American nerves. By the spring of 1920, the emotionally exhausted people wanted to relax. Dangers seemed more remote. And by that time the anti-radicals had overreached themselves. The expulsion of the Socialists in New York . . . offended the sense of justice of conservative men, inducing them to join the broadening movement for civil rights. The election removed the treaty and presidential politics, both often geared to the foreign scare, as issues. Even before the election the calm response to a bomb exploded in Wall Street evidenced the return of sanity.

The foreign scare gravely damaged civil liberties. For those wronged there could be no adequate compensation. More important, a priceless tradition had been despoiled, its continuity destroyed. In the postwar atmosphere the Ku Klux Klan and the American Legion were safely launched. Playing on the hostilities that underlay the foreign scare, the Klan polluted politics for a decade. The immigration restriction law of 1924, Calvin Coolidge, and the company shop embodied the ultimate triumphs of postwar attitudes. Rooted in persistent prejudices, those attitudes had occasioned a fruitless dissipation of national energy as well as a repressive disorder far more dangerous to Americans than the exaggerated threat of radicalism had ever been.

II

POLITICS AND THE WELFARE STATE

7

"THAT KIND OF A LIBERAL": FRANKLIN D. ROOSEVELT*

AFTER half a century, the manner has receded in national memory, and with it so has the man. Americans under sixty—most Americans, that is—cannot hear the voice that spoke the words which history records. Few under sixty can evoke a personal experience of long depression ("I see one-third of a nation ill-housed, ill-clad, ill-nourished") or of sudden war ("Yesterday, December 7, 1941—a date that will live in infamy"). Few have a sense of a living Franklin Roosevelt in their past. He lives for them, if he lives at all, only in history, which strips from his past, as from any past, much of its passion, much of its gaiety, much also of its distorting sentimentality, and some of its immediate truth. . . .

The world Roosevelt knew as President was pervaded by the Great Depression of the thirties with its attendant hardships. There was no general affluence, no plenitude of funds or goods to be distributed to needy people. Recovery, eluding the New Deal's various efforts, occurred incidentally, not

*Adapted from *The Yale Review,* Vol. 6, no. 1 (October 1970), pp. 14–23.

as a product of deliberate national policy but in response to heavy federal spending for defense and war. In theory at least the failure to achieve recovery was unnecessary. Had Roosevelt understood economics, he might in theory have built business confidence and thus stimulated private investment, or alternatively have championed countercyclical spending at many multiples of the volume of the peacetime deficits actually incurred. In fact, the circumstances of the 1930's, the relatively primitive level of economic intelligence, the prevailing hostility to business and industry, and the constrictive possibilities of politics all militated against those theoretical solutions.

Only a minority even of professional economists embraced Keynesian theory until late in the decade. Their attempts to explain the new economics did not quickly persuade the large majority of businessmen and congressmen, who clung instead to the prudential folklore of outmoded analyses even after the experience of war provided ample documentation for Keynes's case. Indeed the proponents of the Employment Act of 1946 met strong resistance on the Hill. Roosevelt, for his part, had moved belatedly, more by hunch than comprehension, to Keynesian formulations, first during the budget crisis of 1938 when he accepted the counsel of the spenders in his official circle ("it is up to us to create an economic upturn"), again in 1945 when he approved the basic outline of the Employment Bill that Congress weakened in the following year. He had moved faster and farther than most Americans of his generation. He had learned from his mistakes, precisely as he had learned, after his adventures in buying gold in 1933, to find a better basis for monetary policy. Roosevelt never understood economics any more than he understood atomic physics. He was not an intellectual; few Presidents have been. But he had a respect for intellectuals, including economists, and a searching zest for new ideas. Too few Presidents have shared those traits.

Recovery failed partly because Roosevelt was resolved to advance his objectives in social reform. He was prepared on his own terms to cooperate with industry but not to boost business confidence if boosting entailed special tax favors or permissive government. Herbert Hoover's reiterated reassurances had not spurred investment. More important, the practices of the business and investment communities during the 1920's did not commend the practitioners for favor. Roosevelt was not content with rhetoric ("money changers . . . in the temple of our civilization" . . . "royalists of the economic order"). The regulatory agencies the New Deal created, each in some measure confined by compromises characteristic of the legislative process, nevertheless for a time imposed refreshingly strict standards of behavior on their charges. Only after Roosevelt's death did appointments to those agencies lead to the substitution of genial collusion for vigorous vigilance. . . .

More than regulation, Roosevelt's labor and tax policies made him enemies on his right. Gradually he became a champion of the unions. He and his advisers in 1933 contrived the National Recovery Administration to bring more order and more government planning to national economic life. Though industry soon dominated planning within the NRA, the provisions of the act also strengthened the union movement and its emerging new and militant leadership. That stimulus, intensified by the Wagner Act, assured unions, for the first time in American history, of a fair chance under the law to bargain collectively with employers. The President, it was said of Roosevelt as it could be said of few others ever in his office, wanted men to join the unions. Since his time, the terms of labor law and the quality of labor leadership have changed to the detriment of American workers but, in his day, labor organizations enjoyed their sunniest and most creative season, while federal fair labor standards and unemployment and old age insurance—innovations Roosevelt sponsored—provided the foundations for a still unfinished structure of equity and security for the laboring force.

Roosevelt sponsored, too, a succession of controversial revenue acts. Given the New Deal's modest level of spending, advancing tax schedules impeded economic recovery. But taxation, for Roosevelt, was as much an instrument for reform as for revenue. The legislation he signed in 1935–1937 lifted income and estate taxes in the higher brackets, closed many of the loopholes through which the wealthy were escaping taxes, increased corporate taxes, and attempted major corporate reforms by imposing an intercorporate dividend tax and a short-lived undistributed earnings tax. Roosevelt meant to soak the rich to help the poor. He achieved less than he wanted to partly, as the critics on his left complained, because he fought less doggedly than he might have, but largely because Congress gave him much less than he asked for. Indeed in 1943 he took the unprecedented step of vetoing a revenue bill because, as he said, it provided "tax relief . . . not for the needy, but for the greedy."

Yet Roosevelt was not and never claimed to be a radical. He was a reformer, a meliorist, much in the tradition of the progressives of the early twentieth century, one of whom he had been as a young man. Like them, he intended to reform capitalism in order to preserve it, to enlarge and strengthen the middle class rather than to abolish it. ("I am that kind of a liberal because I am that kind of a conservative.") He moved therefore to protect farms and homes from foreclosure by providing government loans at reduced rates, loans that also increased the liquidity of banks that held mortgages either defaulted or in arrears. So, too, federal insurance of bank deposits protected depositors from loss and banks from runs. While helping those who owned property to retain it, the New Deal also generated a gradual leveling effect as labor policy moved blue collar workers toward middle-class income and status, and agricultural policy assured many farmers first of a tolerable and later of a comfortable standard of life.

The urban unemployed had the hardest road to travel. In contrast to any previous President, Roosevelt accepted the obligation of the federal government to provide assistance to the destitute. There was never enough relief, never enough money appropriated to hire all those who needed jobs or properly to care for all the shivering and hungry. But as they developed, the relief programs hired more and more men and women, and hired them increasingly in jobs related to their talents and aspirations as lawyers, accountants, engineers, artists, writers, teachers, actors. The New Deal's relief policies ("We are poor indeed if this Nation cannot afford to lift from every recess of American life the dread fear of the unemployed that they are not needed in the world"), sometimes faltering in execution, rarely adequate for unemployables, pointed to the large goals Roosevelt defined for a more prosperous, postwar America—the rights of every family to a decent home, to necessary medical care, to a decent education; the right his generation especially cherished "to a useful and remunerative job."

As his kind of liberal, his kind of conservative, Roosevelt took for granted the need to operate within the tolerances of the American political system and consequently to build not for eternity but for a year or two or ten ahead, when building would have to proceed again. As a tactician, he did not want to tie his hands, he liked to remain on a twenty-four-hour basis, he was ready to concede what he considered marginal in order to gain what he deemed essential. By the standards of a later generation, on some issues his concessions outweighed his gains.

So it was with racial matters. Roosevelt tended not to think in racial terms. He approached questions of Negro rights from a political rather than an idealistic angle. He responded to Negro leaders sympathetically but evasively. Accordingly the New Deal assisted Negroes only in limited ways. Government under Roosevelt ceased being lily-white. The executive departments desegregated their facilities, and particularly in Washington, increasing numbers of Negroes found permanent federal jobs, though disproportionately in menial or clerical roles. In some Northern states, Negroes received a considerable though not an equitable share of relief, and one major relief program trained young Negroes for skilled jobs until Congress eliminated its funds. But Roosevelt delayed establishing the Fair Employment Practices Committee until he was pushed into it. Without reflection, he permitted discrimination against Negroes within the Civilian Conservation Corps and by the Tennessee Valley Authority. Fearful that a Southern filibuster would tie up "must" legislation, he continually avoided taking a strong stand for an anti-lynching bill. For their part, Southern congressmen had no trouble amending the Relief Act of 1935 so as to make appointments of senior administrators subject to senatorial consent, a provision that assured rewards for deserving Democrats everywhere and the triumph in the South of Jim Crow in the distribution of relief.

His spotty record on racial issues reflected Roosevelt's sense of priorities. Questions of political economy commanded his attention until 1940. During the years of war, his preoccupation was victory, to which he subordinated various democratic objectives, often on the basis of supposedly expert but dubious advice. To the dismay of Eleanor Roosevelt, he accepted the hollow argument of the War and Navy Departments that desegregation of the armed forces would impede the progress of the war. He also followed the Army's lamentable advice in incarcerating the Japanese-Americans. Similarly, on the basis of his judgments about the mood of Congress and the politics of the Middle East, he tolerated the State Department's devastating delays in finding asylums for European Jews threatened with extinction by the Nazis. Yet Roosevelt's humanity, projected in his spontaneous warmth, won him the trust and love of men and women who had reason for impatience with those public acts.

When his personal impulses clashed with his sense of political possibilities, Roosevelt suffered seasons of caution or indecision. Detesting Hitler, he foresaw the dangers Nazism posed to Europe and to peace. But he also recognized, as in degree he shared, the disenchantment of Americans with the First World War and their reluctance again to be embroiled. Yielding to that mood, which dominated Congress, Roosevelt until 1940 put forward no significant policy contingent upon public approval to retard aggression or to preserve world peace. Within the area of his executive discretion, he made occasional, inconclusive gestures toward those ends. Concern for the balance of power in Europe and Asia motivated his recognition of the Soviet Union in 1933. His desire to buttress France brought him in 1936 to support technical changes in monetary and tariff policy he had previously opposed. He interpreted neutrality legislation to the advantage of China and of Loyalist Spain. After the Munich conference, he stretched his interpretations further so as to encourage French and British purchases of American military aircraft. But his first bursts of effective energy came only with the fall of France when his constituency at last recognized the vulnerability of the United States. Then in quick succession came the sale of surplus arms to England, the destroyer deal, lend-lease, the use of the

American navy to convoy ships as far as Iceland, and the incremental embargo against Japan.

By the summer of 1941, those limits drawn, Roosevelt's energy abated. By then he had settled in his mind upon the policy of assisting the British and the Russians in the war in Europe first, the Chinese only secondarily, and of continuing, as fast as possible, to arm the United States, still woefully unprepared to fight. There Roosevelt halted. To those eager for outright war against the Axis, he seemed unsure of himself, drifting. Pearl Harbor mobilized his energy again, as it mobilized the temper of America, until then manifestly anti-Axis but still wistfully anti-war.

Roosevelt did not plan Pearl Harbor, an unparalleled disaster for the United States. American officers, civilian and military alike, had misinterpreted the MAGIC intercepts which, if accurately interpreted, would have removed the surprise element in the attack. But those officers were not traitors. They simply erred, just as loyal men in Norway, France, Great Britain, and the Soviet Union had erred in failing accurately to read the evidence of incipient German movements before those movements caught them by surprise.

Roosevelt's policies, however, did challenge Japanese ambitions. Had he raised no objections to the Japanese war against China or Japanese expansion into Southeast Asia, Japan would not have chosen to attack. If the American embargo had not reduced Japan's access to supplies of strategic materials, Japan would probably not have decided to attack in 1941. War came in the Pacific because the Japanese government, committed to its purposes, wholly understood American opposition to them and believed it could prevail by starting a war it expected to win.

By insisting upon the independence of China, Roosevelt demanded more than the resources of the United States could guarantee, but before and after 1941, he committed only a

fraction of those resources to the Chinese. Even that fraction
was wasted by the weak, undemocratic, and corrupt government of Chiang Kai-shek. In spite of growing doubts about
Chiang, Roosevelt retained more confidence in the possibility
of guiding him than conditions warranted. There was no ready
alternative. Repeated American efforts failed to bring Chiang
to necessary social and political reforms. The United States
could not engage in a full-scale land war in Asia, or in the
deliberate subversion of Chiang's regime. Blindly, the
Generalissimo raced to his own destruction which the Japanese had begun by their invasion and the Communists completed by force of arms. Roosevelt's tactic failed, for Chiang
was a weak instrument for achieving the independence or
guiding the development of China. But unlike most statesmen in the West, Roosevelt realized that a strong and independent China would occupy a crucial place in postwar politics.

He realized, too, that the winning of the war and the preservation of the peace depended upon the cultivation of cooperation with the Soviet Union as well as with Great Britain.
Yet jealous of American interests, he conceded to Russia and
England only those matters he deemed expendable for the
sake of victory. He shaped the Bretton Woods agreements to
the economic advantage of the United States. He looked forward to the ultimate independence of India and of other British and European colonies, but he pressed for that eventuality
only as far as he believed he could without disrupting the
Anglo-American alliance. Similarly, he never agreed to Russian expansion in eastern Europe. But because he recognized
the indispensable contribution of Russian armies to the waging of the war and the enormous costs the Russians bore, he
pushed his subordinates to facilitate lend-lease aid to Russia
and he shared Stalin's impatience with British hesitations about
the cross-Channel invasion. He also welcomed the prospect
of Russian engagement on the Asian front where the Japa-

nese, until Yalta and later, seemed capable of prolonged resistance to American offensives.

Roosevelt did not foresee, much less invite, the cold war. On the contrary, he planned after an armistice rapidly to remove American forces from Europe and Asia. He expected also, perhaps with too little sensitivity for the feelings and prerogatives of smaller nations, to base postwar stability, within the framework of the United Nations, upon the influence and continuing cooperation of four major powers—the United States, the Soviet Union, the United Kingdom, and China. Those expectations overestimated Russian friendship and British strength, and underestimated the aspirations of colonial peoples, the distress of Europe, and the mutual suspicions of governing authorities in Washington and Moscow. Perhaps Roosevelt overestimated most of all his own ability to improvise, to patch things over, once the war was won, until the gradual realization of his expectations dispelled the suspicions that threatened them.

While the war raged, Roosevelt was so intent on victory that he made some decisions that worried the Soviet Union and challenged the identification of the United States with democratic forces and causes, with the very freedoms he had pronounced. So, in two revealing instances—American reliance on Admiral Jean-François Darlan and later Therese B. Peyrouton in North Africa, and American collaboration with Marshal Pietro Badoglio in Italy—the United States chose partners whom French and Italian democrats distrusted and disliked. The advocates of those partnerships excused them on the ground of military necessity. Roosevelt agreed, just as he had agreed on the same ground to the War Department's opposition to racial desegregation. As Commander-in-Chief he felt, apparently, that he had no choice. Still, he incurred long-range costs to international amity and to social justice, causes he intended to promote.

Those decisions and others like them persuaded Roosevelt's critics that he was a master of duplicity. Rather, the competing demands of individual freedom and of social and political order shaped his course. He was, after all, a statesman, not a saint; a politician, not a pamphleteer; a man whose chosen role put a premium on doing. He disciplined his consciousness in order to protect his essential capacity to act from the complicating counsels of his democratic sympathies. And though not without occasional miscalculations, he succeeded in being his kind of a liberal, his kind of a conservative.

For most Americans over sixty ("This generation . . . has a rendezvous with destiny") he still lives in their past. A Lackawanna train in April 1945 on which some dozen homeward-bound commuters cheered the death of that bastard in the White House. ("They are unanimous in their hatred for me—and I welcome their hatred.") A small ship swinging into Tulagi harbor where a message told the incredulous crew that Roosevelt had died. "Who the hell is President?" a teenage sailor wondered. He recalled no other President. ("Let me assert my firm belief that the only thing we have to fear is fear itself.") For those over sixty there remain that open Ford, that old gray hat, that tilted cigarette, that wave and grin, those words and their familiar cadence: "The test of our progress is not whether we add more to the abundance of those who have much; it is whether we provide enough for those who have too little." "More than an end to war, we want an end to the beginning of all wars." After half a century, there is that past, and in those words it speaks directly to the present.

8

FIRST LADY:
ELEANOR ROOSEVELT[*]

IN the course of her busy and constructive life, Eleanor Roosevelt wrote three volumes of autobiography which revealed
much about her as a woman and more about her contributions to the many good causes she served. During most of her
life, she was continually visible to the American people, in
the public eye as wife of the President, as his unofficial emissary, as a champion of her own preferred social reforms, and
not least as a public lecturer and syndicated columnist. She
was a woman of whom few Americans of her generation or of
her children's generation were unaware, one whom most of
them admired. Yet the day after she died, students in a history class at Yale University punctuated a lecture about her
with boos. One of her grandsons, a member of that class,
wistfully asked the lecturer an hour later why his friends had
hissed his grandmother. The lecturer, sad and surprised him-

*Adapted from a review of Joseph P. Lash, *Eleanor and Franklin* (New York: W. W. Norton, 1971) in *The Yale Review,* Vol. 61, no. 3 (Summer 1971), pp. 422–28.

self, replied as best he could that the students, like their parents whom they echoed, had never known her. . . .

The daughter of parents from socially prominent and wealthy New York families, Anna Eleanor Roosevelt grew up under the suffocating constraints of late Victorian values and mores. Orphaned as a child, she lived with her maternal grandmother, a pious, prudish old lady who expected her young charge to conform to her own ascetic standards. Eleanor was supposed to acquire, too, the manners and graces of conventional debutantes, and to enter Society as a prelude to an acceptable marriage and an ensuing career of motherhood, domestic management, and unostentatious leisure. Though a strong neopuritanical streak marked her always, Eleanor Roosevelt gradually shed the genteel culture of her childhood. First as a schoolgirl in England, later as her husband's wife and in ventures of her own, she demonstrated an extraordinary capacity to learn from experience. The mature woman little resembled her grandmother's image of a lady.

Experience taught her, for one example, the injustice and irrationality of the antisemitism of her youth. For another, by sheer act of her will she overcame her even stronger prejudice against blacks. For years she would not employ them even as domestic servants. For still longer she called them "darkies." When later she realized that blacks had a right to a full and equal share in American life, she nevertheless for a time drew back from physical contact with them. Resolved to shed that bias, too, she did. By 1941 she had become of all white Americans probably the most spontaneous and generous friend of American blacks and the most influential advocate of the political and social changes their leaders considered essential. Her journey past prejudice carried her far beyond the tolerance of her contemporaries. In the South, "Eleanor stories" gave an obscene cast to her decency. In the

War Department, Henry Stimson and his associates casti-
gated her for attacking their policy of continued segregation
of black soldiers, whom they privately deemed inferior bio-
logically and intellectually. In the White House, her husband, only an opportunistic champion of civil rights, arranged
his schedule to avoid her proddings about that issue.

As with blacks, so with youth, the First Lady offered
understanding instead of her husband's characteristic impatience or jolly evasiveness. Continually she encouraged young
men and women to define and pursue their legitimate goals,
especially those designed to employ the federal government
as an instrument to open for youth avenues of training, education, and employment that would permit the eager and the
diligent to discover their talents, fulfill themselves, and in
the process enrich the nation. In listening to the young, she
provided an audience for radical as well as conventional peti-
tioners. Her critics to the contrary, however, she embraced
neither the Marxism nor the Stalinism of some of those who
attempted to recruit her. Rather she believed that the American system could and should allow, indeed generate, the
changes which she and her true young friends endorsed.

Both as a promoter and as a symbol she pushed that system
toward its limits. No New Dealer exceeded her in zeal for
the fight against poverty. Her projects were many, but her
favorite involved the development of Arthurdale, West Virginia, as a new community where the Appalachian poor, with
federal assistance in the early stages of the experiment, could
find rewarding employment to support decent living and good
schooling and their own self-respect. Because the scheme . . .
seemed to be impractical, her critics considered it visionary.
It was neither. Had the Congress been less parsimonious, the
executive branch less conventional, and both more dedicated
to reform than to palliation, Arthurdale might have received,
as it did not, the funds essential for success. The development

of underdeveloped regions, as Americans have come to learn, could not proceed at bargain basement prices. Too, that kind of development, as Eleanor Roosevelt knew, was essential unless the American people were to imprison one-fifth of their countrymen in poverty. In Arthurdale, as in other instances, her practical idealism fell before the monumental inertia of the federal government even in a period of social reform. Yet at Arthurdale as elsewhere, she symbolized great possibilities.

As a living example of those possibilities she made much of her impact on Americans. Especially did she represent the range of opportunity available to American women. As late as 1920, she had little interest in the ballot and less in politics. During that year, while FDR campaigned for the vice-presidency, she began her education in politics. Under the continuing guidance of Louis Howe, she was to become a master in her own right. As a politician, she worked ordinarily through others, especially with women, and she cherished anonymity; but . . . no woman exerted an influence equivalent to hers on Democratic politics from the mid-1920's through the next two decades. She used her influence to bring other women actively into politics and public life, and to mobilize women for sundry worthy purposes. Of course her political growth and influence depended heavily upon her husband's position, but she helped to reinforce that position. More important, few women of her generation were capable of learning as rapidly as she did or of involving themselves as deeply and effectively in a calling which had for so long been so emphatically male. Concurrently she pursued other callings with vigorous commitment—she was a schoolteacher, lecturer, journalist, and, with less success, entrepreneur in the manufacture of furniture. As in questions relating to blacks, youth, and the poor, so in those relating to the role of women in American life, Eleanor Roosevelt identified herself with what her uncle Theodore, in his better moments, might have called "the progress that conserves." During the next fifty years few politicians gained the wisdom and courage to stand on that whole range of issues where she had stood. . . .

Admirable pioneer, First Lady of her world, Eleanor Roosevelt nevertheless felt she had failed as a woman in love. Through what appears to have been no fault of her own, she sensed no love in her mother, if love there was. That handsome lady, while embracing her two sons, denied her shy and homely daughter a place in her heart. "Granny," she called the child Eleanor, who chilled at the name. Elliott Roosevelt, Eleanor's dashing father, adored his daughter, as she knew. He was the white knight of her fantasies, the center of her child's private universe. But Elliott . . . was sick, unreliable, a lost soul in a Victorian circle where psychoanalysis was unknown and would have been considered as unwholesome as were Elliott's well-known hedonism, uncertainty, alcoholism, and infidelity. His brother Theodore and his sister Bamie banished him. His daughter Eleanor clung to her memory of him, to his letters, and to his sweet promises which, characteristically, he almost always broke.

A hostile mother, a feckless father, a younger brother who ultimately failed her as his father had, all that Eleanor Roosevelt lived with. So, too, did she live closely to a mother-in-law so jealous of her own son's affections that she could not recognize his wife's desire to love her and please her. She had to live, too, with children spoiled by their grandmother and over-indulged by their preoccupied father. On occasion, her puritanical side ascendant, she bent perhaps too far the other way, for one example, in forcing her daughter into a school she despised, for another by punishing one son for several months for an inadvertent indiscretion painful for her. So she felt she had failed, at least in part, as daughter, sister, mother—roles to which she brought her own deep love and in which she wanted desperately to be loved deeply in return.

In some degree that sense of failure reflected her insecurity; in some degree it derived from her relationship with her husband. Had the love between them satisfied her expectations, her other experiences might in time have hurt her less.

At the outset . . . Eleanor and Franklin Roosevelt did love each other, and at the end that love, while altered, had by no means disappeared. Neither, for Eleanor, had the profound hurt Franklin inflicted upon her by his affair with Lucy Mercer. A pretty, young, vivacious woman, Eleanor's private secretary, Lucy Mercer in 1917 became for a time Franklin's mistress. She gave him what Eleanor could not: unquestioning adoration, companionship in frivolity, and apparently spontaneity in sex. Eleanor Roosevelt knew her husband wanted those qualities in a woman. She was by temperament and training unable to provide them. Never unquestioning, she was never adoring; formidably sensible, she was never frivolous or even comfortable with frivolity; wholly unliberated, she viewed sex only as a necessary obligation of marriage, most appropriate for procreation. She suspected that Franklin and Lucy were involved with each other. It was a liaison that Alice Longworth, Eleanor's cousin, encouraged. "He deserved a good time," Mrs. Longworth remarked of Franklin. "He was married to Eleanor." Typical of Alice Longworth, the comment cut because it came close to the truth. Still it was unfair, for Franklin, whatever his needs, knew how Eleanor would react to the discovery of the affair, which he permitted in a callous, even a cruel way.

Franklin Roosevelt, as he once admitted to Henry Morgenthau, was capable of cruelty toward those about whom he cared the most. Louis Howe, Morgenthau, Henry Wallace, among others, at one time or another felt the thrust of that capability. It was devastating for Eleanor. "The bottom dropped out of my own particular world," she later recalled. She rebuilt her world, and she and Franklin continued married on new

terms, one of which demanded his complete break with Lucy.
In the last, weary months of his life, he conspired with some
of his staff occasionally to see Lucy secretly at the White
House while Eleanor was away. The romance was surely gone,
but doubtless he again needed Lucy's quiet adoration. She
was among those at his cottage at Warm Springs the day he
died. Eleanor discovered his deceit when she arrived to
accompany his body to its grave. So the last thing he did was
to hurt her again, cruelly, and to make her feel again inadequate as a wife.

Yet whatever her weaknesses or his, their marriage was not
a failure. Her "services of love," as she called them, contributed to his career far more than did the assistance of anyone else. She was continually his conscience. Without Eleanor,
Franklin Roosevelt would have been a lesser President and a
lesser man. So, too, did he contribute to her career. The
extraordinary growth that marked it owed more to him,
directly and indirectly, than to any other influence. If his
infidelity spurred her to seek her independence, his physical
handicap later and his political needs thereafter channeled her
independent energies into socially creative enterprises. If she
was his conscience, he was her teacher, especially of the art
of the possible. Without Franklin, Eleanor Roosevelt would
have been a different and a lesser woman. In a significant
sense, then, their marriage, a love story of a kind, did succeed. In the equilibrium of their relationship, she was the
champion of human liberty; he was the guardian of public
order. Their incomparable partnership provided the foundation for their memorable achievements alike in politics and
of the human spirit.

9

THE PRICE OF VISION:
HENRY A. WALLACE*

HENRY Agard Wallace wanted to be Vice President of the
United States, mounted no campaign to secure or retain that
office, disliked many of its duties and limitations, and yet
desired renomination and resented those who prevented it.
Those attitudes reflected predictable responses by the kind of
man Wallace was to the nature of the vice-presidency, especially under the conditions that Franklin D. Roosevelt imposed
upon the conduct of business during his administrations. The
President could prescribe political snake oil even to so practical an intelligence as Wallace's. At his ebullient best, Roosevelt could engage Wallace's transcendental faith in progress
and brotherhood. Within the privacy of his person, as his
diary disclosed, Wallace recognized with bemused skepticism his own accepting vulnerability to the combination of
guile and greatness that characterized his chief. In that privacy he also conceded nothing, though officially he had con-

*This essay, reprinted here without its original notes, was first published as the Intro-
duction to *The Price of Vision: The Diary of Henry Wallace, 1942–1946* (Boston: Houghton Mifflin, 1973), pp. 3–49.

tinually to yield, to those decisions of Roosevelt's that bore adversely on policies to which Wallace attached some personal and larger public importance.

During the portentous years of World War II, the relationship of the President and the Vice President of the United States, their common objectives and their intermittent disagreements, deeply affected their party, their country, even the world. In considerable measure those relationships also forecast the more bitter and ominous conflicts that were later, at a critical time, to force Wallace out of public life and deprive American government of his humane sensibilities.

WALLACE'S path into and out of the vice-presidency began in the Middle Border, in the Iowa of the late nineteenth century, where the determining roots of his being grew out of his family, the soil it nurtured, and the culture it both shaped and absorbed. Always a man of that west, Wallace brought to Washington the perspectives and commitments that his western experience fostered continuously from his childhood to his middle life.

He was the third Henry Wallace, the son of Henry Cantwell Wallace and grandson of the first Henry Wallace, "Uncle Henry," who had grown up on the farm of his Ulster-Scot father near West Newton, Pennsylvania. The first Henry Wallace began his westering in search of improved health and of a seminary that offered a liberal Calvinist training. After ordination he continued west to Iowa to find a parish comfortable with his own reformist views. Soon he had to escape the tensions of his over-conscientious pastorate by turning to work the good ground of Winterset, Iowa, where he taught his neighbors about the scientific farming he practiced. Believing, as did thousands of Americans—all spiritual heirs of Thomas Jefferson—that farmers were the special agents of the Lord on earth, Wallace believed, too, that they had a duty to preserve the bounty of the earth. Christian faith, agrarian pride, and a conservationist practicality provided the foundations for the secular sermons that Uncle Henry contributed to his local newspaper during the 1880s. Those doctrines made him, too, a devoted Granger whose editorials attacked industry and the railroads—"the trusts"—that seemed to arrogate hard-won earnings of Iowa husbandmen to monopolistic profits of remote eastern capitalists.

Those messages were the texts also of the ablest farm leaders of his generation, Wallace's friends Seaman Knapp of Iowa State College and James Wilson ("Tama Jim"), another Iowan who was in time to serve the longest term (1897–1913) as Secretary of Agriculture in American history. Together, in sundry ways, they promoted scientific agriculture, sound farm management, and government policies favorable to their constituents. Uncle Henry counseled his constituents primarily through the newspaper he edited, *Wallaces' Farmer,* a farm weekly purchased in 1895 by his eldest son and published first in Cedar Rapids and later in Des Moines. He and his two friends, with others of similar mind, took their texts to the entire nation in their "Report of the Commission on Country Life," prepared in 1908–09 at the instigation of President Theodore Roosevelt. A persuasive summation of the program of agrarian progressives, the report called for redressing the grievances of rural America so as to preserve a "scientifically and economically sound country life." For Uncle Henry, that objective would ensure the future of the nation. "Good farming," he believed, "is simply obedience to natural law, just as good living is obedience to moral law." In 1916 his last will and testament encapsulated his creed: "Religion is not a philosophy but a life."

No one influenced Henry A. Wallace more than did Uncle Henry. Born in 1888, Wallace as a small child lived in Ames, where his father was teaching at the state agricultural college. In 1895 the family moved to Des Moines where the boy began to spend hours almost daily with his devoted grandfather. From Uncle Henry, who delighted in his grandson's quick mind and serious manner, young Henry learned about his family, about pioneering, about the land and plants and beasts. He learned, too, to recognize God in nature and man, and to serve him through work—work at the chores that sustained the land and its tillers, and work at the services that profited mankind. "Be sure," his mother often told her sons, "that you have clean hands. And remember that you are a Wallace and a gentleman."

Those lessons reached young Wallace from every point of his boyhood compass. His mother, a dedicated gardener, showed him the satisfactions of cultivating flowers, which he always loved. "Become gardeners," he recommended to his associates many years later. "Then you will never die, because you have to live to see what happens next year." His father guided him through the laboratories at the college and introduced him to a student he had befriended, a lonely, young black genius, George Washington Carver. The boy, habitually a solitary individual, eschewed his contemporaries to follow Carver, always an encouraging tutor, on botanical excursions. Carver "made so much of it," Wallace recalled, ". . . that, out of the goodness of his heart, he greatly exaggerated my botanical ability. But his faith aroused my natural instinct to excel . . . [and] deepened my appreciation of plants in a way I can never forget." And like Uncle Henry, Carver saw a divine force in all living things.

The boy's father encouraged his son's emerging interests. Henry C. Wallace, "H.C." or Harry to his friends, eldest of Uncle Henry's children, had a professional competence in breeding livestock and improving grains. From one of his friends, his teen-age son received some seed corn to test for productivity. With the seed, in 1904, Henry A. Wallace proved that the contours of an ear of corn did not correlate with its propensity to yield. The shape of the ear did not matter; what did was the genetic quality of the kernel.

At sixteen Wallace had discovered that the symmetry of a plant in no way assured its utility; indeed that in all life appearances could deceive. His characteristically tousled hair and rumpled clothes attested to his own indifference to appearance, as did his vigorous but conspicuously inelegant tennis. More important, he had learned from Carver as well as from genetics the lesson that he was later to label "genetic democracy," a doctrine by no means prevalent in the Middle Border or elsewhere in the United States in 1904.

His other lessons, some yet fully to be absorbed, had similar vectors. The experience of westering, for Uncle Henry and through him for his grandson, was an experience of cooperation, of a mingling of strangers in a common land where essential collective efforts gave individuality a chance to thrive and permitted groups of individuals to bargain with aggregates of distant economic power. The brotherhood of man, an article of Christian faith, was a palpable necessity as a means for surviving the rigors of the receding frontier and for controlling the threatening circumstances of contemporary life. So, too, the application of intelligence to environment, the employment of science to improve the products of nature, the utilization of economic data to manage the otherwise uncertain fluctuations of the market—those acts of mind and will guaranteed an abundance ample for the comfort of all men, truly a land of milk and honey, a new Jerusalem.

At Iowa State College and then on the family newspaper, Wallace refined his understanding of those conclusions. Sober, diligent, ascetic, he made few friends, studied hard, and conducted his experiments with genetics and with techniques for hybridizing corn. His Bachelor's essay demonstrated the importance of soil-building, one form of conservation, for raising livestock. Problems of land utilization were to interest him for the rest of his life. Though uninvolved in politics, he was, like his father and grandfather, an enthusiastic supporter of Theodore Roosevelt and the Progressive Party in 1912. The regulatory state that Roosevelt advocated, Wallace believed, would ultimately prevail even though the Bull Moose failed. Indeed for the sake of a prosperous agriculture, it had to prevail.

Wallace's studies in economics and mathematics convinced him of that. After college he undertook to educate himself in those subjects, as well as to exploit the other resources of the Des Moines Public Library. His children remember him arriving home at night always with a stack of books in his arms. Soon an expert on statistical correlations, Wallace used that method to derive accurate indices of the cost of production of hogs. He began publishing those indices in the family newspaper in 1915. On the basis of other data, he suggested in 1919 that productivity cycles in livestock had a seven-year pattern—higher productivity followed rising prices until the saturation of the market led to falling prices that induced lower productivity. Further study, now of census figures, persuaded Wallace that with industrialization and urbanization, the average size of families diminished. With the domestic market consequently curtailed, farmers would need larger markets abroad for their crops. His book summarizing his work, *Agricultural Prices* (1920), was, in the judgment of one leading economist, "perhaps the first realistic econometric study ever published." Later Wallace mastered even newer techniques for computing multiple correlations and regressions. With a mathematician as his collaborator, in 1925 he published *Correlation and Machine Calculation,* an early venture in the creative march toward computer technology. Statistics, mathematics, genetics, scientific husbandry, economics, demography, all those skills impinged upon the future of his Iowa neighbors, the men and women throughout the state who lived on the farms they worked.

THOSE men and women could control some of the variables that affected them. Wallace proved as much by putting into commercial use his knowledge about hybridization. With some business associates, he founded in 1926 the Hi-Bred Corn Company (later the Pioneer Hi-Bred Corn Company) to produce and sell hybrid corn. Characteristically, he also realized that the establishment of two competing concerns would help to supply the market, which would need all they could furnish. That act of faith in science, abundance, and competitive capitalism reflected no lack of business acumen. Wallace intended his company to make a legitimate profit. More, he intended his customers to profit from the use of his superior product, and in profiting to improve the quality and reduce the price of corn, to the advantage of all who purchased it. During years of agricultural depression the company shrewdly built the market for its seed by offering it to customers without demanding payment in cash on the condition that they plant half their acreage in hybrid, half in ordinary corn, and then repay a portion of the value of the higher yield on the acres growing the hybrid variety. By 1966, the higher yield from hybrid seed accounted for one quarter of the total national corn crop.

That innovative method for selling seed drew upon the example of Wallace's grandfather's friend, Seaman Knapp, who had devised the system of demonstration farming to persuade cotton growers to improve their methods of cultivation. Wallace's readiness to promote hybrid corn by inducing others also to enter the business revealed in some measure his intellectual debt to Thorstein Veblen, the powerful critic of

American capitalism whose books Wallace read with enthusiastic reward. Veblen provided a systematic analysis to support the suspicions of monopoly that Wallace had absorbed from his family and their adherence to the old Granger program. In industries dominated by a few large firms, Veblen argued, management could adjust production to demand in order to sustain prices and profits. That process, administered pricing in the vocabulary of a later generation, held production below capacity. In Veblen's words, it involved the sabotage by managers of the abundance which engineers were capable of creating. It inhibited productive potentialities which, if realized, would assure plenty for all Americans. Veblen imagined a solution in a revolution that would transfer industrial authority to a soviet of technicians, men committed to maximum production and equitable distribution.

Wallace, educated also by other economists, was moving toward a less dramatic formulation, but one from which he expected similar results. Like other western progressives, he advocated a vigorous application of the antitrust laws and other federal controls to limit the size and power of industrial concentrations, and to prevent them from restricting production or retarding technological advances that increased productivity. Like Veblen, he envisaged a technologically dynamic society dedicated to the efficient making and sharing of industrial and agricultural commodities, a society that would need scientists and managers to fashion an abundant life for the common man. In its agricultural sector, that society—capitalistic but not beholden to laissez-faire doctrines—would function according to the model he had created for marketing hybrid corn. Through management, science and technology would overcome poverty and hunger, "Science," Wallace later wrote, ". . . cannot be overproduced. It does not come under the law of diminishing utility. . . . It is perishable and must

be constantly renewed." It was for him the continuing frontier, the limitless source of new plenty and leaping hope.

The selfishness of industrial practices, in Wallace's view,
had its political equivalent in the selfishness of economic
nationalism, of protective tariffs and other artificial restraints
on international trade. That trade, he believed, if unfettered,
would provide the avenue to sharing abundance throughout
the world. Wallace had grown up with the "Iowa Idea," a
plan that called for removing or reducing the protection
afforded products manufactured by large corporations,
including many products farmers bought, like barbed wire
and harvesters. Confronted by European competition, American manufacturers would have to reduce their prices or lose
some of their market. In either case, farmers would benefit.
Just as important, as Europeans gained access to the American market, they would earn dollars which they could then
spend to purchase American agricultural commodities.

Reduction of tariffs, as Wallace saw it, also related to the
preservation of peace. In the absence of restraints on trade,
nations would become more dependent upon each other and
therefore less able to embark upon war. To that issue Veblen
also spoke. Imperial Germany, he believed, constituted the
greatest threat to peace, for the Prussian autocracy and the
military elite formed a combination of purpose and power
committed to domination and conquest. For Wallace, that
grim potentiality could mark the United States if an industrial plutocracy and an ambitious military combined to direct
national policy.

Accordingly Wallace anguished over the future of his country
when he observed during the years of World War II that
Standard Oil of New Jersey, part of a cartel controlled by I.
G. Farben, had manipulated patents to prevent the American
development of synthetic rubber; that oil companies in gen-

eral came to foster that development but oppose increasing natural sources of rubber in Latin America, sources on which the United States would be partially dependent; that industry and the military combined to dampen, almost to eliminate, federal prosecution of firms violating the antitrust laws; that the American cornucopia, sufficient to feed a devastated world, was to be confined, according to the preferences of the same men of money and of arms, to helping only those peoples, whatever their need, whose politics followed American prescriptions; and that the findings of American science were to be similarly contained. Those developments made profits and even plenty the handmaidens of politics. Yet for Wallace politics was only a necessary means for setting policies that would put both profits and plenty within the reach of every man.

WALLACE disliked politics in all its aspects. Never gregarious, he was uncomfortable alike in smoke-filled rooms and noisy halls. Shy but candid and sometimes blunt, he lacked small talk. He detested both the manipulation of men and the prolonged conniving it demanded. He learned to campaign, but his speeches, while often effective, made only clumsy concessions to the harmless blarney that ordinarily punctuated political oratory. "Farmer Wallace," he was called by Alice Longworth, Theodore Roosevelt's daughter and Washington's social doyenne. She did not mean it as a compliment, but as usual her description had some substance. In her salon, in her world of genial conspiracies, Wallace was never wholly at ease.

Yet Wallace entered politics, first as an editor supporting compatible candidates, later as a holder of high office, ultimately as a candidate himself, because he had no alternative except to abandon the public policies he urged upon the nation. Like his Iowa neighbors, as a private citizen he could control only some of the variables affecting his life and theirs. The others fell to the control or misdirection or indifference of the government.

Both major political parties continually disappointed the Wallaces. The Republicans during the Taft years did nothing to help agriculture. The Democrats under Woodrow Wilson proved to be rather stingy benefactors. Congress did reduce the tariff and ease conditions for agricultural credit. Further, the Food Administration under Herbert Hoover during World War I stimulated the production of corn and hogs. But, as Wallace's father continually demonstrated, Hoover—Iowa-born but otherwise bred—paid Iowans meanly for their efforts.

In 1921 Henry C. Wallace accepted appointment as President Warren G. Harding's Secretary of Agriculture. His son, now editor of the newspaper, had also a close view of the operations of his father's department. H.C. recruited a staff of experts who brought unprecedented technical talents to their tasks. He was able, too, with Harding's support, to persuade Congress to enact legislation to assist agricultural marketing and to curb speculation in commodities. But the senior Wallace failed in his program to reach markets overseas. His successful antagonist was again Herbert Hoover, now Secretary of Commerce, whose relentless opposition to promoting agriculture contrasted with his vigorous efforts in behalf of industry. Hoover, so Henry A. Wallace believed, contributed inadvertently to the frustration and fatigue that taxed his father's strength and reduced his resistance to the operation from which he was unable to recover in 1924.

Before his death, H. C. Wallace had endorsed a plan for agriculture for which his son helped thereafter to organize increasing support. Incorporated in a succession of bills sponsored by Senator Charles L. McNary of Oregon and Representative Gilbert N. Haugen of Iowa, that plan proposed a two-price system for commodities. Government purchases

were to sustain the domestic price at the level of "parity"—
the ratio between agricultural and industrial prices that had
prevailed during the years 1910–14, good years for farmers.
The government would sell its purchases abroad at a lower
price while taxing farmer-beneficiaries to cover any losses.
There were shortcomings to the plan. European tariffs, rising
to compete with American protection, would impede the
necessary sales. Europeans were in any case short of dollars
because of the drain of repaying the United States for debts
incurred during the war. More important, the McNary-Haugen plan placed no limits on production, which would increase
to unmanageable proportions if the government guaranteed
farmers a high price on all their crops. President Calvin Coolidge and Herbert Hoover both opposed the plan, which Congress twice passed and Coolidge twice vetoed, primarily on
other grounds. They contended that it would destroy individualism, establish artificial prices, and create a dangerous
federal bureaucracy to administer it. Those objections ignored
the artificial prices, large bureaucracies, and collective rather
than individualistic nature of American corporate enterprise.

A registered Republican, Wallace condemned the GOP for
its callousness toward the farmer, whose share of national
income was steadily falling, and for its acceptance of the
business creed. He urged his readers in 1924 to vote for Robert M. La Follette and his new Progressive party, and in 1928
to vote for Alfred E. Smith, the Democratic nominee who
had endorsed the latest McNary-Haugen bill. Yet so unpol-
itical was Wallace that he neglected to change his party reg-
istration until 1936.

From 1924 forward, he consulted continually with some
of the economists his father had employed in the Department
of Agriculture, in particular Henry C. Taylor, at one time
chief of the Bureau of Agricultural Economics, and two younger
men, Mordecai Ezekiel and Louis H. Bean, who were to con-

tinue fruitfully to advise the department and its head
throughout the 1930s and 1940s. He also came to know the
two leading academic experts on agricultural economics, John
D. Black of the University of Minnesota and later Harvard,
and M. L. Wilson of the University of Montana. After the
onset of the Great Depression, with its devastating consequences for markets at home and abroad, Black and Wilson
worked out the Domestic Allotment Plan, the program that
Wallace and like-minded farm leaders endorsed in 1932 as a
preferred substitute for the defeated McNary-Haugen proposals. The new plan, the basis for the Agricultural Adjustment Administration of the New Deal, looked to the federal
government to pay farmers to withdraw acreage from cultivation and thus curtail their production of crops. The withdrawal of marginal land and the rotation of cultivation of
fertile soil applied the principles of conservation. More
immediately, reduction in supply to the domestic market
would lift commodity prices, while government payments
would enlarge farm income, with parity in purchasing power
again the goal.

Especially after the crash of 1929, farmers had other crush-
ing problems. Land values had fallen during the 1920s and
now shrank further, while the interest payments on mortgage
debts incurred during the prosperous war years remained cruelly
high. The deflation in commodity prices made the weight of
debt intolerable, led to more and more foreclosures, and
embittered the countryside. Wallace came to advocate federal
action for mortgage relief and controlled inflation. Influenced
by Irving Fisher, the foremost American economist of his
generation, Wallace served as vice president of Fisher's Stable
Money League. It demanded a commodity dollar, a dollar
valued not on a fixed ratio to gold but by a constant relationship to purchasing power, in itself elastic. *Wallaces' Farmer*
educated its readers in those ideas, while Wallace became a

familiar figure at conferences concerned with preserving a healthy rural America.

Like his father and grandfather, Wallace became a reformer without becoming a radical. He saw the need for strong federal action and for a large federal establishment to protect the existence of the independent farmer. Price supports, mortgage relief, and managed money were adventurous departures from past policy. As their advocate, Wallace contemplated major institutional change. But he did not approve farmer strikes to withhold crops from market, or the sudden liquidation of mortgages, or an undisciplined recourse to printing paper or coining silver money. Those more radical measures had their many champions by 1932, for an angry impatience naturally flowed from the desperation of American farmers. But Franklin D. Roosevelt, the successful aspirant for the Democratic nomination that year, by temperament a moderate, found the reforms with which Wallace was identified compatible with his own sense of proper remedy. Wallace, one of the experts whose advice Roosevelt solicited, supported him both before and after his nomination. Once elected, Roosevelt decided, after reviewing several other possibilities, that Wallace had the confidence of the farm leaders and the qualities of mind and purpose that he wanted in his Secretary of Agriculture. Wallace accepted the position. Now, in spite of himself, his commitment to agricultural reform had drawn him into politics, both the politics of decision-making within the federal government and the politics of competition between the parties.

THERE was a part of Henry Wallace that Franklin Roosevelt recognized but never criticized. Some of his less sympathetic associates worried about what they considered Wallace's mysticism, a quality they considered disturbing and unpredictable in its consequences. Yet Wallace was not a mystic, unless that description, as he once said, applied to any man of Christian faith. What made him seem a mystic to those who called him one was primarily his indomitable curiosity, a curiosity that led him to explore everything that caught his interest, religion not the least.

Essentially Wallace's religion was the Christianity common in the Middle Border. It had its foundation in faith rather than theology. Like Uncle Henry, Wallace concluded that the rigid tenets of orthodox Calvinism clashed with his generous belief in the pervasive goodness of God. Those tenets were at variance, too, with his sense of the presence of God in nature and life. He did not use the vocabulary of transcendentalism, but he shared the convictions of that creed about the immanence of God in man. Still he also tried continually to find God, not palpably but spiritually, whether in the beauty of growing things, in the symmetry of genetic patterns, or in the evocations of religious rituals. Consequently he experimented with religion, just as he experimented with corn, seeking the most satisfying yield.

Wallace tested his responses to various churches. He was conscious of the spiritual excitement that Methodism could stir but too private a man to find continuing fulfillment in collective rhapsody. The gorgeous rituals of Catholicism also moved him, but Catholic dogma and hierarchy put him off. He tried to feel what the saints had felt by practicing one kind of ascetism or another, but for him deprivation of the flesh or spiritual removal from the world divorced religion too much from life, which he was resolved to serve. He was at times fascinated by the occult and he studied oriental faiths, but they, too, failed to answer his needs, though his reading led him to a concept of Confucius, a "constantly normal granary," a phrase he adapted for his own use. He settled in the end for membership in the Episcopal church, which he attended regularly during his years in Washington. Here, particularly in the communion service, he received as much as formal religion could offer him. He interpreted the Lord's Supper his own way. "It is the function of the church," Wallace said at one communion breakfast, "to emphasize the ties which draw men together no matter how much finite differences may appear to separate them. . . . Weak as is the church . . . it is a synthesizing, centripetal force . . . on behalf of the sacredness of the individual and the unity of humanity." It was the symbol and the agency of the brotherhood of man.

That brotherhood had a special psychological importance for Wallace. Just as he was not a hail-fellow, so, outside of his immediate family, he was not an intimate man. His aloneness in life fostered his need for brotherhood in spirit, a need he recognized in other men, particularly those who lived on the soil. He put it best, perhaps, in discussing the people of Soviet Asia: "All of them . . . were people of plain living and robust minds, not unlike our farming people in the United States. Much that is interpreted . . . as 'Russian distrust' can be written off as the natural cautiousness of farm-bred people. . . . Beneath the . . . new urban culture, one catches glimpses of the sound, wary, rural mind." Those wary men and women Wallace discovered everywhere he went, in Siberia, China, throughout Latin America, as well as in the countryside of the United States and beneath the skins of Americans in labor unions or military regalia or governmental suites. Not their spiritual comfort only, but also, in the shadows of an awful war, the prospects for a genuine peace depended upon a centripetal force that would assure the sacredness of every one of them and the unity of mankind.

Essential though it was, the church was not enough. Always a Calvinist in part, Wallace had a sense of duty, even of mission, to accomplish the work of the Lord. His continual recourse to biblical metaphor was more than the rhetorical habit of a minister's grandson. He was an austere moralist, impatient less with impiety than with sloth, deceit, selfishness, and materialism. More, he cast himself often as prophet or witness, now in the role of Joseph husbanding his people's resources, now as Micah beating swords into ploughshares, now as Gideon attacking a wicked citadel. That last role he assumed in 1948, in his predictably futile campaign for the Presidency as the candidate of a disorganized new party, against the advice of his family and his loyal friends, indeed against his better judgment. He had, he felt, to bear witness against the policies he had attacked and for the beliefs he had broadcast.

Yet the compulsions of mission that inhered in Wallace's religion were balanced by a contemplative gentleness. It was not just that he loved his family, which he did, deeply though undemonstratively. It was also that when he crossbred corn or strawberries, he had more at stake than productivity. He loved the plants, just as he loved grasses—grasses, as he described them, growing quietly taller, silently dropping their seeds onto the earth and into the winds, full fields of grasses bending with the prevailing breeze, full fields observed from the air in huge patterns of contrasting greens and browns. He loved the soil, the way it felt between the fingers, its pungent darkness. Without direct contact with growing things, he lost touch with the universe and its creator. His Washington victory garden, planted in his sister's yard, provided a useful crop, but more important, gave him when he worked in it a serenity he could capture no other way. In the soil he found his ultimate communion. His was strongly a Social Gospel, but he tempered that gospel with a tenderness that displayed his natural charity. Joseph he could emulate, or Gideon, but at the core he was more akin to Paul.

To the secular mind, Wallace's faith seemed outmoded, his witnessing quaint, his spirituality incomprehensible. To the urban mind, his affinity with nature appeared irrelevant and distracting. As for his inquiries into the occult, secular and urban Americans took them for an eccentricity. Washington was filled with the polished, the urbane, and the fashionable, so in Washington Farmer Wallace, spiritually as well as culturally uncomfortable, felt often bored and out of place. As Roosevelt realized, that did not matter. He needed Wallace to manage the Department of Agriculture and its programs, and for that task, Wallace, practical scientist and progressive reformer, was admirably equipped.

DURING his eight years as Secretary of Agriculture, Henry A. Wallace accomplished more than did any one else who has ever held that office. Each of the many programs the department initiated, as one of its officers later attested, "had Wallace's close attention and support." Each profited, too, from the support Wallace solicited from the President and from the skills of the administrators, lawyers, economists, and agronomists to whom the Secretary delegated responsibilities for the detailed supervision and the technical research without which the department could not have functioned. They were impressive men, several of whom became Wallace's lifelong friends. Among the most effective were Rexford G. Tugwell, Wallace's first Under Secretary, one of Roosevelt's original brain-trusters, who, like Wallace, had studied Veblen; Mordecai Ezekiel, senior economic adviser, and his talented associate, Louis Bean; Paul Appleby, chief administrative officer, and Milo Perkins, who ran various special programs like the Food Stamp Plan for the distribution of surplus commodities to impoverished Americans; Chester Davis, who for some years managed the Agricultural Adjustment Administration; and, for a brief period, Jerome N. Frank, a brilliant young New York lawyer.

The Agricultural Act of 1933, a keystone in Roosevelt's recovery program, made national policy of the various proposals with which Wallace had been identified before the election. Among the provisions of the act, one founded the Agricultural Adjustment Administration within the Department of Agriculture to manage the Domestic Allotment Plan. In developing policy under that plan, Wallace confronted two major crises which he resolved with a practical opportunism that revealed both a disciplined toughness and a political sensitivity surprising to his critics.

The earlier episode arose because the Domestic Allotment program was established too late to affect planting or husbandry in the spring of 1933. Farmers in the south had already started their cotton, farmers in the west had already bred their hogs, before the Agricultural Adjustment Administration (AAA) could begin to make payments for the withdrawal of acreage or the limitation of production. Yet cotton and hogs, glutting the market, were selling at historically low prices. To remove the glut, to prevent it from carrying over to 1934, to raise prices and to increase farm income, Wallace deliberately violated his own profound belief in abundance and its distribution. He mobilized the Extension Service of the department to enlist cotton farmers, in return for bountiful payments ($100 million in all), to plough up a quarter of their crop. Less drastic measures assisted grain farmers. As for hogs, on the advice of local committees throughout the west and of the Farm Bureau Federation, the department purchased and slaughtered six million little pigs. Much of the baby pork was given to the hungry on relief, but Wallace deeply regretted the conditions that had forced his hand. "The plowing under . . . of cotton . . . and the slaughter of . . . pigs," he said, "were not acts of idealism in any sane society. They were emergency acts made necessary by the almost insane lack of world statesmanship . . . from 1920 to 1932." He had to play, he explained, the cards that were dealt him; industry had limited production artificially for many years, and "agriculture cannot survive in a capitalistic society as a philanthropic enterprise."

The unavoidable destruction of crops in 1933 prepared the stage for the successful operation of AAA and in later years for new directions of policy, but a second crisis intruded before Wallace could embark on those new directions. Recourse to the Extension Service, as Wallace knew, reinforced the position within the department of one of its most conservative sections, for the Service had long fostered the interests of the Farm Bureau Federation, an organization dominated by large commercial farmers, whose needs often conflicted with those of small, independent farmers, tenants, and farm laborers. Further, Wallace had had temporarily to accept as head of the AAA George N. Peek, a father of the McNary-Haugen scheme, who remained committed to dumping surpluses abroad rather than controlling production at home. Soon able to get rid of Peek, Wallace replaced him with Chester Davis who, like his predecessor, had the confidence of the Farm Bureau Federation. Wallace felt he needed that group's large influence in Congress, but the price proved high. In 1935 Davis and Jerome Frank clashed over AAA contracts which Frank and his young associates had written to protect farm tenants and sharecroppers in the south. Either he or Frank, Davis told Wallace, would have to go.

Wallace regretfully fired Frank and most of his group in the General Counsel's office. Frank was shocked, as was Rex Tugwell, for they believed they had been following the Secretary's wishes. Years later, others believed Wallace had acted to purge the department of communists, of whom a few were in Frank's office. The latter issue simply did not occur to Wallace. The former pained him, for, as with the little pigs, he realized that he had departed from principle in order to preserve his ability to move ahead, albeit with reduced speed, toward larger goals. He had already concluded that the habit of dissent, typical in his experience of the western Democrats who had jointed La Follette in 1924, obstructed a practical approach to solving urgent problems. "It seems," Wallace wrote in 1935, "as though . . . Progressives are splendid critics but very poor builders."

The episode of the purge, perhaps especially Tugwell's angry disappointment with the Secretary's expediency, had a double impact on Wallace. It persuaded him, under the tutelage of Will Alexander of his staff, more thoroughly to examine the wretched circumstances of southern croppers, white and black, and of the displaced and miserable migrant farm laborers of the west. He proceeded then more aggressively to seek effective remedies for their problems. He added his own support to the efforts to create the Resettlement Administration (under Tugwell and later Alexander) and the Farm Security Administration (under Alexander, Milo Perkins, and C. B. Baldwin). Those agencies began, though belatedly, to help the downtrodden in American agriculture. Wallace had earlier sponsored the Rural Electrification Administration that carried inexpensive electricity to farm homes, an objective first defined by the Country Life Commission. As Ezekiel wrote, REA "revolutionized the face of rural America." Further, Wallace's growing concern for eradicating rural poverty and his growing suspicions of the Farm Bureau Federation sensitized him to the problems of urban poverty and of American blacks, and rekindled his apprehensions about big business and its privileges. By the time of World War II, he had become the champion of the common man alike on the streets and on the land. He had become, too, an opponent of the demands not only of arrogant industrialists but also of the equally arrogant Farm Bureau.

The episode of the purge had also a more personal effect

on Wallace. Because he had to decide between Davis and Frank, he had no escape from the politics of allocating power. Because he accepted a short-run loss in order to try to win long-run gains, he had to bend principle to expediency. In so doing, he had to wound an able and trusting subordinate. Later, during World War II, Wallace may have recalled the pains of 1935 when Roosevelt in effect fired him first from the chairmanship of the Board of Economic Warfare and later from the vice-presidency. In both cases the President sacrificed some principle to more expediency; in both he sacrificed a valued colleague to his own assessment of political exigencies. In both instances, Wallace, though gravely wounded, remained loyal to Roosevelt, whom he still preferred to any other chief. The problem, Wallace realized even in 1935, grew out of the New Deal's style of administration. "In this administration," he wrote, "the objectives are experimental and not clearly stated; therefore, there is certain to be, from the White House down, a certain amount of what seems to be intrigue. I do not think this situation will be remedied until the President abandons . . . his experimental and somewhat concealed approach. There are . . . many advantages to this approach but it does not lead to the happiest personal relationships and the best administration." Roosevelt never abandoned his approach. In the politics of the New Deal, as Wallace discovered, one had on occasion to dish it out, and on other occasions to take it.

The game was worth the anguish if the stakes were high enough. For Wallace they were, for during the middle 1930s he succeeded in advancing his most cherished objectives. The Supreme Court's invalidation of the Agricultural Adjustment Act of 1933 forced the department to devise a constitutionally acceptable alternative. The Soil Conservation and Domestic Allotment Act of 1936 and the Agricultural Adjustment Act of 1938 preserved the practice of managing production. Those

measures also put a new emphasis on conservation, on withdrawing acreage not only to reduce crops but also to follow a
rational system of land utilization. From 1936 forward, as
Wallace said, "the Department launched a positive attack on
the dual problem of soil destruction and unbalanced crop-
ping."

The dreadful dust storms of the years immediately preceding had attested to the indispensability of protecting the
"voiceless land." Those disasters also reminded Americans of
the vulnerability of agriculture to nature and of the possibility of shortages in foodstuffs. The act of 1938 gave Wallace
the opportunity he had long sought to create an "ever-normal
granary," to employ government purchases, storage, and sales
so as to assure adequate supplies without future gluts or
shortages. The resulting program provided food for Americans and their allies during the extraordinary years of World
War II and the early postwar period. As Wallace admitted,
he had not foreseen the war when he formulated his program,
but his success led him to hope, as he wrote in 1942, for the
establishment of an ever normal granary on a worldwide scale.
That concept underlay the plans recommended in 1946 by
Sir John Boyd Orr, Director-General of the Food and Agricultural Organization of the United Nations, plans Wallace
energetically endorsed. He had earlier adopted comparable
policies to build up American strategic reserves through the
Board of Economic Warfare.

Just as the accumulation of reserves depended upon sources
abroad, so, as Wallace saw it, did the efficient functioning of
the American economy. Contending during the 1930s, as he
long had, that "America must choose," he related the choice
to national prosperity. The option lay between domestic self-
sufficiency, which would inhibit and distort economic growth,
and open international trade, which would encourage the
United States to produce and export what it did best and to

import goods produced more efficiently elsewhere. Wallace took the side of maximum growth, for it would provide employment for men and capital and permit the elimination of want. The New Deal's reciprocal trade treaties took a limited step toward freer trade, but Wallace envisaged much more dramatic changes that would open all markets and all shipping and air routes. The war spurred him to urge even more insistently interrelated policies to promote free trade, economic growth, and full employment.

WALLACE'S objectives, accomplishments, and expanding sympathies marked him by 1940 as one of the country's outstanding statesmen. He had demonstrated the personal loyalty to the President that John N. Garner, Vice President since 1933, so stubbornly withheld. Wallace had, too, the liberal credentials that Roosevelt wanted for his running mate in 1940. And during the first six months of that year Wallace had taken a position on the war in Europe that answered Roosevelt's political needs.

The President, in the view of his isolationist critics, was leading the nation too close to the conflict abroad. In the view of those, still a minority, who wanted at once to join the endangered British cause, the President had delayed too long in taking steps to supply Great Britain and to develop American armed forces for employment overseas. Privately Roosevelt may have shared the latter assessment but politically, he believed, he could not afford either to increase his pace or to give the isolationists further cause for complaint. Wallace stood about where the majority of Americans did after the Germans had overrun most of western Europe. He detested Nazism, which he continually attacked, as he always had. He saw potential danger to the Americas in Germany's advance. He therefore preached hemispheric solidarity and national preparedness—the mobilization of the economy and of a strong and balanced military force. "We must," he told Roosevelt, "be in a position to command fear and respect." Yet Wallace also opposed American entry into the war and resisted the thought that it was inevitable. Further, he believed that mobilization need not entail a surrender of policy to generals and financiers, and that a good neighbor should sponsor democratization along with friendship in Latin America. Indeed with the spread of fascism in Europe, the new world more than ever before had to provide a persuasive example of effective democracy.

Wallace, as Roosevelt insisted, suited his needs, but few of the President's counselors or of the party leaders agreed. Wallace had always ignored the powerful captains of the great Democratic city machines. He disliked and distrusted, perhaps even despised, men like Edward J. Kelly of Chicago and Frank Hague of Jersey City, who felt the same way about him. His increasing zeal for civil rights for black Americans and for relieving the poverty of the sharecroppers of the South, many of them black, offended most of the influential senior southern Democrats in the Senate. Like many of their northern colleagues, they considered his ideas radical, his religion puzzling, and his manner remote.

Wallace also lacked the confidence of Roosevelt's circle of immediate advisers, particularly those whom Felix Frankfurter had recruited. They knew he was learned, but he was not one of them, and by their standards he had none of the polish the White House required. For his part, Wallace did not quite trust them. He called them "connivers" and considered them preoccupied with power, though he knew they had made significant contributions to reform. Even Ben Cohen, perhaps the gentlest and ablest man in the group, operated too guardedly for Wallace's taste. Cohen, along with some others, feared for a time in 1939 that Paul McNutt, a handsome but vacuous Indiana Democrat, might be Roosevelt's choice for the vice-presidency. Against that chance, Wallace observed that "the New Dealers"—he used the phrase pejoratively—resisted taking a "position of too great an opposition against McNutt. . . . The New Dealers . . . don't like the McNutt possibility but feel they must prepare for it as a contingency." Wallace did not feel that way, nor did he have any enthusiasm for a Vice President selected from the inner circle of the White House or from its outer fringe, perhaps Harry Hopkins, the President's éminence grise, or William O. Douglas. They were little to be preferred, he felt, to Secretary of State Cordell Hull, a favorite of conservative Southerners, or National Chairman James A. Farley, whom the city bosses liked.

Farley, an active candidate, felt that Roosevelt was blocking his ambitions. Always on pleasant terms with Wallace, Farley early in 1940 complained to him about the President. "Farley was incorrect," Wallace judged, "in calling the President a sadist although there is a certain amount of that element in his nature. The predominant element, however, is the desire to be the dominating figure, to demonstrate on all occasions his superiority. He changes his standards of superiority many times during the day. But having set for himself a particular standard for the moment, he then glories in being the dominating figure along that particular line. In that way he fills out his artistic sense of the fitness of things."

In spite of that insight, in spite of the opposition he knew he provoked, Wallace was a completely receptive, though never an active, candidate for nomination. He organized no movement on his own behalf because, as he told a cabinet colleague, "I did not look on myself as very much of a politician." He did not think that nomination as Vice President would lead to the Presidency, for unlike Farley, he expected Roosevelt to live out a third term. "The President," Wallace observed, "is more likely to maintain his vitality by being President than by retiring." Nor did he expect Roosevelt to retire. One of Wallace's Iowa friends asked him if he "was interested in having my name presented to the national convention in case the President did not run. I told him that it was scarcely worth thinking about because I was so certain the President was going to run. I said, of course, if the President did not run, I would be interested." As for the vice-presidency, "I said that would depend altogether on what the powers that might be might think would best insure victory."

Roosevelt was the power that was. To a reluctant convention he dictated the choice of Wallace as his running mate. He even contemplated withdrawing himself if the convention should reject his selection. It almost did, but Roosevelt's adamancy, the energetic politicking of Harry Hopkins, the President's emissary on the floor, and the timely appearance of Eleanor Roosevelt as her husband's special ambassador for Wallace brought the unhappy delegates around.

Roosevelt made Wallace Vice President in 1940. Four years later, when Wallace had far more support within the party, Roosevelt dumped him. He announced his personal preference for Wallace but he also expressed his satisfaction with several other possible candidates and then let the party leaders move the convention to a decision he had previously approved. That change in Roosevelt's tactics, as Wallace realized, constituted a complete reversal. The President again had been the dominating figure, filling out, now to Wallace's disadvantage, "his artistic sense of the fitness of things."

RECEPTIVE though he had been to nomination as Vice President, Wallace discovered little satisfaction in that office when he entered it in January 1941. Usefully busy almost every day for the eight preceding years, he now had almost nothing to do. Presiding over the Senate's meandering debates bored him. Often he appeared to doze in the chair. More often he turned the chair over to a colleague. The Democratic Majority Leader, Alben Barkley, an engaging Kentuckian, ran the business of the Senate. Most of the members of that body respected Wallace but few welcomed him to the informal gatherings, the Senate's club, which by temperament he had no desire to join.

He had, Wallace said, more time for tennis than ever before in his life, but seldom had the nation faced more urgent issues. For their resolution Roosevelt intended to harness Wallace's talents, but he was slow in finding an appropriate role for him, for he was slow in establishing offices properly geared first for mobilization and then for war. While the President procrastinated, Wallace educated himself in the problems of national defense and of the defense economy by discussing them regularly with experts on the staffs of the White House, the departments, and the defense agencies. At Roosevelt's initiative, he was among the few originally to learn about S-1, the then infant project to develop an atomic bomb. In July 1941 the President gave him a first assignment as chairman of the Economic Defense Board, established at that time as a "policy and advisory agency" to deal with "international economic activities" including exports, imports, preclusive buying, shipping, foreign exchange, and similar matters.

That mandate, as it turned out, was as broad as the agency's actual authority was narrow. Power over its supposed functions remained dispersed among the executive departments, and decisions, when they were made, remained the prerogative of the White House. So, too, with the Supply Priorities and Allocations Board that the President created in August 1941 with Wallace as chairman. In characteristically Rooseveltian fashion, it was superimposed upon the Office of

Production Management, which had been crippled by friction within its staff and by its rivalry with the War and Navy departments. SPAB was to serve as the coordinating center for defense mobilization. It failed for the reasons that had vitiated the Economic Defense Board and OPM.

Even before the Japanese attack on Pearl Harbor, those responsible for mobilization chafed at Roosevelt's reluctance to delegate and centralize authority. The advent of war forced the President to act. At least in theory, real authority over the domestic economy was granted in January 1942 to the new War Production Board under Donald Nelson, a former vice president of Sears, Roebuck who had been executive director of SPAB. Wallace was to sit as chairman, along with various Cabinet officers as members, of WPB's governing committee. He liked and admired Nelson, but he did not, as one friend observed, "find it congenial to work with the big businessmen who dominated that organization, nor with the admirals and generals who were their military counterparts."

Far more satisfying to the Vice President, Roosevelt had also made him chairman of another new agency, established by executive order on December 17, 1941, the Board of Economic Warfare. It was to assume the responsibilities of the Economic Defense Board but with strengthened authority— as it turned out, less than enough—to deal directly with foreign governments in the procurement of strategic materials and related functions. Wallace now had a mandate, one he believed he could use both to abet the war effort and to influence postwar policy.

As he had in the Department of Agriculture, Wallace in the Board of Economic Warfare devoted himself to questions of policy and delegated responsibility for daily administrative and technical decisions. The major weight of that responsibility he assigned to his executive director, Milo Perkins, an old friend and associate and an energetic promoter of Wallace's own purposes. Under Perkins were the three sections of BEW: the Office of Imports, charged with procuring strategic materials and with preclusive buying all over the world, but especially in Latin America where neither the Germans nor the Japanese had become a military threat; the Office of Exports, which was to use its licensing authority to prevent goods from reaching Axis nations; and the Office of Warfare Analysis, which selected targets of economic importance for strategic bombing. The first of those sections commanded most of Perkins's and Wallace's attention, and its operations were the bases for the controversies that were to mark the history of the agency.

About two months after the establishment of BEW, with those controversies in their first stages, Wallace resumed keeping a diary. Twice before he had initiated and abandoned that practice, on both occasions initiating it when political events in Washington especially involved him. He had kept a diary briefly during the Davis-Frank episode, and he had again for the months preceding his nomination for Vice President. Now he began once more, with few lapses until he left public office. The content of the diary revealed his continual engagement in political developments within government and in the policies that politics affected. More than an outlet for reflection, it served, as its author intended, as a record of his activities. Such was also the case with the diaries of so many of Roosevelt's Cabinet, Henry Stimson, Henry Morgenthau, Jr., Harold Ickes, and James Forrestal in particular. With varying degrees of self-consciousness, they recorded an account of what they had said and heard and done, an account to which they could refer should some colleague challenge their consistency or veracity. Such challenges emerged from the personal frictions engendered by Roosevelt's style of administration. As Morgenthau, speaking from experience, warned Wallace, relationships with Jesse H. Jones especially imposed on a prudential man the self-protective task of keeping a full record. Like the diaries of his colleagues, Wallace's diary, while incidentally convenient for history, had a more contemporary and expedient use.

While he kept the diary for himself, Wallace in 1942 also took his thoughts to the American people with greater frequency and moment than ever before. No member of the administration except the President made more public speeches or attracted more continual attention. Roosevelt probably planned it that way. In the interests of national unity and of harmony within the Grand Alliance, the President during the war years moved with more than his customary caution. But Roosevelt typically was less cautious privately than he appeared to be in public. By no means averse to examining bold policies for adoption once the war had been won, he needed a scout to test the responses of both national and international audiences, a semi-official spokesman whose proposals he could embrace if they were well received or repudiate if they were not.

The President did not have to cast Wallace in that role, for the Vice President without prompting seized every occasion he could to publicize his hopes for the postwar world. Indeed Wallace was restless with the failure of the American government to set forth in clear detail a plan for the future that would lift the spirits and galvanize the wills of men everywhere. He fretted not the least because the relative silence from the White House permitted other voices to seem louder and more persuasive than in his opinion they should have. So, for one example, though he shared many of the sentiments of Wendell Willkie's *One World,* he distrusted Willkie's instincts in domestic policy. So, for another, he detested the confident chauvinism of Henry Luce's "American Century." Like Archibald MacLeish, the eminent poet who served for a short and unhappy season as the head of the Office of

Facts and Figures, Wallace believed that Roosevelt was for-
going a commanding opportunity to define the war as a vehicle for practical idealism. The President, preoccupied with
military problems and the conflicts among the nation's major
allies, emphasized victory above all other considerations. After
victory, he told MacLeish, he would speak more concretely
about the nature of the peace. Wallace, for his part, while
always committed to the eradication of Nazism as a first
priority, was determined, too, to stir the blood of democrats
everywhere, to prophesy, as he did, the coming century of
the common man.

His rhetoric in that cause gave a testamental cast to the
sundry objectives that engrossed him. As his diary disclosed,
his activities on the Board of Economic Warfare aroused the
quick opposition of two of the most powerful conservatives
within the administration, both noted for their influence on
the Hill, Secretary of State Cordell Hull and Secretary of
Commerce Jesse Jones, who was also head of the federal lending agencies. Both men had a long record of defending any
apparent invasion of what they jealously considered their personal domains. Now Hull resented any independence from
State Department supervision of BEW representatives negotiating with foreign governments. Jones was even more
indignant over Milo Perkins's efforts to arrange loans for the
development abroad of sources of strategic materials without
proceeding through the dilatory, sometimes obstructionist,
lending agencies. Enlisted by Perkins, Wallace tried to persuade Roosevelt to grant BEW independence from Hull and
Jones, but the President, under pressure also from Wallace's
antagonists, gave BEW more the semblance than the sinew
of what it sought.

The bureaucratic struggle merely clothed fundamental disagreements about policy, particularly in Latin America. There
Wallace and Perkins had two large goals. "International trade,"

Wallace had earlier written, "has always been closer to economic warfare than the American people have been trained to think." Through international trade he endeavored in Latin America to develop sources for essential materials of war—rubber and quinine for two—which the United States had previously obtained from areas the Japanese had conquered. Preclusive buying also denied those and other materials to the Germans. The procurement of adequate supplies, Wallace believed, depended upon increasing the productivity of Latin American workers, whose physical strength and morale suffered from malnutrition, disease, miserable sanitation and housing, and skimpy wages. Efficiency demanded social reform, as did the first step toward a decent future for the laborers. BEW tried to take that step by writing into procurement contracts obligations on the part of Latin American governments or entrepreneurs "to furnish adequate shelter, water, safety appliances, etc." to consult with BEW "as to whether the wage scale is such as to maximize production," and to cooperate "in a plan to improve conditions of health and sanitation," a plan for which the United States would pay half the costs.

Hull attacked that policy indirectly. The State Department endorsed some of BEW's conditions for contracts, but it also complained that the conditions as a whole constituted interference in the domestic affairs of a foreign nation, a course the department claimed to eschew. Noninterference, as practiced by the State Department, had special connotations. The doctrine served for several years as Hull's excuse for protecting the pro-Nazi but officially neutral government of Argentina from the disciplinary measures of economic warfare recommended continually by Army Intelligence and the Treasury Department. Too, the State Department helped to arrange shipments of Lend-Lease arms to Latin American governments, non-fighting allies against the Axis, that were openly repressive toward workers and peasants. Hull knew that Wallace welcomed social change in Latin America. Indeed Wallace had identified that change with peaceful revolution. The Board of Economic Warfare did not demand that Latin American states alter their laws; it attempted only to write contracts to help Latin American workers. But that was too much revolution for Hull, and therefore by his standards too much interference.

Like Wallace, Hull was a dogged proponent of freeing international trade from artificial restraints. Like Wallace, he was eager to enlarge American markets abroad in the postwar period, temporarily by advancing generous credits. But the Secretary of State and most of his colleagues equated that objective with the spread of American institutions, political and economic. They expected their trading partners to be or to become capitalistic republics in the model of the United States. When the war ended, they attached political conditions to commercial negotiations. Wallace did not. He sought postwar trade with any nation, whatever its system of government or pattern of property ownership. And, during the war, he wanted American credits, trade, and contracts to turn the calendar toward the century of the common man. He lost.

As much as Hull, Jesse Jones contributed to that defeat. The delays and the parsimony of Jones's lending agencies retarded procurement, as Wallace and others demonstrated and Jones self-righteously denied. Wallace found just as aggravating the political objections to BEW contracts, which Jones claimed were needlessly costly. Preoccupied with prices and interest rates, Jones never grasped the greater importance, during the crisis of war, of productivity, one of Wallace's goals. He did understand and reject Wallace's long-range social concerns, which he scoffed at as an international WPA. He scoffed, too, at Wallace's worries about the postwar implications of American policy on synthetic rubber.

Wallace feared that federal assistance for the synthetic rubber industry, which he knew was essential for wartime supply, would lead to postwar tariff protection for that industry, and consequently inhibit postwar natural rubber developments which BEW was nurturing in Brazil and elsewhere. As ever, Wallace argued that without a market in the United States, those natural rubber producers would be unable to survive, and unable, too, to purchase American products. Jones fixed his interest on the postwar profits of the domestic rubber industry.

Jones had the sympathy and support of like-minded senators, including senior southern Democrats like Kenneth McKellar and Harry Byrd, who chaired powerful committees. They gave him a platform from which to attack BEW, its policies, and the concessions to it that Roosevelt had made. Where Hull ordinarily expressed his negative opinions in colorful but private invective, Jones habitually broadcast his vitriol. He both offended and infuriated Milo Perkins, who regrettably struck back in kind. Provoked largely by Perkins, so did Wallace, with little more circumspection. After several public skirmishes, the open warfare between two of his subordinates, a circumstance Roosevelt would not tolerate, led to the President's decision in June 1943 to abolish BEW. He transferred its functions to a new superagency, the Office of Economic Warfare, and appointed to the chairmanship of the body Leo Crowley, whose ability to flatter the President and to placate Congress considerably exceeded his taste for reform or his personal probity. Perkins left the government. Wallace remained, his authority and status severely diminished, his spirit undeterred.

WALLACE'S "Century of the Common Man," a major address he delivered in May 1942, set forth themes which he repeated and elaborated for the next several years. They grew out of his previous ideas, some partially formed even in his youth, and they foreshadowed the disagreements between him and others in government during his last year in office. Yet his speeches, book, and articles said less about his precise objectives than did his diary, and his written words communicated his purpose only in the context of the actual issues to which he adverted daily. Each theme he associated with the century of the common man had hard correlatives in the questions that occupied wartime Washington.

Peace, the essential first condition for the future of mankind, meant different things to different Americans during World War II. For Wallace, the establishment and preservation of peace demanded a true internationalism, a world community of nations and peoples linked economically and politically through the agency of a United Nations. His vision included his familiar convictions about trade and economics, and his expectations for the economic development of underdeveloped areas along the lines that BEW drew. As he saw it, with the end of the war the United Nations would assume the bulk of that task. It would first have to concentrate on the restoration of areas devastated by war, a function which devolved before the end of hostilities to the United Nations Relief and Rehabilitation Administration. An enthusiast for that agency, Wallace recognized that it had to rely in its early work primarily on American resources, for the United States alone of the great nations was emerging from the war with an ebullient economy. But Wallace believed that American wealth should not give the United States a proportionate influence either in UNRRA or within the United Nations. Those agencies, in his opinion, had to bend to multilateral direction and to serve multinational interests.

The internationalizing of responsibility for providing nourishment, relief, and development throughout the world depended upon political internationalism, which Wallace stressed. It could eventuate only with the end of European imperialism and with the abandonment of balance-of-power politics. On that account, he was especially critical of the British, particularly Winston Churchill. Continued British domination over India, in Wallace's understanding, violated the whole purpose of the war, as did Churchill's impulse for empire, his unabashed belief in Anglo-Saxon superiority, his disdain for China and distrust of Russia, his preference for secret negotiations, and his manifest intention to hold the reins of world leadership, whatever the semblance of world government, in British, American, and, unavoidably, Soviet hands.

Roosevelt, too, expected the great powers to dominate the UN and enjoyed and exploited his secret conferences either alone with Churchill or in the larger company that included Stalin. But the President seemed to Wallace to share his anti-imperialism and even some of his other doubts about the British. So also, Roosevelt was determined to get along with the Russians. Further he was as emphatic as was Wallace in calling for the withdrawal of British and European, as well as Japanese, political influence in East and Southeast Asia. They looked forward there not to American encroachments but to the independence, in most instances after a period of transition, of the various Asian peoples. In the case of China, as they both realized, Chiang Kai-shek could expect to rule only if he cleared out the corruption of the Kuomintang, embarked upon major social reform including distribution of land to the peasantry, and reached a modus operandi with his communist opponents, whose growing strength fed on the discontent his policies fostered.

Still, Roosevelt's concern for victory first and victory as fast as possible resulted in wartime decisions that struck Wallace as ominous for the future. The United States, Wallace believed, had to align itself unequivocally with the forces of democracy everywhere. On the ground of military expediency, Roosevelt did not. He authorized the negotiations and arrangements in North Africa and Italy that made notorious fascists the approved local agents of Anglo-American occupation. The State and War departments nurtured those policies which Wallace came privately to oppose.

Wallace also parted with the President, though without public or private acrimony, over the question of the peace-keeping role of the United Nations. Roosevelt talked in general terms about a postwar international police force to prevent aggression, but while the fighting continued, he deliberately postponed serious consideration of the nature and structure of such a force. Indeed he seemed often to regard it as a convenient substitute for the positioning of American units abroad. Further, he was too busy with grand strategy to give time to detailed postwar planning. More important, he did not want predictable British, American, and Russian disagreements about postwar policies to impede the functioning of the wartime alliance. He sensed, too, that the Congress and the American people were loath to approve much more than the principles of international organization, and he dreaded a divisive domestic debate that might generate the kind of opposition to a United Nations that had defeated Woodrow Wilson's League of Nations. Roosevelt had not wholly decided about his course. He did expect after victory rapidly to withdraw American forces from Europe and Asia. He had no apparent sympathy for postwar American military adventures overseas. Yet his announced descriptions of postwar world organization, at best opaque, appeared to presume a political stability founded on a balance of influence among the strong.

Wallace for his part advocated wartime planning for a United Nations that would exercise responsibility for peace and for disarmament. Like Undersecretary of State Sumner Welles, he saw regional agreements as a necessary foundation for the larger mandate of the UN. Regionalism, as he later admitted, could provide a cloak for spheres of influence—of the United States in the Americas, of the Soviet Union in eastern Europe, and of the British, French, and Chinese in areas of their traditional concern. But he counted on the United Nations to prevent regionalism from becoming colonialism. Further, to stop aggression of any sort he advocated endowing the United Nations with its own army and air force, and with authority to impose economic sanctions.

He contemplated a degree of surrender of national sovereignty to an international body larger by far than was acceptable to any but an insignificant few in high offices in any of the governments of the major partners in the war against the Axis. Indeed few Americans who understood Wallace's purpose fully supported it. The senior members of the State Department especially looked upon his proposals as fanciful. So did the senior Democrats in the Senate, while the Republican leadership was even more chary of international commitments. For those critics, as for most of their constituents, peace, in whatever international garment, implied primarily "freedom from fear"—from threats to the security of the United States. That security was to be assured essentially by American power alone or in willing alliance with demonstrably trustworthy friends. As Wallace realized, from that position the step was short to unilateral American adventurism undertaken in the name of peace.

As in international, so in domestic policies, Wallace by 1944 had advanced well beyond the consensus of the American people and their congressional representatives. That gap reflected their conservatism, for Wallace, by no means alone in the forward sector, had not departed from the traditional objectives of American reform movements or the growing body of economic doctrine of the time.

The bases for the political democracy that Wallace associated with his century of the common man were so conventionally American that he did not need to spell them out. The nuances of his speeches and the thrusts of his activities indicated that he meant by political democracy representative government, universal suffrage, and the civil liberties guaranteed by the Constitution of the United States. Those conditions did not wholly obtain during the years of World War II. He worried particularly about the distortions of representation that resulted from the disfranchisement of blacks in the South, from the power of Democratic machines in the North (Chicago especially bothered him), and from the influence that wealthy individuals and corporations exerted on Congress and on some executive agencies. He also despised the redbaiting techniques of the Dies Committee in the House and the McKellar Committee in the Senate. Obsessed with fears about radicals, those committees, reckless in their accusations, bullied the witnesses they disliked. Again and again in his diary Wallace expressed his own reservations about "Communists" or "reds," but in his distress about the tactics of the witch-hunters in Congress and the FBI, he constantly also expressed a discriminating opposition to professional anticommunists.

Only men with the truncated mentality of Martin Dies or Kenneth McKellar could discover, as they did, sinister and radical tendencies in Wallace's ideas about economic democracy. Wallace simply incorporated his understanding of wartime developments into his long-standing proposals for promoting and distributing an economy of abundance. The experience of the war provided a telling verification of the theories of John Maynard Keynes and his American interpreters and disciples. The enormous federal deficits of the war years spurred private investment and employment, and achieved at last the full recovery that had eluded the New Deal. To Wallace, as to the Keynesians he regularly saw, it was patent that properly managed federal fiscal policy could sustain prosperity in the postwar years. Accordingly he believed, with Roosevelt, in the ability of the government to establish and preserve the conditions that would provide sixty million jobs, a figure that seemed outrageously high in 1944 to the adherents of conventional economics. In order to achieve that goal, as Wallace understood, the government had systematically to employ experts to study the economy and its performance, and to make continual recommendations about federal fiscal and monetary policies to sustain maximum employment. To that end he supported each of the series of bills introduced by Senator James E. Murray of which the last was passed, after revisions, as the Employment Act of 1946.

The long years of depression had whetted the interest of all Americans, however much they disagreed about means, in achieving an economy of plenty. Americans, however, disagreed profoundly about how and to whom to allocate shares of prosperity. Debates about the particular aspects of that general question proceeded through the war years. After the Democratic reverses in the elections of 1942, a coalition of Republicans and southern Democrats controlled congressional decisions. While that coalition tried, with considerable success, to roll back the New Deal, the President accepted most of the defeats his policies suffered without more than token protest. Eager for the support of the conservative coalition for his military and foreign policies, he deferred battle over domestic issues. "Dr. New Deal," Roosevelt told the press, had been succeeded by "Dr. Win-the-War." Depressed by the resulting situation, Henry Morgenthau commented that he could put all the remaining New Dealers in his own bathtub. He exaggerated. There was in Washington a group of young liberal Keynesians who were eagerly planning a new postwar New Deal. They had the significant cooperation of the leadership of the CIO and the Farmers' Union. In the Senate they had influential friends like Claude Pepper of Florida and Robert Wagner of New York. And they had visible champions in high office, of whom Wallace was the most senior in rank and most articulate in speech. His program for economic democracy reflected their thinking, as well as his own.

As he had for so long, Wallace during the war combated the power of big business. In the continuing struggle for control of the War Production Board, he sided with Donald Nelson, a protector of small industry, against Ferdinand Eberstadt, the ingenious investment banker who represented the preferences of the armed services and their corporate allies. Increasingly in 1943 and thereafter, Wallace also consulted the lawyers in the antitrust division of the Justice Department, serious young attorneys who were frustrated by the President's suspension of antitrust proceedings at a time when bigness was growing rapidly. With them, Wallace attacked American corporate giants that had been (and would again be) associated with international cartels, and, like them, he searched for ways to revise the patent laws so as to prevent monopolies based on patent rights, especially patents developed at large cost to the federal government. He was not anti-business but anti-bigness; he was not an opponent of capitalism but a proponent of competition.

So, too, Wallace allied himself with the workers against their employers. He had earlier applauded the success of the CIO in using collective bargaining to increase the share of labor in corporate profits. Unions, he believed, would have to function to that end after the war. Though he deplored wartime strikes that retarded production, he recognized the validity of many of the demands of the strikers and he opposed congressional efforts to punish union labor and its leadership. Supporting Roosevelt, Wallace also advocated holding down wartime agricultural prices so as to prevent inflation from eroding the gains in income that labor had achieved. To his satisfaction, the strength of the unions, the impact of wage and price controls, and the incidence of wartime taxes resulted during the war years in a significant redistribution of income favorable to working men and women.

Wallace stood behind other programs to assist industrial and agricultural workers. He advocated federal support for education, especially in technical and scientific subjects, so as to make learning available to qualified candidates who could not otherwise afford it. He praised the proposals of the National Resources Planning Board (an agency which congressional conservatives dissolved out of spite) and of the Social Security Administration for postwar increases in old age and unemployment benefits, and for postwar extension of coverage to millions of Americans then still outside of the Social Security system. Eager to improve the delivery of health care within the United States, he commended the program Henry Kaiser had devised for the collective care of workers employed by his firms. Wallace applauded, too, the less adventurous but still controversial plan of the Social Security Administration to include medical insurance within its province. "Socialized medicine," as the American Medical Association called it with characteristic imprecision, stirred up so much opposition that Roosevelt would not attach his prestige to a Treasury measure sponsoring it. He could not, the President argued, take on the AMA in the middle of a great war. Wallace could and did, as did Bob Wagner and the other authors of the unsuccessful Wagner-Murray-Dingell bill for revising Social Security to encompass medical insurance.

For Wallace, then, economic democracy directly affected

the common man. It would increase national income by utilizing fiscal policy to encourage economic growth and antitrust policy to discourage monopolistic restraints on production. It would increase the share of the common man in national income. It would also provide him with protection against the trials of unemployment, old age, and illness. Taken together, those purposes constituted what Roosevelt meant by "freedom from want." Taken together, they also constituted what Wallace's critics called either communism or socialism or the welfare state. They were anathema to the still formidable number of businessmen and their lawyers, accountants, and clerks who believed, in spite of all that had happened since 1929, in something they called "the American system," by which they meant the political economy of the Harding-Coolidge-Hoover years.

Wallace disturbed an equally large constituency by his advocacy of "genetic democracy," another major facet of his century of the common man. The phrase was peculiarly his own. His experiments in hybridizing corn had led him to an adjective for which most other men substituted "racial." He meant that and more. He urged equal opportunities for black Americans in voting, employment, and education, but he sought the same objectives for women of whatever color. Further, he envisaged in the not distant future equal political and economic opportunities for Asians and Latins, not only for American citizens. In the case of the Jews, he came before 1944 to agree with the Zionists that a prosperous and dignified future for European Jews, particularly after the ghastly experience of Nazi persecution, could materialize only in an independent Jewish state in the area of Palestine, then British-controlled. His were politically dangerous convictions. Even during a war against Nazism, most white Americans remained openly prejudiced against men and women of darker skins, most were uneasy about directly assisting European

Jews, most were indifferent about the rights of women. Indeed Roosevelt disagreed with Wallace. The President had doubts about Zionism, little patience with militant women, and little respect for most women in public life. Further, he had condoned the incarceration of the Japanese-Americans, and he had erected a bureaucratic barrier of personal aides to spare him from having to listen to the legitimate demands of American blacks. Wallace's genetic democracy put him in a lonesome salient far out ahead of the army of American voters and of their elected commander.

He had a related vision still further from the American consensus. It was a prospect incomprehensible except to those few who shared Wallace's belief in the brotherhood of man, his faith in the experience of westering as an avenue to that brotherhood, and his conviction that commerce brought and held societies together. When first he met Ambassador Vyacheslav Molotov, he described to him, as he later did in print for American readers, a huge stretch of highways and airports reaching northward from the west coast of South America to Alaska and across the Bering Sea westward through Siberia to European Russia. Along that line he saw potentialities for a vibrant commerce. When he reflected about strategy in the Pacific, Wallace gave Alaska a high priority for defense, for he viewed Alaska as the last American frontier. But the larger frontier, the one he postulated for settlement and development in the late twentieth century, made Alaska only one part of a vast area that also included Soviet Asia and Mongolia. There he believed a commingling of peoples from America, Siberia, China, and Mongolia could build a new center of civilization, a center founded on agriculture, the commerce to sustain it, and the industry that would follow population and employ the extraordinary resources of the northern Pacific triangle. That prospect beguiled him before his visit to Soviet Asia and China. The observations he made on that trip, recorded in his diary and in his *Soviet Asia Mission,* confirmed his sense of the possibilities for realizing the prospect. The rivalries of international politics made it only a dream in 1944, but it was precisely those rivalries which Wallace believed had to be tempered and contained so that the century of the common man could begin in the northern Pacific as in all lands.

Wallace's beliefs provoked the opposition to his renomination that was virtually universal among Roosevelt's advisers and the Democratic party leadership. He knew they did not want him. He knew, too, that thousands of rank and file Democrats shared his kind of aspiration and supported his candidacy. But in 1944, as in 1940, he did not campaign. By default rather than by direction, he left his chances to a few friends who were almost as clumsy and uninfluential as they were ardent and dedicated. At Roosevelt's request, Wallace even left Washington for Asia during the critical weeks before the national convention. Again, as in 1940, he knew his presence or his activity made little difference. The decision about the nomination was the President's to make. And Roosevelt dropped him. The President's disingenuous remarks during their discussion of the nomination wounded Wallace at least as much as did the President's decision. Once he became aware of it, Wallace fought, too late and with too few allies, to hold his office, but he accepted defeat in good grace and campaigned hard for the ticket. That earned Roosevelt's gratitude and Wallace's nomination as Secretary of Commerce.

The episode confirmed Wallace's sense of the President's style. Eager to dominate yet reluctant to offend, Roosevelt hated to tell a loyal friend the simple truth when that truth was bound to hurt. Instead he fenced, he turned to humor, evasion, and half-truths. He would have been kinder in 1944 to tell Wallace the truth, for Wallace had the character to accept it. The truth was that the renomination of Wallace would probably have hurt the ticket. Wallace admitted as much in 1951 in conversation with an interviewer who asked him what would have happened if he had been renominated and then succeeded to the presidency after Roosevelt's death. "Anyone with my views," Wallace answered, "would have run into the most extraordinary difficulties. . . . It would have been a terrific battle for control of public opinion. . . . It's quite possible that I would not have been able to get the support of Congress."

Indeed, it was quite probable, for the Senate, with the Democrats bitterly divided, in 1945 barely approved Wallace's appointment as Secretary of Commerce, and then only after stripping that office of the lending authority Jesse Jones had exercised. As for public opinion, in 1944, as Wallace realized, it was running against him. In his own retrospective assessment, the American people were "prosperous, fully employed, complacent." They were weary of controls, weary of shortages, eager for victory and for postwar security and personal comfort. They were not seeking new obligations, new causes, or strange adventures. Accordingly they were uncomfortable with the implications of Wallace's century of the common man. In Wisconsin the voters had eliminated Wendell Willkie, Wallace's closest Republican counterpart, from the race for his party's nomination. Roosevelt, accepting the counsel of his advisers and of his own instincts, removed Wallace, who had taken positions the President was willing to have tested but, in the President's judgment, had failed the test. Wallace had said in 1940 that the question of his nomination was subordinate to the best interest of the party. In 1944 he had not changed his mind. Though he and his friends thought that his renomination would strengthen the ticket, he had to defer to Roosevelt's contrary conclusion. He would have found it more palatable if the President had been more candid.

AFTER Roosevelt's death, Wallace remained in the Cabinet because he expected, as Secretary of Commerce, to initiate programs to expand both the American and the world economy, and because he hoped to exert a liberalizing influence within the government. As he confided in his diary, he did not trust the new President. Harry Truman, though his own record was clean, had ties to the corrupt Pendergast machine in Kansas City. His sponsors included men like Robert Hannegan and Edwin Pauley whose motives and methods Wallace suspected. Further, in Wallace's view Truman had followed a devious course in winning the vice-presidential nomination. In time, Wallace was to consider his suspicions confirmed. Where Roosevelt had been engagingly disingenuous, Truman, in dealing with Wallace, became transparently dishonest. But at first, though he did not much like Wallace, the President was disarming. His apparent openness, his earthiness, his self-effacing eagerness to master his new office and its problems persuaded Wallace that they might be able to work together productively.

They remained within reach of each other on domestic policies. Truman approved Wallace's plans for reorganization of the Commerce Department, though he kept Wallace off the governing board of the Export-Import Bank. After some hesitation, the President gave his full support to the employment bill. With less commitment than Wallace, he also supported the continuation of the Office of Price Administration and its efforts to retard inflation. He recommended continuing wartime policies designed to provide equal employment opportunities for blacks. He opposed Republican measures to cripple labor unions, but he had limited sympathy for the postwar militancy of the CIO, and he recommended punitive action against the railroad brotherhoods when they walked out on strike. Recognizing his own political weakness in labor circles, Truman, as he later disclosed, kept Wallace in the Cabinet primarily to placate the unions. He listened to Wallace's advice about labor issues and on occasion used him as an emissary to CIO leaders. That role pleased Wallace, who also knew that Truman as a senator had voted consistently for New Deal measures. As President, he now urged Congress to expand Social Security, to provide for national medical insurance, and to increase minimum wages. No more than Roosevelt could he be faulted for the conservative coalition in Congress or for the yearning for "normalcy," so like the mood of the early 1920s, that infected so many Americans, war veterans not the least.

To Wallace's growing disillusionment, however, the President acted in a manner at variance with his rhetoric. It was not the conservatives in Congress but Truman himself who altered the profile of the Cabinet. Like any President, he naturally wanted his own men around him—men loyal to him, not to the memory of FDR. But most of those he chose struck Wallace, as they did others, as less able than their predecessors, less liberal, and often meaner in personal and public spirit. Wallace had never found James F. Byrnes, the new Secretary of State, a sympathetic colleague. He had liked Henry Morgenthau and valued his spontaneous enthusiasm for myriad good causes, but after Morgenthau resigned, Fred Vinson and John Snyder, both personal friends of Truman, brought to the Treasury Department a narrow view of both domestic and international issues. Wallace had had his problems with Harold Ickes, but he cheered Ickes's opposition to the nomination of Edwin Pauley, another Truman crony, as Assistant Secretary of the Navy. The Senate blocked that appointment, for Pauley's associations with the oil industry made the prospect of his control over Navy oil reserves ominous. Still, Ickes resigned, dubious as was Wallace about Truman's concern for the conservation policies Roosevelt had nurtured. Even more disheartening had been the President's earlier selection of Howard McGrath to replace Francis Biddle as Attorney General. A political hack from Rhode Island, McGrath filled the Justice Department with nonentities who vitiated the antitrust division that Biddle's men had energized. The incompetence as well as the permissiveness of many of the newcomers to the Justice and Treasury departments led to the series of episodes of petty corruption that later gave Truman's cronies a deservedly shoddy reputation, one that hurt the President, too. Wallace, who saw government gradually losing its indispensable integrity before those scandals occurred, lamented equally the concurrent loss of constructive social purpose. The President's selection of associates, in Wallace's opinion, cost him much of his credibility.

The last of the New Dealers to remain in the Cabinet, Wallace held on primarily because of his overriding concern about military and foreign policy. Truman let him stay in order to appease the restless liberal intellectuals and labor leaders. Wallace symbolized their hopes, and as long as he was there, though they might grumble about Truman, they were unlikely to desert him. Only slowly did Wallace learn that he was just a symbol, that he had no influence, that Truman from the outset had had no intention of taking his advice. The President let him talk, but he made him an outsider. As they moved apart from each other, Truman contributed to the ultimate separation by dissembling in what he told Wallace. Though Wallace would probably have dissented anyway, he could not be expected to understand, much less to approve, policies about which he was at least partially misinformed.

Still, the failure of communication between Truman and Wallace counted far less than did their fundamental disagreement about the role of the United States in world affairs. They started with different assumptions. The President and his closest advisers believed that national security depended upon military strength and position, on a large and poised strategic air force that could retaliate in the event of an attack, on the availability of safe bases from which both bombers and naval aircraft could operate, and on a large reserve army ready for quick mobilization. They were, in a sense, preparing for the war that had just ended, for defense against another blitzkrieg or another attack upon Pearl Harbor. They were fashioning a system of deterrence (before that word had become the vogue), a system to which the American monopoly of the atomic bomb gave unparalleled power. But there was no point in building that system of defense in the absence of an enemy. They identified the Soviet Union as that potential enemy. That identification rested on several premises. Those who made it considered Russian policy in Poland and in the eastern zone of Germany evidence of an expansionist purpose at least as extensive as were historic Russian ambitions in the Black and the Mediterranean seas. They tended to forget or to ignore the natural concern for their own security that the Russians felt, especially about Poland through which the Germans had attacked twice within one generation. They tended, too, to overlook the Russian need for reparations to replace capital equipment destroyed by war and unavailable from the United States in the absence of a credit which the State Department would not approve. Too, suspicions of the Soviet Union fed on American fears about communism as a doctrine and about Stalin as a dictator, as a mad and evil genius who quickly replaced Hitler in American demonology. The Soviet Union did intend to protect its interests as it defined them, but Truman's counselors exaggerated the dangers to the United

States inherent in that intention. Truman's own tough talk to Molotov early in his presidency expressed his real opinion of the Soviet Union better than did his more placatory public pronouncements. And more and more the President accepted as fact the presumptions about a Soviet menace that were advanced with rising emphasis by Secretary of State Byrnes, Ambassador Averell Harriman, and their staffs.

Wallace proceeded from a different set of assumptions. National security, in his view, depended not on American arms but on a strong United Nations, on the abatement of international hostilities rather than the deployment of American forces, on comity, not deterrence. A large reserve army, a powerful strategic air force and navy, the bomb, and a global ring of American bases, he argued, served only to alarm the Soviet Union, obviously the only potential target for American strength. So alarmed, the Russians in their turn were bound to be hostile. It was not some demoniacal quality in Stalin or in communism, as Wallace saw it, but ancient Russian fears that accounted for their policies in eastern Europe. New anxieties about American encirclement would provoke them to an arms race that no nation could afford and the peace of the world might not survive.

As before, like some others in Washington, Wallace accepted the existence of spheres of influence as at least a temporary circumstance of the postwar period. He did not expect the Soviet Union to intrude in Latin America, and he did not expect the United States to intrude in eastern Europe. Probably he underestimated the repression that accompanied Soviet domination; certainly he did so in 1947 and 1948. But at no time, his critics to the contrary, did Wallace condone repression by any nation. Rather, he believed that the elimination of international tension would, over time, lead both to a softening of Soviet foreign policy and a relaxation of police methods within areas of Soviet control. To encourage that relaxation he advocated more patience in diplomacy than Byrnes or Truman ordinarily displayed. He urged, too, energetic cultivation of Soviet-American commerce, first of all by the extension of a credit to Russia, exactly the policy Harriman and the State Department blocked. The establishment of a basis for trade, Wallace predicted, would serve the economic advantage of both nations and help gradually to convert suspicious hostility to tolerant rivalry between two different political and economic systems. He wholly expected the American system to prove its greater worth.

Truman's stance toward the Soviet Union was the most continual but by no means the only source of distress to Wallace. He worried, too, about relations with Great Britain, with Latin America, and with China, as well as about decisions affecting the control of the atomic bomb. With respect to China, he had no quarrel with Truman's attempt, unsuccessful though it was, to work out an accommodation between Chiang Kai-shek and the communists. In contrast to Truman, however, Wallace held that the presence and deployment of Soviet troops in Manchuria, which militated to the advantage of the Chinese communists, accorded with agreements between Roosevelt and Stalin. Still, Wallace and Truman agreed that the United States had done and was doing all it could for the Generalissimo; if he fell, the fault would be his.

They came close to agreement, too, about domestic control of atomic energy, though not about related international policy. Wallace, who had known from the beginning about the project to develop the atomic bomb, turned for advice about its control to the nuclear scientists who had created it. Informed by those physicists, whom he trusted as the experts in their field, he concluded that atomic weapons were far too destructive to be left to the control of the military. Too, the development of atomic science was far too important to be removed from control of the physicists. Wallace realized there was no secret about atomic energy. European scientists had played indispensable roles in the American project; the Germans and Japanese had built cyclotrons during the war; the Soviet Union, whose scientists were first-rate, had an atomic bomb within its reach if it was prepared to defray the enormous costs of making one. But the prospect of a nuclear arms race appalled Wallace. He envisaged instead the utilization of atomic energy as a source of power and a field of research, in both thrusts as a boon instead of a threat to mankind.

Those considerations accounted for his opposition to the May-Johnson bill which would have left the military with authority over American atomic development. With many of the nuclear scientists, with the essential assistance of Director of the Budget Harold Smith, and against the devious opposition of General Leslie Groves, Wallace encouraged the drafting and enactment of the McMahon bill. It provided, he felt, even after unfortunate amendments designed to mollify congressional saber-rattlers, acceptable assurances of civilian control over the domestic atomic energy program.

The McMahon Act could not guarantee that civilian authorities, the President included, would not yield to military counsel. In Wallace's opinion, many of them already had. Vannevar Bush had supported the May-Johnson bill, as for a time had other scientists and administrators of organized science including James B. Conant. Even Robert Oppenheimer had not enlisted against it, and until Harold Smith and others persuaded him to reconsider, Truman had gone along with Bush and thus with General Groves. In the end the President did exert his influence for the McMahon measure, but he accepted, with far more equanimity than did Wallace the amendments to the bill that gave the military a stronger voice than most of the veterans of Los Alamos deemed safe or wise.

With too few exceptions to matter, congressmen felt a kind of panic at the thought of sharing the supposed secret of the bomb with any nation, especially with the Soviet Union. Yet science recognized no national borders. Passionately, therefore, Wallace advocated a policy of openness about American scientific information, as his communications to Truman and others disclosed. That policy would ease apprehensions about American intentions, a politically desirable eventuality. It would also avail people everywhere of knowledge with which they could harness atomic energy to build an abundant society. That view, close to the opinion of Secretary Stimson and a few others in the Cabinet, was neither radical nor irresponsible. The sharing of basic scientific information did not imply the disclosure of technical details about the production of fissionable materials or the triggering mechanism for an implosion weapon. But the sharing of basic scientific information seemed to the timid and the ignorant equivalent to the loss of a precious secret on which national security depended. So thought Secretary of the Navy James Forrestal. So thought enough congressmen and ultimately, with less intensity, the President himself, to limit American flexibility in approaching the issue.

Privately Truman concluded that Wallace's opinions about atomic policy were unsafe. He also took pains not to venture beyond what Congress would approve. He could not obtain that approval without Republican support, so in atomic, as in all foreign policy, he paid the high price of bipartisanship. At the least that price involved continual concessions to the outsized vanity of Senator Arthur Vandenberg, senior Republican on the Foreign Relations Committee. On that and other accounts, Truman found it necessary often to employ anticommunist rhetoric, which he seemed not to consider distasteful. Further, he drew back without any prodding from offering the Soviet Union anything, even basic scientific information that he could not long keep secret, without receiving in return something he felt he had been denied. In the case of atomic energy, he moved to circumvent the Soviet position on the use of the veto in the Security Council of the United Nations. The proposals that he had Bernard Baruch put forward in the UN were less liberal than the preliminary recommendations drafted by David Lilienthal and Dean Acheson, who was by no means soft in his view of Moscow. As Wallace complained, the Baruch plan, unlike Acheson's, eliminated the veto as it applied to questions of atomic energy while it also guaranteed for a decade American monopoly of atomic weapons, and offered the Soviet Union information only on the installment plan, with each installment conditional upon Soviet good behavior during the previous period. A proud and powerful nation, capable of mounting an atomic energy program on its own, was bound to reject the Baruch proposals. A more generous offer, Wallace believed, would have won Soviet trust and acceptance. As he saw it, men like General Groves, Secretary Forrestal, and Baruch had infected American opinion and warped American policy. As for Truman, who had seemed to wobble for months, he struck Wallace, as he did Eleanor Roosevelt, as a weak and vacillating man.

By Wallace's standards, the President also appeared cynical. Truman looked upon Latin America as a counter in the game of world politics. To hold the nations to the south to a hemispheric coalition dominated by the United States, the President through his spokesmen at San Francisco arranged the admission of Argentina, then manifestly a fascist country, to the UN. That maneuver aroused the suspicions of the Soviet Union, which had been no less cynical in its role in the politics of the conference. It also presaged the meretricious manner of the State Department in Latin American relations— the appointment of ambassadors content to cooperate with the conservative forces of the military, the church, and the large landholders; the arming of those governing coalitions which used the weapons they received to stifle opposition; the abandonment of the objectives the Board of Economic Warfare had advanced. Wallace had seen Latin America as the first beneficiary of the policies he advocated for the common man. Now he watched the President and State Department revert to the neocolonialism of the 1920s, to a policy pitched to the alleged needs of national defense and the palpable advantage of American investors, a policy impervious to the woeful conditions of daily life which he believed the United States had an obligation to mitigate.

Wallace also interpreted as cynical Truman's early approach to the Palestine question. Disinclined to alienate Great Britain, the President yielded to London's anxieties about placating the Arabs and protecting British control in the Middle East. The definition of Palestine's borders and the limits on Jewish immigration on which British and American negotiators first agreed left Palestine too small and weak for economic development or military security, and left thousands of displaced European Jews without access to a permanent home. Wallace, who urged Truman to demand a solution more favorable to the Jews, played on the President's political sensitivities. British convenience and prospects for American oil investments in the Middle East came gradually to count less with Truman than did the Jewish vote. But Wallace had meanwhile concluded that the President had little more humane concern for the Jews of Europe than for the impoverished in Latin America. He also considered the President's original position on Palestine as typifying an unfortunate course of American relations with Great Britain.

That issue disturbed Wallace as much as did any other. He admired the heroic role of the British common people in their resistance to the Nazis. But like so many middle west-

ern democrats, he despised the British upper classes for their
haughty manner and their arrogance about race, national origin, and social position. Further, he blamed them for British
imperialism, which he wished to eradicate. On that account
he distrusted Churchill, alike for his aristocratic ways and his
imperialistic sentiments, so freely expressed whenever the Prime
Minister visited Washington. Even after the election of a Labor
government, Wallace feared that Great Britain would remain
Churchillian in purpose, would continue to hold the uncrit-
ical affection of Anglophiles in the Department of State, and
would induce the United States to assume a partnership in
world politics. He had trusted Roosevelt to resist that role,
but Truman was more vulnerable to British influence, partly
because he shared Churchill's fear of Russia, partly because
among his closest advisers were men like Dean Acheson, who
characteristically associated American with British interests.

From April 1945, when Roosevelt died, through the
remainder of the year, Wallace grew more and more restive
with the international policies of the administration. Increasingly he realized that Truman in private conversations gave
him assurances that the President's public actions contra-
dicted. Still Wallace allowed himself to hope that Truman
might change. During 1946 he lost that hope. The Baruch
plan alarmed him. So did the hard line toward the Soviet
Union that Averell Harriman advanced upon his return from
Moscow to Washington, the tough policy that Secretary of
State Byrnes pursued in his negotiations with the Russians,
the tough talk of State Department Russian specialists like
Charles Bohlen and George Kennan. They read Stalin's monitory address of February 9, 1946, as a trumpet of hostility,
of communist militancy and Russian expansionism. Wallace
read it as a regrettably inimical response to threats that Stalin
perceived in his exaggerated interpretation of American policy. According to that reading, there was still room for recip-

rocal understanding. But then at Fulton, Missouri, with Truman on the platform, Churchill delivered his celebrated "iron curtain" speech, that called for a fraternal alliance of the English-speaking people. It was precisely the alliance Wallace most opposed. Involving, as it did, the fading grandeur of the British empire and the implicit threat of the atomic bomb, it was addressed aggressively against the Soviet Union. It portended the rejection of spheres of influence in Europe that had been defined by the deployment of troops at the end of the war. It invited Anglo-American penetration of the Soviet sphere. Speaking at Stuttgart, Germany, in September, Secretary of State Byrnes sounded the first notes of that new policy which would gradually make the United States the catalyst, initially in the economic and later in the military reconstruction of West Germany as a part of a larger anti-Soviet bloc.

There were provocations, as Wallace knew, for Byrnes's address. The Soviet Union had permitted no democracy in the areas it ruled; it had seized German industrial equipment and commandeered German labor in its eastern zone; it had broken promises made at Yalta and at Potsdam; it had disregarded human rights in Poland and elsewhere in eastern Europe; it had been intransigent in preventing a common policy for occupied Germany as a whole. But the United States had been intransigent, too, in its unilateral control over occupied Japan, in its deployment of strategic air power, in its manipulations in Latin America. American occupation authorities in Japan had wantonly destroyed the Japanese cyclotron. Washington officials, while denying a credit to Russia, had arranged one for Great Britain, possibly on harder terms to the Labor government than they would have extended to the Tories.

Politically and ideologically, the world had begun to polarize by September 1946. Wallace's hopes were evaporating for the kind of world he had associated with a century of the common man. At Madison Square Garden on September 12, he tried again to put his message across, to warn against Churchill's proposals and to urge another approach to the Soviet Union. He criticized alike British imperial and Russian political practices, and the communists in the audience booed him, for he was pleading not for Russia but for peace. Truman, who had read and approved the speech, disavowed it after Wallace's opponents opened fire and Byrnes and Vandenberg insisted that the speech impeded their diplomacy at the ongoing conference of foreign ministers. On Truman's order, Wallace promised to speak no more until that conference was over. But that tenuous arrangement only postponed the obvious solution. Byrnes, dissatisfied, demanded that Truman fire Wallace, and Truman did. The President had, after all, issued the directions Byrnes was following. As Wallace and Truman both knew, there could be at any one time only one American foreign policy. Once the issue was openly joined, Wallace had to go.

THOUGH Truman's administrative decision was incontestably correct, his foreign policy was not. Like his critics at the time, so critics since have questioned both his presumptions and his tactics. Wallace was only one of the first to do so. In the absence of access to the Soviet archives, there can be no sure assessment of Wallace's case. American provocations may only have confirmed fixed Soviet decisions about postwar policy. But provocations there certainly were, as Wallace argued. At least until the time of Fulton, the possibility existed of a practical accommodation between the United States and the Soviet Union, of a temporary coexistence of mutually suspicious spheres of influence, of a gradual lessening of hostility and a gradual movement, as Wallace recommended, first toward commercial and scientific and then toward political cooperation, all within the framework of the United Nations. Even after the Fulton speech, the United States could have assisted the countries of the Southern Hemisphere more on an altruistic and less on a political basis. American records, easy of access, disclose that Truman never expected a rapprochement with the Soviet Union. Wallace had reason to disagree. He had the prescience to realize that the hard line abroad would generate hysterical reactions to dissent at home, lead to the postponement of urgent domestic reforms, and encourage military adventures costly alike of men and morale. He had the foresight to propose alternatives to which the United States government turned only after a quarter century of terrible waste had made accommodation more attractive to most of the American people.

Yet in the months immediately following his departure from public office, Wallace's insights were cloudy. As his fears about Truman's policies grew, so did his vulnerability to those who were urging him to run for the presidency on a third party ticket. He was tempted to embark on that unhappy course on several counts. Out of government, he was removed from the councils of state to which he had often contributed and from which he had often also learned. He was removed, too, from easy access to the kinds of experts who had given him such influential assistance in earlier years, for one example in the making of agricultural policies. He had to rely instead more on his intuitions and hopes than on hard data and salient technical knowledge. Further, those who now advised him lacked the experience and judgment of his former counselors. Many of the men in the group around him were naive; some were eager to use him to advance their own interests; none had much political insight. Yet their pressure moved Wallace less than did his own temperament. Believing that Truman was leading the country and the world toward war, committed to a contrary view of the new century, Wallace disregarded the warnings of his family and old friends and followed his own compulsion to stand political witness to his faith.

In his eagerness to find a rapprochement with the Soviet Union, he blinded himself to the mounting evidence of Russian tyranny in eastern Europe. In his determination to resist redbaiting, he became indifferent to the debilitating tactics of communists within his Progressive Party of 1948. For several years, his passion overcame his practicality.

Even so, he remained perceptive. Long an advocate of American assistance in the rebuilding of the European economy, he urged employing international agencies to administer aid programs and granting aid exclusively on social and economic rather than political bases. These considerations led him to underestimate the responsibility of the Soviet Union for keeping eastern Europe out of the Marshall Plan. Earlier, however, he had protested against the Truman Doctrine and its applications in Greece and Turkey. As Wallace then said, that doctrine ignored and weakened the United Nations, substituted unilateral for multilateral aid, and gave military assistance unfortunate priority over economic assistance. Worse, the anticommunist rhetoric of the doctrine expressed a universal commitment to antirevolutionary interventions. As Wallace foresaw, both the precedent and the rhetoric had ominous portents.

Indeed Wallace's fundamental trepidations about American policy, all of them prominent before he left office, had become by the early 1970s common criticisms of the history of the interceding years. The collusion of the military with those industrial interests that depended upon defense expenditures had resulted in enormous waste and bureaucratic inefficiency. The military-industrial establishment against which Dwight D. Eisenhower warned his countrymen in 1961 had worried Wallace two decades earlier. Indeed the military, as Americans learned by 1970, had proved unable to maintain the standards of financial probity and disciplined warfare on which professional soldiers liked to pride themselves. Unilateral military intervention, as Wallace had feared, had become something of a national habit, with the war in Vietnam only the most recent and most dreadful example of the corrupting dangers of American adventurism. Too, war and preparation for war, deterrence and its cost, balance-of-power politics with their related expenditures—even bribes—for the purchase of allies, had debilitated the UN and absorbed national income needed for domestic social programs, the very programs Wallace had urged for relief of poverty, conservation of the land and its resources, education of the young, the delivery of health care, and the protection of the aged. The inversion of national priorities, attacked in 1968 by Eugene McCarthy and Robert Kennedy and in 1972 by George McGovern, had drawn Wallace's criticisms in 1942.

In other ways also Wallace proved prescient, a man far ahead of his times, as he had so often been. After the revolution in Cuba, Washington recognized Latin America again as a continent full of people, not just a reservation for private investment and seductive military aid. The Alliance for Progress that John F. Kennedy launched in 1961 had as its social targets precisely those of the Board of Economic Warfare. Even Richard Nixon discovered what Wallace had always maintained, that communist ideology did not constitute an insuperable hurdle to communication. In 1971 Nixon went to China, which he had condemned as demoniacal for more than two decades, and in 1972 to Moscow, there to suggest that the encouragement of commerce between the Soviet Union and the United States would benefit both nations and ease their political relationship. For saying such things Wallace had been called a red or at least a pink from 1946 through

1948, as were others of his opinion, with Nixon one of their most fervent accusers.

The irony of history should have restored Wallace's reputation, but in the early 1970s he was still remembered more for his occasional fallibility than for his extraordinary foresight. Three decades earlier he had imagined a splendid century which still had yet convincingly to begin. He would have welcomed a century of the common man, as he welcomed the New Deal, whenever it began. He would have lost none of his verve for administering the agencies to promote it, shed none of his worries about the persisting impediments to it, surrendered none of his zeal for opposing the enemies of it. While he found armor for his missions in his faith, while he preached his best hopes, Henry A. Wallace sought their fulfillment less in his message than in the hard labor of learning and doing. By his works, he believed, practical Christian that he was, men would know him.

In his works they would find a good man.

10

UNITY AND STABILITY
DURING WORLD WAR II*

DURING the Second World War the American people united against their enemies in a measure greater than they had ever united for any other national purpose. That unity provided an essential ingredient for fighting physically remote but ruthless foes. Nevertheless wartime intensifications of emotions on the home front ordinarily whetted rather than dampened antecedent divisions within American society. In their ethnic rivalries, class conflict and political partisanship, Americans continually united against each other. To be sure, Churchill was right for Americans, too; war did demand blood and sweat and tears. But war also demanded social stability. War did not alter the human condition, and among Americans, as among other peoples, the war at once aroused and revealed the dark, the naked and shivering nature of man.

Commercial radio, in the observation of one analyst in 1942, ordinarily provided a twisted treatment of military news. "The

*First published as "United Against: American Culture and Society During World War II," Harmon Memorial Lectures, no. 25, United States Air Force Academy, Colorado, 1983.

war," he wrote, "was handled as if it were a Big Ten football game, and we were hysterical spectators." He should not have been surprised. All social units, nations included, ordinarily achieved cohesion largely by identifying a common enemy against whom all their members could unite. Sensitive to that phenomenon, Franklin D. Roosevelt, while an undergraduate at Harvard, had attempted to whip up school spirit for the Yale game. In the Ivy League as well as the Big Ten, the cohesion of each university community had long reached a peak during the annual contest with a traditional rival, a peak in which a sense of common identity in a common cause imbued not undergraduates only but also alumni and even faculty, dedicated though the last constituency theoretically was to an unemotional pursuit of truth.

Within the federal government, during the period before American entry into the war, the Office of Facts and Figures (OFF) had a large responsibility for achieving a similar national unity. In that time, Americans were divided about the war. A significant majority came to believe in helping to supply the victims of Axis aggression, but a considerable minority opposed that policy as needlessly inviting direct involvement in the war itself. The head of OFF, the talented poet and Librarian of Congress, Archibald MacLeish, attempted initially to let the facts tell the necessary story. That tactic failed. Several eminent authorities about public opinion advised, as one of them put it, that the agency would have to employ "a large element of fake," the proven technique of American advertising. MacLeish continued to hope that the splendid goals embodied in the Atlantic Charter, from which he drew inspiration, would also inspire the public. After Pearl Harbor, that hope, already fading, surrendered to the banalities and hoopla of commercial practice. The resulting propaganda struck some veterans of Madison Avenue as unpersuasive. One of them called openly for a propaganda of hate. MacLeish balked. He stood, he declared, in accordance with the Christian doctrine of hating sin but forgiving the sinner, not for hatred of the enemy but for hatred of evil. That laudable distinction made few converts, and soon MacLeish resigned.

MacLeish had overlooked a different distinction, one made by Walter Lippmann in his classic study of 1922, *Public Opinion,* a book hewn by its author's experience with propaganda during the First World War. An understanding of "the furies of war and politics," Lippmann wrote, depended upon the recognition that "almost the whole of each party believes absolutely in its picture of the opposition, that it takes as fact, not what is, but what it supposed to be fact." Indeed the adjustment of people to the environment in which they lived occurred "through the medium of fictions." The product of both acculturation and manipulation, those fictions served as facts, albeit counterfeit facts, and determined a large part of behavior.

No counterfeit was required to bring together for a time the factions which for two years had confronted each other about the question of whether the United States should go to war. The Japanese attack on Pearl Harbor ended that debate, as did the ensuing declarations of war on the United States by Germany and Italy. "The suddenness of the . . . attack," in the words of Isaiah Berlin, the British official in Washington charged with informing the Foreign Office about American conditions, ". . . came as a great shock to the nation. . . . The immediate effect has been to make the country completely united in its determination to fight Japan to the end. . . ." Formerly dissident elements, he added a week later, recognized that the country was "in the war for good or ill, and that all should unite their efforts to bring about the defeat of the totalitarian powers. It is also gradually felt that Hitler is the ultimate enemy. . . ." Those were sound analyses, but as the initial trauma of the Japanese attack subsided, Americans at home yielded to habitual sentiments. In the United States the same observer later recalled, "political and economic life to a considerable degree continued as before, and . . . some of the pressures and internecine feuds between individuals and . . . blocs, inherited from the New Deal and even earlier times, continued." In the spring of 1942 surveys indicated that some seventeen million Americans "in one way or another" opposed the prosecution of the war. That summer, after a series of American defeats in the Pacific, public morale sagged. It would turn around, Isaiah Berlin predicted, only with the broad engagement of American troops in the fighting.

That forecast contained a telling insight. As Gordon Allport, a master of the study of prejudice, later demonstrated, "the presence of a threatening common enemy" cemented the loyalties of aggregates of people. There was to be no attack on the United States, but when American troops in large numbers did meet the enemy, they united against their foe with less need for artificial stimulation than was the case with their countrymen at home.

Whether or not there were atheists in American foxholes, there were few men in combat in any of the services who did not know danger and fear and a resulting hatred. Bill Mauldin, writing in Italy during the long campaign there, spoke to the essential condition of every front: "I read someplace that the American boy is not capable of hate . . . but you can't have friends killed without hating the men who did it. . . . When our guys cringe under an SS barrage, you don't hear them say 'Those dirty Nazis.' You hear them say, 'Those goddam Krauts.' " So also in their expletives about the Japanese with the crews in P.T. boats in the Solomons, or the Marines on Iwo, or the airmen over New Guinea.

The common cause each combat unit joined owed much to the shared danger of a group of men fighting side by side. As

Ernie Pyle noted about the air corps, "basically it can be said that everything depended on teamwork. Sticking with the team and playing it all together was the only guarantee of safety for everybody." In that respect the aviators were no different from the doggies. The G.I. fought at once against the enemy and for his buddies. Robert Sherrod phrased it well: "The Marines . . . didn't know what to believe in . . . except the Marine Corps. The Marines fought . . . on esprit de corps." The services deliberately inculcated a sense of unit—of platoon and company, of ship and task group, of pilot and crew and squadron. Training exercises in themselves required a quick responsiveness and spontaneous cooperation that fostered a needed togetherness. But danger provided the strongest cement.

In the backwater of the fighting, behind the lines, esprit was therefore harder to sustain. Like the marines, most soldiers and sailors had little awareness of the Four Freedoms. They were young Americans prepared to defend their country but eager to get it over with and go home. For the supply service in the Chinese-Burma-India theater or the garrison in Greenland, the enemy was far away. They found substitutes in their hatred of the natives, or the heat or cold or dirt, or the inescapable unfamiliarity of their stations. John Horne Burns described that phenomenon as it affected G.I.'s in Naples, Italy, J. D. Salinger as it operated on Attu. In the tragicomic novel, *Mr. Roberts,* the men of a ship assigned to dull errands in the South Pacific expressed their cohesion in their common detestation of their irascible captain. The officer hero of the novel, who understood the crew, deliberately defied the captain before obtaining the release he wanted, assignment to a combat ship, on which he later was killed. The fiction was rooted in fact, in the coming together of real crews of platoons far from danger in their dislike, sometimes persecution, of a tough drill sergeant or C.O., or of an outsider in their ranks, a teetotaler or a socialist, a black or Hispanic or Jew.

American civilians behaved in much the same way. Few doubted that the war had to be won or that they should do their part in contributing to victory. But that commitment often flagged as individuals, impatient for the fruits of victory, shopped in the black markets for consumer goods the government was rationing. Others, tense because of the absence of a husband or brother, or because of long hours on the job or long lines awaiting cigarettes, spent that tension by blaming neighbors or politicians or even phantoms whom they had never liked. But civilian morale was much sustained in a vicarious battle, a hatred of the enemy informed, not without cause, by the malign characteristics attributed to the Germans and Japanese. American civilians characteristically described the Germans as warlike and cruel, though also misled and probably amenable to postwar cooperation. American racism, spurred perhaps by Japanese fanaticism in the field, produced a more negative picture of the Japanese, who were usually viewed as treacherous, sly and fierce, and probably a poor risk for postwar friendship.

Those attributions of generalized national characteristics, those counterfeit facts, emerged, as in all wars, both from prior prejudice and from current propaganda, public and private. So it was that American blacks harbored less animosity toward Asians than did American whites. Yet even whites during the war had a benign opinion of the Chinese, the nation's allies, though few Americans could easily differentiate on sight among different Asian peoples. Indeed at other times, earlier and later, as one authoritative study showed, the American image of the Chinese alternated between the villainous figure of Fu Man Chu and the amiable symbol of Charlie Chan. *Time* magazine endeavored to help its readers tell friend from foe. The Japanese, the journal asserted, with no basis in fact, were hairier than the Chinese; "the Chinese expression is likely to be more placid, kindly, open; the Japanese more positive, dogmatic, arrogant. . . . The Japanese are hesitant, nervous in conversation, laugh loudly at the wrong time. Japanese walk stiffly erect . . . Chinese more relaxed . . . sometimes shuffle." Comic strips drew a similar picture, and even the War Production Board called for the extermination of the Japanese as rats. As did the Germans with the Jews, so did Americans with the Japanese, and to a lesser extent the Germans, enhance their own sense of unity by hating an outside group to which, in each case, they applied stereotypes sustained, as Allport wrote, "by selective perception and selective forgetting."

Though officially the federal government did not consider the United States a party to a racial war or a war of hatred and revenge, official rhetoric sometimes conveyed those feelings. The responsible spokesmen were genuinely angry and more, gravely concerned about spurring civilian participation in wartime programs. So it was that the Treasury Department, adopting a tactic which its analysts recommended after extensive study, endorsed advertisements for war savings bonds that depicted the Japanese as "ungodly, subhuman, beastly, sneaky, and treacherous," in one case as "murderous little ape men."

So, too, the War Department in its preparations for the trials at Nuremberg pursued retribution at a large cost to Anglo-American law. The attorneys who worked out the trial procedures proposed from the first to charge the Nazi government, party and agencies with "conspiracy to commit murder, terrorism, and the destruction of peaceful populations in violation of the laws of war." The conviction of individual Nazi leaders would implicate Nazi organizations that had furthered the conspiracy, and lesser German officials would then be convicted in turn if they had been associated with those agencies. That proposal, with its presumption of guilt by association, ran directly counter to the Anglo-American tradition of presuming innocence until guilt was proved. No such thing existed, moreover, as an "international crime of conspiracy to dominate by acts violative of the rules of war." Indeed conspiracy law had no place at all in European practice. Recourse to the conspiracy doctrine made the Germans targets of an *ex post facto* proceeding, even a bill of attainder of a kind. The British Lord Chancellor, unlike the American Secretary of War, preferred to hew to the "Napoleonic precedent" which called for political rather than judicial action to resolve what was essentially a political rather than a legal problem. But the Americans prevailed even though, as one critic later wrote, "the whole of the war-crimes policy planning was shot through with excess . . . combined with . . . overmoralizing." Those were precisely the qualities that marked wartime American reportage, fiction, propaganda and public opinion about the Germans.

Those qualities also characterized the language and behavior of various groups within American society which, throughout the war, united against each other with venom and occasional ferocity. Like troops behind the lines, they found familiar targets close at hand for antagonisms that predated the war but drew new force, often with official sanction or indifference, from wartime developments. In the name of wartime necessity, racial prejudice sparked the most blatant official violation (except for chattel slavery) of civil liberties in American history—the confinement of Japanese Americans, American citizens as well as immigrants, in barren camps in the interior western states.

The Japanese Americans, of whom the overwhelming majority were loyal to the United States, were innocent of any proven crime, but after the attack on Pearl Harbor, anti-Japanese sentiment, especially on the west coast, reached hysterical proportions. Within weeks the noxious counterfeits of the Native Sons and Daughters of the Golden West had become official doctrine. The congressional delegations from the Pacific slope and the Attorney General of California demanded the evacuation of the Japanese Americans from the area, with internment the predictable sequential step. General John L. DeWitt, commanding general there, announced that a "Jap is a Jap. . . . It makes no difference whether he is an American citizen or not." Secretary of War Henry L. Stimson backed DeWitt. The "racial characteristics" of the Japanese, he held, bound them to an enemy nation and required their evacuation. The Attorney General of the United States, after some hesitation, supported Stimson, as also vigorously did President Roosevelt. Almost universally the American press endorsed the policy. The head of the War Relocation Authority, charged with administering the internment camps, attributed a few, rare protests to "liberals and kind-hearted people" who did not understand wartime necessity.

That argument proved barren after the war when returning Japanese American veterans met open hostility in Washington state and California. The whole policy disregarded the experience of Hawaii where Japanese Americans, too numerous to be incarcerated, remained, with insignificant exceptions, exemplary citizens throughout the war. Yet even the Supreme Court in the Hirabeyashi case upheld the constitutionality of the evacuation on the ground that "residents having ethnic affiliations with an invading enemy may be a greater source of danger than those of different ancestry," though neither German nor Italian Americans were locked up. Two later wartime cases resulted in only inadequate modifications of the ruling, which was effectively overturned only many years later. The court's record, its disregard for the wholesale deprivation of liberty without due process of law, provoked just one contemporary rebuke from a distinguished member of the bar, the stinging retort of Eugene V. Rostow. The treatment of the Japanese Americans, he wrote in 1945, "was in no way required or justified by the circumstances. . . . It was calculated to produce individual injustice and deep-seated maladjustments. . . . [It] violated every democratic social value, yet has been approved by the Congress, the President and the Supreme Court."

The attack on Pearl Harbor afforded a partial explanation for the persecution of the Japanese Americans but not for its counterpart, the "truculent anti-Negro statements" that "stimulated racial feeling," as Isaiah Berlin observed, in the South and in northern cities. He also reported a less but growing anti-Semitism and mounting hostility, not least among servicemen, toward Hispanic Americans. The movement of blacks into industrial areas to find employment in war industries, the shortage of housing, schooling and recreational facilities in those places, and resulting rivalry of whites and blacks for various kinds of space, those and other wartime conditions intensified historic prejudices and, just as Allport postulated, sparked episodes of violence. Major race riots occurred in Mobile, Alabama, in Los Angeles (where the victims were largely Chicanos), in Harlem and, most destructively, in Detroit. The motor city, as a Justice Department investigation disclosed in 1943, was a "swash-buckling community. . . . Negro equality . . . an issue which . . . very considerable segments of the white community" resisted. Among whites and blacks, truculence was growing. There had been open conflict in 1942 between Polish Americans and blacks over access to a new federal housing project. There followed sporadic episodes of fighting, often involving alienated teenagers. In the deep heat of a June weekend in 1943 a clash between blacks and whites in a park escalated into a riot that for two days rocked the city where thirty-four people, mostly blacks, were killed. Federal troops, summoned by the Michigan governor, restored a superficial quiet, but blacks and whites remained united in their suspicions of each other.

Predictably the press in Mississippi blamed the riot on the insolence of Detroit's blacks and on Eleanor Roosevelt for proclaiming and practicing social equality. The NAACP pleaded for a statement from the President to arouse opinion against "deliberately plotted attacks." Roosevelt did condemn mob violence in any form, but he ducked the racial issue as he did generally during the war.

Those developments conformed to the pattern of that issue in that period. The South opposed any threat to segregation. The presumed threats arose from the continued efforts of American blacks, during a war directed in part against Nazi racism, to fight racism at home, too. The federal government moved reluctantly, when it moved at all, under political pressure from black leaders. Only the imminence of a protest march on Washington persuaded the President to establish the Fair Employment Practices Commission which thereafter made small and erratic progress toward its assigned goal. Blacks did obtain jobs in war industry but less because of federal action than because of a shortage of workers, and then usually in semi-skilled positions and as members of pro forma affiliates of segregated labor unions. Worse, no protest succeeded in stirring the armed forces to desegregate the services. Secretary of War Stimson supported segregation, as did Army Chief of Staff George C. Marshall, partly because they would not, in Stimson's words, use the army in wartime as a "sociological laboratory." But Stimson also believed that blacks lacked courage, mechanical aptitude, and the capacity for leadership. Consequently, though Roosevelt now and then scolded the army, black troops served primarily under white officers and in service of supply assignments. There were token exceptions, such as a black fighter squadron, as also within the navy, where almost all blacks performed menial duties. Those policies gave the lie to the government propaganda showing happy black workers at lathes in model factories or contented black soldiers poised for combat. The persisting inequality and humiliation of blacks impelled their leaders to unite their fellows, along with some sympathetic whites, against bigotry and official indifference. The war years saw the founding of CORE and the first modern freedom rides and sit-ins, some of them successful, all portentous, all fraught with interracial tension.

Like ethnic animosities, class conflict persisted during the war. In his reports about American morale, Berlin referred most often to industrial unrest. "Anti-labour feeling," he observed in November 1942, "has risen to a considerable height. Public indignation at . . . strikes in war industries . . . comparisons between industrial workers' wages and those of soldiers and farmers, all continually whipped up by predominantly Republican and anti-labour press." In June 1943 he noted a "rising tide of anti-labour feeling among armed services" stationed within the country. Several months later, as he wrote, that feeling reached the top when General Marshall, during an off-the-record press conference, "struck the table and said with genuine anger that the behaviour of the labour leaders . . . might easily prolong the war at a vast cost in . . . blood and treasure." That outburst was not typical of Marshall, though the opinion may have been, as it surely was among almost all business managers, most Republicans and conservative Democrats, and many senior officials in the federal bureaus and agencies responsible for the conduct of the war, particularly those involved in production, manpower, and wage and price control. Their biases led them to exaggerate the satisfactions of working men and women and to resist and overestimate the power of the unions.

The wartime growth of the economy did carry with it significant gains for industrial workers. Demand for labor pulled into the factories previously ostracized blacks, displaced rural workers, and unprecedented numbers of women. Real wages rose, full employment at last returned, and government fiscal policy under those conditions effected a considerable redistribution of income downwards. The War Labor Board's adoption of its "maintenance of membership" policy assured a substantial growth in the unions. But workers nevertheless continually expressed their legitimate discontent. Only a part of rising wages reached weekly pay envelopes which were reduced by deductions for union dues, an unaccustomed charge for the recently unemployed; for the federal income tax, for the first time collected on a pay-as-you-go basis; and for war bonds, which social pressure induced almost everyone to purchase. In crowded industrial cities even rising wages could buy only squalid housing. Rationing limited the availability of choice foods. "To the workers it's a Tantalus situation," a *Fortune* reporter observed: "the luscious fruits of prosperity above their heads—receding as they try to pick them." Other frustrations characterized the work place—the unfamiliar discipline of the assembly line, inequities in job classifications and, especially for women, in pay and in the extra burdens of domesticity. The resulting anxieties and alienation took the form of recurrent absenteeism, particularly among women, and of wildcat strikes, particularly in the automobile, steel and railroad industries. Yet those activities seemed like sabotage to business managers and harassed federal officials, few of whom had ever known the daily burdens of industrial life.

That imperception, a manifestation of both a cultural difference and a latent hostility between social classes, informed angry editorials, provoked military table-pounding, and fostered repeated demands within Congress, among middle-class voters, and ironically, among communists in the labor movement, to discipline or to punish or even to conscript striking workers. Often labor union leaders were the objects of that animosity, though the workers in the troubled industries were usually more restless than were their representatives. Indeed, almost all the leaders had made a no-strike pledge in return for the maintenance of membership policy, and they had thereafter continually to strive to restrain the workers while they negotiated with responsible federal officers for increased wages to match the rising cost of living. In that mediating role they confronted the growing power within government of captains of industry and finance who had been brought to Washington to staff the war agencies and the Navy and War departments. Among those recruits labor had few friends.

In the circumstances, most labor leaders moved with caution, but not John L. Lewis, the head of the United Mine Workers (UMW), whose militancy made him the despised symbol of establishment hostility. Lewis had never believed in the no-strike pledge, disliked the President, and did not trust the government to effect a significant melioration of the still wretched conditions of work in the mines. Yet Lewis was no radical. He remained committed to business unionism, to the traditional objectives of collective bargaining. At least one cabinet member, Harold Ickes, who had a special responsibility for fuel, understood as much. Lewis seemed radical because his wartime tactics, often clumsy and usually strident, appeared to his opponents and were made to appear to most Americans, to be unpatriotic and unreasonable.

During 1942 and 1943 Lewis orchestrated a series of strikes and wildcat strikes to advance his purpose, the unionization of all mine fields and the improvement of wages, benefits, and safety conditions. In considerable measure he succeeded. But his ventures, colliding with the intransigence of the mine owners, did threaten necessary coal supplies for industry and therefore inspired a temporary government take-over of the mines. They also made Lewis and the UMW the undesignated but identifiable targets of the Smith-Connally bill which Congress passed in 1943. Roosevelt vetoed the measure because he recognized its ineffectuality, but immediately Congress overrode the veto. Essentially useless as a device to impose industrial stability, the act increased the President's power to seize plants in war industries, made it a crime to encourage strikes in those plants, and outlawed union contributions to political campaigns, long an objective of Republicans and conservative Democrats. Its political influence challenged, organized labor could take no solace in Roosevelt's veto message which recommended drafting workers who took part in strikes in plants in the possession of the government. In 1944, prodded by the War Department, the President went further and urged a national service law which, he said, would prevent strikes. Though Congress did not approve that expedient, Roosevelt's recourse to it revealed how little influence labor any longer had in Washington. Lewis had united his miners against the owners, but in the process, he galvanized opinion at home and among servicemen against himself. The actual and the emotional imperatives of war produced a retaliation potentially damaging to the entire labor movement.

The leadership of the CIO, eager to retrieve their losses, had no one to turn to but the President who still stood in 1944 for most of the causes they embraced. The Republicans, in contrast, had a long record of hostility to unions and to progressive measures. Denied the ability to contribute union funds to the Democrats, Sidney Hillman and his associates formed the Political Action Committee to raise money from workers and their liberal friends, and to get out the vote. Even so, the influence they exerted was too small to effect the renomination of their most outspoken champion in Washington, Vice President Henry A. Wallace. Indeed, the class and ethnic enmities of the war years underlay the rejection by the Democrats of Wallace, and by the Republicans of Wendell Willkie, his counterpart within the GOP. Both men had attacked business management for its narrowness of vision; both endorsed the aspirations of American blacks.

Divisive issues affected politics throughout the war years. A coalition of Republicans and southern Democrats rolled back the New Deal, opposed progressive taxation, forced Roosevelt to move to the right. Those developments had begun before the war and might well have occurred without it. But politics was never adjourned; political rhetoric was, as ever, intemperate; and both parties stooped to a contentious meanness during the campaign of 1944. Governor Thomas E. Dewey of New York, the Republican nominee, exercised a patriotic generosity in excluding from his campaign any reference to MAGIC, the American compromise of Japanese codes which, had he chosen to mention it, would have assisted the enemy and raised with refreshed force the question of the Administration's culpability for the surprise at Pearl Harbor. Dewey also kept foreign policy out of the campaign in order to avoid premature controversy about the structure of the peace. Nevertheless, the Democrats gave him no quarter; identified him, in spite of his record as governor, with the reactionaries in his party; mocked him for his small physique and little moustache. Early and late, the Republicans, including Dewey, identified the Democrats, often openly, with communism, and employed anti-Semitic innuendos to attack Hillman and through him, Roosevelt. Meanness often emerged in national campaigns. In 1944 the form it took again reflected class and ethnic issues.

The war did not create those issues but neither did it subdue them. In one sense, the remoteness of the battle fronts permitted the expressions of divisiveness that might otherwise have militated against victory. In a larger sense, Americans behaved much as they always had and in a manner not markedly different from other peoples, even those exposed to immediate danger and defeat. Social and political factionalism crippled Italy and France where outright treason, as in Norway and the Netherlands, contributed to German victories. Even in Germany, apart from the victims of genocide, hundreds of decent men and women spent the war in concentration camps, dozens in clandestine subversion, and a group of disenchanted officers, good soldiers all, attempted to assassinate Hitler. In Great Britain the government interned German Jews, civilians grumbled far more than official propaganda admitted, and the Labour Party prepared to win the political triumph it enjoyed before the end of hostilities against Japan. The Soviet state imprisoned or killed many ethnic Germans and dissident Ukrainians, systematically murdered Polish soldiers who were allies but not communists, and stood aside while the Germans demolished the resistance in Warsaw. Thousands of Chinese collaborated with the Japanese, more thousands engaged in civil war, and factionalism vitiated the Kuomintang.

In every warring nation, whatever the degree of its unity against the enemy, men and women also united against their fellows, often with the ferocity of prejudice and hatred. In their dealings with each other, Americans at home exhibited a moderation at least equivalent to that of any other peoples. No inherent superiority of the national soul accounted for the difference. Rather, the intensity of internal strife within the belligerent nations correlated strongly with the proximity of attack, invasion and occupation. Defeat, or the close prospect of defeat, excited a search for scapegoats or a scramble for survival of an intensity Americans were spared. In the dozen years after the war, when Americans first came to recognize their national vulnerability to devastating attack, they united against each other much in the patterns of the war years but more savagely and with more lasting damage. Then, as during the war and at other times, the city on the hill, to the sorrow of some of its residents, did not rise much above the plain.

III

POET,
PHILOSOPHER,
JUDGE

11

ARCHIBALD MACLEISH:
ART FOR ACTION*

ART encompassed experience, so believed Archibald Mac-
Leish; and since politics was part of experience, art encompassed politics. On the contrary politics encompassed art; so
contended the Fascists and Communists of the 1930s and
their spiritual successors who used the power of the state to
brutalize art and artists. MacLeish condemned them for what
they thought and what they did. He also exhorted his fellow
American artists to abandon their posture of political neutrality and accept the responsibility of art for action. Only
action would protect the freedom of the individual and of the
states that nurtured that freedom from the attacks of the new
barbarians ravaging Europe in 1940. Later MacLeish again
exhorted Americans, artists not the least, to protect their
tradition of freedom from the barbarians among their countrymen who were ravaging the politics of democracy in the
postwar decades. As MacLeish saw it a poet had no other

---

*Adapted from a review of Scott Donaldson, *Archibald MacLeish: An American Life*
(Boston: Houghton Mifflin, 1992), in *The Yale Review,* Vol. 81, no. 2 (April 1993),
pp. 106–33.

choice. A responsible artist, a man or a woman of letters, had to be a man or a woman of action.

MacLeish, who was born in 1892 and lived to be ninety, reached that conclusion before his fortieth year. Then and later it gave unity to his life. Though he arrived at it in stages it inhered in the restless and precocious versatility of his youth, even in the influences of his parents. . . . Each in a different way, MacLeish's parents had towering expectations for him. His father, a wealthy Chicago merchant fifty years his senior, brought a stiff Calvinism with him from his native Scotland. Archibald, the second child of his third marriage, found him as remote and formidable as Jehovah. ("If God is God he is not good. . . .") MacLeish had his father's financial support for his extensive education and years of apprenticeship in Paris but never his father's love or even his praise. That deprivation may have accounted for MacLeish's lifelong striving for approval from the fellow poets and critics he most admired. But MacLeish's mother, the descendant of Puritan forebears, believed in striving, too. Before her marriage the principal of Rockford Seminary, Martha Hillard MacLeish, a devout Christian, dedicated herself to good causes, social and religious as well as educational, and expected her children to follow her example. Her earnest liberalism marked her son more deeply than did the contrary patrician smugness he encountered at the Hotchkiss School, which he hated, and at Yale College, which he loved.

At Yale, then "deep in the blue sweater era," MacLeish excelled at everything he undertook. He made the varsity football team and Phi Beta Kappa, was editor of the *Yale Lit,* and was elected to the most prestigious of senior societies, Skull and Bones, whose initiates considered themselves the most accomplished and respected sons of Eli. Then and thereafter, MacLeish was socially most comfortable with such men and women. Yet he was a democrat. In his own mind he invested Yale, as he did his country, with an ideal democratic spirit. And as R. W. B. Lewis observed, though no one seemed to know him intimately, almost everyone he met quickly called him Archie.

In 1917, with American entry into World War I, Mac-Leish, who led his class at the Harvard Law School, interrupted his studies to volunteer for the Yale Mobile Hospital Unit. After arriving in France, he moved to the field artillery where he saw action as a captain. In 1917 he also published *Tower of Ivy,* his first book of poetry. That early verse displayed a sentimentality that enveloped many aspects of his life—his love for his wife, for her rival for his affections, for his own and his mother's vision of America, for Woodrow Wilson's vision of a war to end all wars and to save democracy. MacLeish's poetry at that time dwelt on memories of love and thoughts of death, on "laughing mouth . . . uplifted lips," and on collegiate landscapes. He believed, he wrote, "that beauty is attainable, that the world of the mind is real, that men are in nature seekers of the true God," and that the war was being fought to preserve those verities from destruction by the Germans.

Those sentiments made MacLeish especially vulnerable to the general disillusionment that grew out of the brutality of the war and the selfishness of the terms for peace. He was unsettled even more by the accidental death in Belgium of his younger brother Kenneth, a naval aviator. As so often with MacLeish, the particular merged with the general. "Men become the symbols of ideas by losing their familiar and personal qualities," he wrote his mother in 1920, two years after Kenny's death. "And Kenny as the symbol of brave youth content to die for the battle's sake will really exist when Kenny . . . has a little paled and faded into oblivion." Then, on a visit to Kenneth's grave in 1924, the particular changed and with it the general: "It seems to me grotesque . . . that that beautiful boy should be lying under the sand in a field he never saw—for nothing. . . . It is horrible. . . . It is very still. The sky has become black and threatening. I feel nothing except the numbness of the earth, its silentness. . . . It is absurd to die anyhow. What difference does it make when you die. It is ridiculous to lie quite still. . . . Perhaps you will understand my feeling about the war that creates my feeling about Kenny. It was an awful, awful, failure. A hideous joke."

MacLeish realized that his emotions had "a way of crystallizing around some sensuous object." Kenny's grave affected him, but so did the funeral of Woodrow Wilson. "Does it strike you," he wrote Dean Acheson, his Yale classmate and lifelong friend, "as whimsical that a man who spent most of his public life, all his popularity and the greater part of his health in the fight for peace should be loaded onto a gun carriage as soon as he is past resistance and put away to a tune of gun fire and brass? But they can't get rid of him that way. Hot air through a bugle will do for H. C. Lodge." MacLeish's feelings about the war, then, did not damp his belief in Wilsonian ideals, in a "peace without victory." Like other liberals of the 1920s, he blamed Lodge and the Republicans for the American rejection of the League of Nations. He was disillusioned with the outcome of the war, not with Wilson's avowed purpose. And not wholly with the fighting itself, for he never forgot the experience of a brotherhood of arms: "Those are as brothers whose bodies have shared fear/ Or shared harm or shared hurt or indignity./ Why are the old soldiers brothers and nearest?/ For this: with their minds they go over the sea a little/ And find themselves in their youth again. . . ."

After the war, back in Cambridge at the Harvard Law School, where he said he received his education, MacLeish went on to practice law, teach political science to undergraduates, worry about the state of the world, join the campaign for justice for Sacco and Vanzetti, and dither about his future. He had always had doubts about a career as a lawyer, at best a "compromise" allowing some leisure for writing. Law had its fascination, as in the dissent of Justice Oliver Wendell Holmes, Jr., in the *Abrams* case, a majestic plea for liberty of speech and opinion. As he wrote Acheson, MacLeish had a large regard for "the law as a social instrument" and for "the infinite capacity of the human brain to shape that instrument." In his mother's path, he also believed a man "must . . . act upon the world." But poetry still attracted him. Unlike the law, poetry "must not prove, must not explain," though the poet had to have an expressible idea. "The high function of the human mind," MacLeish wrote Acheson, was "its own expression . . . the expression of its ideal of life" which was "not important as a reforming agency" but as "an act of creation." Obviously MacLeish was torn. "The question," he proposed, "is how to work at reality. . . . We can be amateur philosophers . . . but that won't do. What you and I are fitted for is the serious . . . study of political and social science . . . as the means of salvation." Though law and poetry were "eternal irritants," political science "and such poetry as I really wish to write will fuse." In that sense, he could have it both ways.

Declining a partnership in a prestigious Boston law firm, MacLeish, thirty-one years old in 1923, took his family to Paris, there to read and write poetry and to find his own personal and artistic world. Once there, he realized he shared the estrangement of other literary exiles, his contemporaries and soon his friends, who had preceded him. "The arts," as he put it later," . . . were discovering . . . that an age ended with the First World War . . . that the city of man was now a heap of stones. . . . A generation born in the century of stability and order . . . could still . . . see the old safe world behind the war. . . . It was not the Lost Generation which was lost: It was the world out of which that generation came." That understanding, MacLeish maintained, produced the great art of T. S. Eliot, Ezra Pound, John Dos Passos, Ernest Hemingway and other Americans who were expatriates because their *patria* was "no longer waiting for them anywhere."

In Paris MacLeish developed the poetic voice that characterized his best work then and thereafter. He put himself through a course of readings defined by the personal curricula previously pursued by Pound and Eliot. He made friends with the foremost artists of the glittering Parisian scene. And he explored his inner self without fully revealing it. He had been "remiss in the practice . . . of religion," he admitted to his mother, but he retained "that gravitation of the spirit which is properly called faith." Partly to find himself "in that direction" he needed "this time for real work." His work, his religious work, was poetry. He concluded, not surprisingly, that the proper techniques of poetry were consonant with those of Pound and Eliot: "To create an emotion by the imperfect representation in words of objects which are imperfectly associated with the emotion desired. That is . . . the problem. . . . Grammatical construction beyond the absolute minimum is not desirable. The effort is the direction of attention. . . . But beauty of rhythm and sound are tremendously desirable because they are the greatest possible aids in *the creation of the emotion desired.*" He admired "a compact, precise edged poetry which could be terribly poignant." He wanted to "arrive at a direct statement. . . . I want lucidity and concreteness."

Those qualities made memorable the poems collected in *New Found Land* (1930). Fusing thought and emotion, they received deservedly glowing reviews. They brought a sensuous musicality to themes which had occupied poets for centuries. "Immortal Autumn" and "You, Andrew Marvell" became and remained standard choices for anthologists. The collection in itself validated MacLeish's decision to make poetry his calling. Supplemented by the best of his later work, the book provided impressive evidence for the view of perceptive critics—among others, R. W. B. Lewis, Louis Martz, Howard Nemarov and Richard Wilbur—that of all the things MacLeish was, he was first a poet.

Self-consciously he hewed to the conventions of his art. Though he knew that the world of his youth, the world of stability and order, had vanished, his poetry spoke of the order inherent in nature as he observed it. Joyce and Proust and others he read wrote with a revolutionary sense of time and space. Not so MacLeish. He found inspiration in the rhythms of the day and of the year. "Immortal Autumn" was one of many poems that used the seasons as the objects he described to evoke the emotions he wanted to express: "I praise the fall: it is the human season . . ." To the same end, "You, Andrew Marvell" used the diurnal: "To feel the always coming on/ The always rising of the night." MacLeish knew what he was doing. "Why should the time conception so move our generation," he asked Wyndham Lewis. "Why do I . . . respond to images of the turning world as to nothing else? . . . When the posts of religion are knocked out does the whole flood come down of necessity?" Since MacLeish made a religion of nature as he made a religion of poetry, the latter question answered its predecessor. But great poetry, after all, had always explored identities of mood and time.

Though he wrote some beautiful poetry, MacLeish was not a great poet. He fell especially short of that stature in his longer works, for two early examples, *Nobodaddy* (1925), a play in verse, and *The Hamlet of A. MacLeish* (1928). In both, as in several of his later long works, MacLeish went about "the business of poetry . . . to make sense of the chaos of our lives. . . . To compose an order which the bewildered . . . heart can recognize. To imagine man." *Nobodaddy,* his contorted version of the story of "the Fall," put Cain and God's curse on Cain in center stage. Burdened by his knowledge of good and evil, Cain, "a fugitive and a vagabond," had to endure on earth outside the Garden of Eden. That was also the burden of mankind—to endure in spite of the knowledge of human depravity, a lesson imparted to MacLeish by World War I. But MacLeish did not mention the war even by implication, and he did not express in any way what he meant by evil. The play anticipated his responses to later demonstrations of a lost past of "golden innocence," but it did not succeed either as drama or as blank verse.

The Hamlet also failed. Here MacLeish exposed his own bewildered heart, blamed himself for seeking fame, and urged himself to set more selfless goals. He bared his grief over the death of a son, his brother and several friends, and he lamented the fear he felt in danger. But there was a shallowness about his lamentations. He seemed to bewail his sins without recognizing the possibility of evil within the human heart. Critics, many of whom had found MacLeish's lyric poetry derivative, repeated and expanded that charge in their reviews of *The Hamlet*. Conrad Aiken, a major poet himself, considered MacLeish enslaved to Eliot and other modernists. Edmund Wilson wrote his savage parody, "The Omelette of A. MacLeish." MacLeish acknowledged the influence of Pound and Eliot but defended himself from Aiken. "The experience . . . was mine," he wrote, "the emotion mine, the poetry mine." But for a long season the negative voices damaged MacLeish's reputation, as did *The Hamlet* itself. In that work, he did not make poetic order of the chaos in his or any life.

Between 1929 and 1932, MacLeish's life and his poetry were both changing. The collapse of the stock market and the ensuing depression cut off the income from his father's estate that had supported his residence in Paris. That loss precipitated his departure from Europe. Even sooner, early in

1929, before returning to the United States, MacLeish began to plan a celebration of America that turned away from Europe and rested on a poetry neither lyrical nor internalized. Valuing his privacy as he did, he believed that the subject matter of poetry did not have to involve the poet's personality, to be introspective. The poignancy and beauty of a poem, he proposed, depended "in very large part upon its faithfulness to the earth and to moral life." Nature and human nature provided essential ingredients for his next major venture, *Conquistador* (1932). In fifteen "books" or parts, that poem retold the story of Cortes' conquest of Mexico through the voice of a common Spanish soldier who spoke for all of his compatriots and with them "looked to the west." The long poem read as an artistically stated saga of brutal heroism. The march westward across Mexico moved over terrain MacLeish had explored in 1929, land he now described with affection and precision. Their journey took Cortes and his men away from the old world toward a new world of imagined riches. Cruel conquerors though they clearly were, they were also adventurers moving with the sun and with a kind of freedom from the confining civilization of Spain. Then European civilization followed them: "And the west is gone now: the west is the ocean sky. . . ."

A critical success, *Conquistador* won the Pulitzer prize for poetry. Delighted by that recognition, MacLeish nevertheless complained that critics had missed the point of his long poem. The text prompted most of them to see it as a drama of brave men and brave, albeit horrid, deeds. MacLeish meant it otherwise, as a metaphor: ". . . it is a lot more about OUR TIME than most of the daily papers." The content of the poem did make a metaphor of westering, of America as westering, and westering itself had been an experience of high expectations, of hope as well as adventure and danger and despoliation. MacLeish had wanted to suggest more. Still, hope and courage did have special connotations for the daily papers in 1932 and for the political campaign of Franklin Roosevelt in that desperate year. And in the 1930s a poetry faithful to life, as MacLeish decided, could properly be a political poetry.

IN order to support himself and his family, MacLeish went to work in 1932 for his Yale contemporary, Henry Luce, as an editor of *Fortune,* then a new monthly magazine. He wrote most of the text for many issues and all of several series, like one on housing, later published as books by "the Editors of Fortune." An able journalist, MacLeish gave most of his time to his new responsibilities. Nevertheless he continued to write poetry and drama. Further, his position with *Fortune* gave him access to men in positions of authority in government, and his assignments took him on journeys through the nation so he could see for himself the traumatic social effects of the Great Depression. His experience as a journalist reinforced his liberal views and both his observations and his politics continually informed his poetry.

Toward the end of the presidential contest of 1932 *The New Republic* published MacLeish's "Invocation to the Social Muse," a poem soaked in irony that rejected both the avid capitalism of Herbert Hoover and J. P. Morgan and the communist doctrines then gaining converts in the United States. MacLeish had earlier warned his banker friends that communism appealed to the emotions of working men and women; capitalism had therefore to identify itself with hope, or lose the world. But in this poem about the calling of the poet, he refused to take sides. Here in America there were, the poem said: "Progress and science and tractors and revolutions and / Marx and the wars more antiseptic and murderous / And music in every home: there is also Hoover." He lampooned both capitalism (among the "handful of things a man likes Mister

Morgan is not one") and communism ("Besides, Tovarishah, how to embrace an army?") and concluded that for poets, • "There is nothing worse . . . than to be in style." The poem antagonized the *New Masses* and other arbiters of literature of the Communist Party of the United States. It would have had the same effect on many of *Fortune*'s subscribers had they read and understood it.

So, too, with *Elpenor* (1933), MacLeish's Phi Beta Kappa poem at Harvard, which took its title from the name of a companion of Odysseus whose spirit, after his death, had descended "into the gloomy shades" of Hell. Visiting Elpenor, Odysseus found Hell like the America of 1933 with "Millions starving for corn with/ Mountains of waste corn and/ Millions cold for a house with/ Cities of empty houses. . . ." In Hell were "fools booming like oracles,/ Philosophers promising more/ And worse to come. . . ," also "Kings, dukes, dictators . . . ranting orations from balconies," but Elpenor had not lost his head. Replying to Odysseus' request for directions about how to go home, Elpenor urged him not to return but to adventure further: "For myself—if you ask me—there's no way back . . . There is only the way on." The advice resembled the theme of westering in *Conquistador*. "Bring yourself to a home:/ To a new land. . . ." That was the New Deal's way, MacLeish believed, the way of social experimentation, a turning from the failed theories of 1920s capitalism to build a new nation more equitable than ever before. He had learned about the New Dealers' many plans and he praised their execution in months to come.

Later in the year MacLeish pilloried the New Deal's enemies on the right and on the left in his *Frescoes for Mr. Rockefeller's City* (1933). The title for the poem grew out of the public controversy over the Rockefellers' decision to fire Diego Rivera, the talented Communist artist whom they had hired to paint murals for their new buildings. MacLeish's poem had six parts, each separately entitled, each a fresco in words, each describing the kind of relationship that different groups of Americans had to the land. He began with "Landscape as a Nude," praising the American land—so often the vehicle by which he expressed his feelings about democracy—as if it were a lover's body or a work of art: "She lies on her left side her flank golden: / Her hair is burned black with the strong sun. / The scent of her hair is of rain in the dust on her shoulders: / She has brown breasts and the mouth of no other country." Then he went on to Crazy Horse, the victor over General Custer: "Do you ask why he should fight? It was his country." In contrast to Crazy Horse and the Sioux, whose hearts were "big with the love [they] had for that country," stood the railroad barons: "It was all prices to them: they never looked at it: / why should they look at the land? they were Empire Builders." The true builders were not the bosses but the laborers, "all foreign-born men," who died on the job and whose bodies have become part of the land they worked. The poem continued with scorn for Commodore Vanderbilt, J. P. Morgan, Andrew Mellon, and Bruce Barton, the symbols of high finance and deluding advertising whom he called "the Makers Making America": "They screwed her scrawny and gaunt with their seven-year panics: / They bought her back on their mortgages old-whore-cheap / They fattened their bonds at her breasts till the thin blood ran from them."

Like FDR, MacLeish welcomed the hatred of the economic royalists without hating capitalism as a system. He also scorned "the Marxian" left and its doctrines. "Background with Revolutionaries," the last part of "Frescoes," satirized those who embraced the Communist Party: "For Marx has said to us, Workers what do you need? / And Stalin has said to us, Starvers what do you need? / You need the Dialectical Materialism!" Americans were too tough for those deceptions, MacLeish concluded, as their land was tough, and anyway,

"There is too much sun on the lids of my eyes to be listening." Communist critics, Mike Gold for one, retaliated, calling MacLeish "an unconscious Fascist" and a bad poet. "Those Frescoes," MacLeish wrote a friend, "seem to have gotten way under the Marxian hide."

Distressed as he was by the wretchedness of the impoverished, MacLeish was tempted now and then by the claim of the Communist Party to be the sole agency for social justice. On several counts he was able to resist that temptation. As "Frescoes" suggested, he rejected both dialectical materialism as a theory and Stalin as a leader. The economic determinism of dialectical materialism made no allowance for the significance in history, as in life, of the individual, a significance in which MacLeish believed deeply. And Stalin, as totalitarian a dictator as were Mussolini in Italy and Hitler in Germany, had arranged the starvation of millions of peasants in order to advance industrialization in the Soviet Union. Like all Communist Parties, the Communist Party of the United States took its orders directly from Moscow, from Stalin. That dependency was far more than MacLeish could tolerate. Answering the criticisms of Communist poet Rolfe Humphries, MacLeish wrote: "I am not a Fascist. . . . I am as strongly opposed to a dictatorship of the Right as of the Left—more strongly in fact since a dictatorship of the Right is an actual possibility in America. . . . My warm distaste for fascism does not in the least cancel my equally warm distaste for those spiritually insufficient members of our society who join (or do not quite join) The Party as their prototypes joined (or did not quite join) the Masons or the Elks or the Church. And for the same reasons."

One of those reasons was fear—fear of loneliness, fear of freedom, fear of individual life in a difficult world. That kind of fear had characterized American industrial leaders in their response to the early years of the Great Depression. "They have been fearful . . . bewildered and void," MacLeish wrote Henry Luce. ". . . They are sterile." Like the Communists captives of their own theories, they lacked the imagination to meet the economic crisis. Those ideas provided the theme for *Panic* (1935), a play in verse, in which MacLeish created a protagonist, J. P. McGafferty, a businessman who had the courage to act until he lost confidence in himself and, like others, yielded to the grip of financial ruin and then committed suicide. He should have fought on, as his wife and a friend urged him to: "Trouble's no unexpected guest in these parts. The new thing's not the trouble. . . . It's you. It's your kind waiting for the great disaster." The real hero of the play was "the free man's choosing of the free man's journey," for "it's always one man makes a world."

When MacLeish later rewrote *Panic* as a radio play, he identified his message of courage explicitly with Franklin Roosevelt. But when *Panic* played in New York in 1935, that meaning was lost on an audience irritated by MacLeish's criticism of big business. The play was to run only two nights, but the Communist Party sponsored a third performance followed by a symposium in which three party intellectuals berated MacLeish for not taking as his theme the inevitable doom of capitalism. But he never intended to write a Communist tract. His real failure was literary. The characters in the play lacked definition either as people or as symbols, and the plot lacked drama.

In *Public Speech* (1936) his poetry reached the level of excellence he wanted to get across the political truths he cherished. The poem "Pole Star" defined love as the only remaining light guiding men and women. For: "Liberty and pride and hope—/ Every guide-mark of the mind/ That led our blindness once has vanished." There was no justice where tyrants ruled; the lamp of liberty had burned out. In "The German Girls! The German Girls" MacLeish used irony to indict the

Nazis as the bringers of darkness: "Are we familiar with the mounted men!—/ The grocery lot with the loud talk in restaurants,/ Smellers of delicatessen, ex-cops,/ Barbers, fruit-sellers, sewers of underwear, shop-keepers,/ Those with fat rumps foolish in uniforms . . ."

Both the Nazis and the Communists constituted threats to democracy. "The real issue," MacLeish wrote Carl Sandburg in 1936, "is whether or not we believe in the people." Both poets did. "No revolution," MacLeish continued, "will succeed in America which professes to take the government away from the people and create the kind of cabinet tyranny which we see now in its intrigues and its jealousies in Russia in this fantastic trial"—a reference to Stalin's rigged trials of his Trotskyite opponents within the Communist Party, so recently his collaborators. "You and I," MacLeish went on, "have a considerable responsibility. We are poets but we are also men able to live in the world. We cannot escape our duties as political animals." Sandburg had fulfilled his duty with his recent poetry and the first volumes of his adoring biography of Abraham Lincoln. Sandburg's work, a "basis for political action," made the issue of democracy clear. Both poets had now to act "politically to drive this issue into the forefront of the sensitive minds of all men. . . . We must now become pamphleteers, propagandists."

In referring to "the people" and "democracy," MacLeish was using the vocabulary of the liberalism of the time. Those abstractions were his basis for political action, for his resulting poetry and speeches. Then and later his letters and publications included references to the objects that evoked his democratic emotions, but those objects suggested not so much a program as a political position and its surrounding state of mind. MacLeish believed in Franklin Roosevelt and the New Deal. He praised some programs: the refinancing of farm mortgages, federal support of needy artists, national codes for industrial cooperation between management and labor. He shared the view of those New Dealers who recognized the economic interdependence of capital, labor and agriculture, and of all industrialized nations. But those specific matters did not inspire his poetry or provide it with useful metaphors. In his poetry, he embodied his beliefs in individuals, especially Jefferson and Lincoln, not as they may really have been in history but as their names evoked American democratic values. In MacLeish's usage Jefferson connoted the western reach of free land, the individual liberties guaranteed by the Bill of Rights and representative democracy. Lincoln connoted the universal freedom of men and women and of their labor, the mystical meaning of the United States as a nation "conceived in liberty and dedicated to the proposition that all men are created equal," and the identification of America with opportunity and brotherhood. By implication, the New Deal contained those values. Nazism and Communism explicitly denied them.

In 1937 fascism and communism clashed in the civil war in Spain. As MacLeish saw it, that war arose from "an inexcusable and unjustifiable act of aggression by reactionary forces against a popular government." Franco and his fellow fascists, the aggressors, received vital material assistance from Hitler's Germany and Mussolini's Italy. In retaliation, the Soviet Union provided aid to the Spanish Loyalists. Like many of the Loyalists themselves, MacLeish underestimated the subversive intentions of both Spanish and Soviet Communists. He cared more about the Loyalist cause than about the company he kept in supporting it. As part of that support, he helped to found Contemporary Historians, Inc., a corporation that raised funds to make and distribute *The Spanish Earth,* a film about the war as seen from a Loyalist perspective.

But MacLeish was not fooled by the revised Communist Party doctrine that called for a "popular front" of cooperation with socialists and liberals to fight fascism. To be sure, he contributed to the *New Masses,* a Communist journal, but on his own terms which included forthright criticism of both the magazine and the party. He also joined the pro-Loyalist League of American Writers, a group of prominent literary folk of whom some were members of the Communist Party. "The man who refuses to defend his convictions," he told a congress of the League, "for fear that he may defend them in the wrong company, has no convictions." That statement began his reply to those, the F.B.I. included, who considered him a "fellow traveller." He continued his mission in his poem "Speech to the Scholars" at the Columbia Phi Beta Kappa exercises. Like the artists who held that the search for beauty and for truth precluded politics in art, many scholars believed in a deliberate political neutrality. "I say the guns are in your house," MacLeish told them. ". . . Arise O scholars from your peace! Arise! Enlist! Take arms and fight!"

In writing as he did, MacLeish explained to Walter Lippmann, he interpreted the conflict between fascism and communism as "superficial and temporary in comparison with the profound conflict between the conception of intellectual and moral freedom on the one side and on the other, the conception of the totalitarian state." That insight positioned MacLeish far in advance of most American intellectuals. He and his like-minded literary friends also displayed extraordinary courage in openly opposing fascism at a time when the establishment in the United States and much of western Europe, fearful of communism and anxious to preserve even a superficial and uneasy peace, was looking the other way in order to avoid admitting the danger and the barbarity of Hitler. MacLeish risked the censure of his Ivy League acquaintances. More important, he invited criticism from some of the very poets—Yeats and Frost for two—whose approbation he craved.

In 1937 MacLeish completed *The Fall of the City,* the first play in verse ever produced for radio and a part of his propaganda for freedom. "The city of masterless men," said the prophecy at the start of the play, "will take a master." An orator addressed the crowd. Resist, he recommended in the spirit of an apolitical idealist, not with spears but with scorn. Reason and truth would prevail without recourse to arms. A messenger, a defeatist, then warned of the strength of the approaching conqueror. A general tried to inspirit the timorous crowd: "There's nothing in this world worse . . . than doing the Strong Man's will! The free will fight for their freedom. . . . You can stand on the stairs and meet him! You can hold in the dark of a hall! You can die!—or your children will crawl for it." But overcome by fear, the citizens concluded that the city was doomed, that "Freedom's for fools: Force is the certainty! . . . Men must be ruled." So the city fell to the conqueror who marched in, huge in his armor. But his visor fell open, revealing emptiness: "The helmet is hollow! . . . The armor is empty." The citizens, lying silent on the pavement, saw nothing: "They wish to be free of their freedom: released of their liberty." Their voices roared: "The city of masterless men has found a master. The city has fallen." As a work of art the play was wanting, but as a tract for the time it was germane. In a new preface, MacLeish later wrote: "Too many nations had walked away from freedom . . . and accepted tyranny in its place."

Tyranny rode to power on the destruction of the innocent, but too many decent people could not conceive of the brutality of fascism. That was the message of MacLeish's *Air Raid* (1938), another radio drama in verse, inspired by Picasso's "Guernica." Like that painting, it described the "new and

unspeakable horror of war." The play opened on an unidentified town, "very quiet and orderly," the men working in
the surrounding fields, the women busy with laundry and
gossip, scoffing at their men's talk of war. They ignored a
siren warning of an airplane circling overhead. They paid no
heed to a policeman urging them to take cover. Perhaps the
plane was coming, one old woman said: "But if it is/ It's not
for housewives in this town they're coming./ They're after
the generals . . . the cabinet ministers . . . the square." The
policeman tried again: "This enemy kills women." The women
laughed, but a formation of planes banked to attack. Still
incredulous, the women called: "Show it our softness! . . .
Show it our womanhood!" Then curtain, with "the shrieking
voices . . . the shattering noise of guns . . . the diminishing
drone of the planes."

MacLeish was using a powerful and popular medium, radio,
to issue a warning unwelcome to his American audience. In
1938 he also used another powerful medium, photography,
to respond to declining popular support for the New Deal
and its ideals. The economic recession of 1937–38 shook
confidence in New Deal policies. Roosevelt largely failed in
his efforts to help liberal Democrats defeat their conservative
opponents in party primaries in 1938, and that year the
Republicans gained enough seats in Congress to form, with
conservative Democrats, a coalition that blocked progressive
legislation. But MacLeish spoke from the left in the sparse
text he wrote for *Land of the Free* (1938)—his "sound track"
he called it—that accompanied photographs commissioned
by the Farm Security Administration, a New Deal agency
created to assist displaced and impoverished farm families.
Both visually and verbally, the book anticipated *Let Us Now
Praise Famous Men,* by James Agee and Walker Evans: both
works used a medium previously little explored; in tone and
content, both focussed on the powerless and dispossessed. In

his volume, MacLeish associated freedom with the unspoiled land and the spirit of westering Americans of an earlier era. He praised their individualism, contrasted their democratic condition to the indignity of the itinerant farmers and embattled labor organizers of his own time, and by implication referred to the New Deal as the vehicle for restoring the freedom and equality Lincoln had celebrated.

MacLeish returned to those themes in "America Was Promises" (1939): "America was promises to whom? / Jefferson knew: / Declared it before God and before history: / . . . The promises were Man's: the land was his— / Man endowed by his Creator: / Earnest in love : perfectible by reason: / Just and perceiving justice . . ." The promises to man were land and liberty, humanity, self-respect and common decency. But "The Aristocracy of Wealth and Talent" also grabbed for the promise of America. So the people had to reach to control their own destiny, for: "unless we take them for ourselves / Others will take them . . . America is promises to / Take!"

Those domestic themes resonated to the same chords as the clash MacLeish described between democracy and authoritarianism in Europe. His political poetry called upon Americans to protect freedom both at home and abroad. As his critics contended, his political verse lacked the intimacy, the tenderness, the melodiousness of his lyrical poetry. But early and late, as he had said in his youth, he was expressing his particular self and therefore, in the late 1930s, the urgency he felt about the perils confronting the nation. His political poetry was action. It needed a vocabulary and cadence different from those required by intimacy. The nature of MacLeish's preoccupations had changed, and with it, so had his techniques.

MacLeish changed himself. Uncomfortable with the politics of Henry Luce's publications, he resigned from *Fortune* and took a part-time position at Harvard as curator of the Nieman Foundation, a program for promising young journalists. But that was a way-station. While registering his usual qualms about any responsibility that would interfere with his writing, in 1939 he accepted appointment as Librarian of Congress. He had moved at last directly into Franklin Roosevelt's capacious political tent. The appointment aroused predictable opposition from professional librarians who wanted one of their own in charge of the nation's most important library; from the Communist Party, long inimical to MacLeish; and from conservative congressmen who considered his political opinions dangerous and un-American. The librarians were wrong. MacLeish proved to be a tactful, innovative, successful administrator. But MacLeish's ideological opponents were correct in their fears. His position enhanced his public stature and provided a platform from which he could broadcast his political messages with increased effect.

Roosevelt had not talked with MacLeish about world affairs, but he put him in a place from which he could reach a larger audience just in time. With the Nazi-Soviet pact of August 1939, Hitler and Stalin joined in an alliance of convenience to divide Poland between them. The ensuing invasion of Poland, which Britain and France had promised to defend, marked the start of World War II and exposed the Nazis and Communists as common aggressors and common enemies of freedom. When MacLeish arrived in Washington, few of Roosevelt's political family were sufficiently articulate and foresighted to challenge the isolationist mood of the nation, to explain that the war in Europe involved American interests, to persuade their fellow citizens that Hitler could not be defeated unless Americans sided with his victims. Macleish joined Secretary of the Interior Harold Ickes and Secretary of Agriculture Henry Wallace in taking that word to the country. He had been doing so for several years. Now he continued particularly to address artists and scholars of whom many still regarded World War I as a disaster, war in any cause as an ultimate horror, and the European conflict as no business of the United States.

That stance, self-deluding in MacLeish's view, could not be sustained after the Nazis overran much of western Europe in the spring of 1940. In June France fell and England fought alone against the Nazis. The civilization of the west, built over two millennia, stood close to a new dark age. Two months earlier, MacLeish had addressed "The Irresponsibles," the intellectuals still committed to a deliberate neutrality. They had a responsibility, he asserted, to defend "the common inherited culture of the West" by which they had lived, a culture now "attacked in other countries with a stated . . . purpose to destroy." In Germany the use of force "in the name of force alone" was destroying the "self-respect and . . . dignity of individual life without which the existence of art and learning is inconceivable." The revolution of Nazism was "a revolution of negatives . . . of despair . . . created out of disorder by terror of disorder . . . a revolution of gangs . . . against . . . the rule of moral law . . . of intellectual truth. . . . Caliban in the miserable and besotted swamp is the symbol of this revolution." The beneficiaries of democracy now had the duty to fight back.

MacLeish had also indicted the Nazis for their racial theories. Hitler's crimes against Jews helped MacLeish outgrow the anti-Semitism inculcated at Hotchkiss and at Yale. In 1939 his "Colloquy of the States" added ethnic pluralism to his roster of democratic values. There was talk "in the east wind," the poem said, about how Americans married: "We marry Irish girls . . . Spaniards with evening eyes . . . golden Swedes . . . Jews for remembrance . . . We're mixed people." Americans were unlike the "blood we left behind . . . the blood afraid of change . . . afraid of strangers" that stayed home "and married their . . . cousins who looked like their mother." Race did not bother Americans, MacLeish said in a speech in 1940: "They were something a lot better than any race. They were a People . . . the first self-constituted, self-declared, self-created People in the history of the world."

In the great and continuing debate of 1940–41 between those who urged assistance to the British and those who advocated American isolation, MacLeish made it his task, now largely in speeches, to remind Americans that the Nazis attacked not with planes or tanks alone "but with violence of belief." The enemies of liberty, he said in one address, confused democracy with a way of owning property or a way of doing business. That was not what Jefferson had thought democracy meant, or what John Adams thought, "or those who took it westward." They meant "the simple man's belief in liberty of mind and spirit." So MacLeish condemned the isolationists, particularly their organization, America First. The most ardent voices of that group included the reactionary Chicago *Tribune,* the aviator-hero Charles Lindbergh who had accepted a Nazi decoration, and his author-wife, Anne Morrow Lindbergh, who praised fascism as an irresistible "wave of the future." That famous woman, MacLeish said, assured us "in a beautiful and cadenced prose that democracy is dead in every country," and she accepted instead the "alternatives of terror and despair." She was wrong. Americans "knew which way to take to reach tomorrow," the way of democracy and freedom.

MACLEISH had become a leading propagandist for democracy before the president made his role official in the fall of 1941 by appointing him director of the newly established Office of Facts and Figures (OFF). MacLeish took that position without salary and in addition to his responsibilities at the Library of Congress. From the outset he was crippled in his task. Roosevelt, remembering the hyperbolic propaganda of World

War I, had created OFF only under pressure from his wife Eleanor and Mayor Fiorello La Guardia of New York. Even then the president defined the purpose of the agency narrowly: "To disseminate . . . factual information on the defense effort and to facilitate a widespread understanding of the status and progress of that effort." He gave OFF no authority to extract information from other governmental agencies. Consequently MacLeish, committed as an individual to increasing American participation in the war against Hitler, found himself as a bureaucrat forced to operate within the restrictions of his mandate which called for data, not passion. He said so in announcing a "strategy of truth." "Democratic government," he added, "is more concerned with the provision of information to the people than it is with the communication of dreams and aspirations." On the basis of the facts, the people would judge.

But MacLeish was a man of dreams, and OFF could not produce the facts. As the United States moved closer and closer to war in the Atlantic, federal defense agencies controlled information so as not to release details about shortages or plans for military and naval deployment. Though MacLeish could not change that policy the press blamed OFF for censorship. Uninformed himself about military matters, MacLeish was as surprised as other Americans by the Japanese attack on Pearl Harbor. In the next months, with American, British and Russian forces suffering severe defeats, the War and Navy Departments refused to release the depressing facts about losses, facts that would have helped the enemy. OFF continued largely to produce pamphlets about the war effort. MacLeish's staff urged him to use the agency as well to dramatize the war, but the radio programs OFF then generated, one of them about FDR, struck Republicans in Congress as partisan propaganda.

Believing, as he put it, in "human liberty and . . . the

moral order of the world," MacLeish held that the United States was defending "not the American continent" but "the American idea and the world in which the American idea can live." That was a difficult conception to get across to the public either by the release of information or the dramatization of FDR. At OFF MacLeish was playing the wrong part.

In the spring of 1942 Roosevelt abolished the agency and replaced it with the Office of War Information (OWI) under the journalist Elmer Davis with a larger, though still restricted, authority. MacLeish remained as one of several men on Davis' advisory board. But MacLeish soon became restless with OWI's policy, the policy Roosevelt intended, of reporting information rather than promoting a Wilsonian postwar internationalism. OWI, he wrote Davis, should "accept responsibility for the job of putting before the people . . . the principal issues which must be decided, in a form which will excite and encourage discussion." Others in the agency, Davis included, decided OWI should maintain a "policy of objectivity," present the facts and not "make policy." MacLeish, who disagreed "emphatically," soon resigned.

He was ready also to leave the Library of Congress, as he told Roosevelt, who accepted his resignation in November 1944 and at once appointed him Assistant Secretary of State for Cultural and Public Affairs. In that position MacLeish, the only liberal in the group of new State Department officials the president named, was to direct public relations in behalf of the United Nations, not yet officially created but anticipated by the Dumbarton Oaks Conference. As the president knew, MacLeish had been speaking in public about the nature of the postwar peace. He rejected the idea of a war for empire—Henry Luce's "American Century." Instead he associated himself with the "Century of the Common Man"— "the long democratic revolution of which Henry Wallace has so movingly spoken." The war, MacLeish also said, "must be a war . . . for the freedom of mankind, and the peace must be a peace for liberty in fact." The nation and the world owed that debt to "The Young Dead Soldiers": "They say: We leave you our deaths. Give them their meaning. / We were young, they say. We have died. Remember us."

To help to build that monument, MacLeish, assisted by Adlai Stevenson, publicized the workings of the San Francisco Conference that founded the United Nations. He participated in the drafting of the preamble of the UN charter and later in writing the charter for the United Nations Educational Scientific and Cultural Organization (UNESCO). But like thousands of Americans, he had lost the leader he revered when Franklin Roosevelt died in April 1945. MacLeish memorialized FDR quietly in one stanza of "Actfive." It was the title poem of a short book of poetry which, so MacLeish wrote, "sought to interpret the events of the war as an expression of the heroic struggle of humanity to 'endure and live.' " He portrayed Roosevelt as he had seen him at the end of his days: "The responsible man, death's hand upon his shoulder, / knowing well the liars may prevail / . . . tired tired tired to the heart / . . . Does what must be done: dies in his chair / Fagged out, worn down, sick / With the weight of his own bones, the task finished, / the war won, the victory assured, / The glory left behind him for others."

FOR MacLeish by 1948 there was nothing of glory in the failure of liberty in much of the world, in the collapse of the wartime alliance, in the inception of the Cold War. In spite of the UN, Wilsonian internationalism had yielded to rival Soviet and American imperialisms. As MacLeish saw it, the Cold War threatened freedom everywhere. No apologist either for the Soviet Union or for communism, he nevertheless argued that American policy supported governments abroad only because they opposed the Russians—support extended in the name of freedom but rendered to oppressive and undemocratic regimes. Worse, fear of communism lent credibility to American demagogues who exploited that fear for personal and partisan ends, and in so doing violated the liberties guaranteed by the First Amendment. MacLeish's liberal vision of a free people under a just government—of a world of such peoples and governments, was under heavy assault.

To feel whole MacLeish, as always, turned to poetry—"the process of reducing to a form at once sensuous and intelligible the fragmentary, reluctant, and inarticulate experience of man . . . the one known process, by which men present to themselves an image of their lives and so possess them." His wartime and early postwar poetry expressed his literary and political sensibilities, both melancholy as the poems in *Actfive* (1948) attested. "Voyage West" offered a melodious but bitter-sweet commentary on an ended love affair, and "Brave New World" expressed anger as well as disappointment: "Freedom that was a thing to use / They've made a thing to save / And staked it in and fenced it round / Like a dead man's grave."

"Freedom," MacLeish wrote Henry Luce, "is not something you *have:* it is something you *do.*" Yet the Luce magazines, MacLeish continued in another letter, had been "largely silent on the great critical issues within the United States affecting the realization of this dream of responsible individual freedom—the issues of freedom of the mind and freedom of the press and freedom of education which are now not only urgent but dangerous—dangerous to speak out about: dangerous to be silent about." Speaking out about freedom was not the work of any church but remained the work of poetry. So MacLeish dedicated "That Black Day" to the memory of Laurence Duggan, a former State Department officer, who had been vilified just hours after his death by two members of the House Un-American Activities Committee (HUAC),

Representatives Karl Mundt and Richard Nixon: "God help that country where informers thrive! / Where slander flourishes and lies contrive / To kill by whispers! Where men lie to live!"

"It is truly to testify we are here—to bear witness—those of us who are artists," MacLeish wrote a friend. And he continued to bear witness while Boylston Professor of Rhetoric and Oratory at Harvard, a position he accepted in 1949. He openly attacked Senator Joseph McCarthy, whose name came to connote the whole atmosphere of deliberate political slander that Mundt and Nixon and HUAC had contrived. In 1952 MacLeish naturally supported his good friend Adlai Stevenson, then Governor of Illinois, who had the courage as the Democratic presidential candidate to condemn McCarthy and his vile accusations. Replying to Stevenson's invitation to help draft a speech for delivery to the American Legion, MacLeish discussed the "ideal of patriotism." It held the Legion together but "it is also the mask behind which some of the most dangerous and evil influences of our day conceal themselves—in the Legion and outside it." Patriotism was love of country but not just of the land: "No, of the people . . . their accomplishments, their endurance, their hopes." Stevenson's campaign, as MacLeish knew, spoke to the "critical issue of individual freedom in a frightened world."

When Stevenson ran again in 1956, McCarthyism had spent most of its force, but now MacLeish called for an attack on the complacency of Americans and the "flatulent fat-headedness in Washington." "What is at stake," he wrote Stevenson, "is our greatness as a people." Communism was "as evil as ever" and the Soviet Union "enormously powerful," but communism had obsessed Americans too long. They should begin "to think in terms of the great world revolution which is sweeping across Asia and will inevitably reach every 'backward' area," a revolution with "infinite possibilities for human good" and human hurt. "We cannot live defensively," MacLeish continued, ". . . in a time of enormous change, a great nation . . . must shape the change." That was the counsel of a liberal who had retained his ideals and moved with the times. So had Stevenson. He again lost the election but his foresightedness and inspiration sustained MacLeish's hopes.

Shed of his melancholy, MacLeish brought his refreshed convictions to his poetry and essays. He defined his liberalism more clearly than he ever had in a critique of 1955 of Walter Lippmann's *Public Philosophy*. In that book Lippmann argued, in MacLeish's paraphrase, that since 1917 in western countries "there had been too much democracy and . . . too little government." The alternative, so Lippmann wrote, demanded "popular assent to radical measures which will restore government strong enough to govern . . . to resist the encroachment of assemblies and of mass opinion and strong enough to guarantee private liberty against the pressure of the masses." Those radical measures required democratic societies to accept the values of Natural Law which would free government from subservience to mass opinion. MacLeish considered that proposal elitist, the antithesis of "the idea of the greatest possible individual freedom to which we have been committed . . . since the end of the eighteenth century." In contrast to Lippmann, he believed it had been essential to involve the people "in the determination of the great issue of war or peace" in 1917 and again in 1941. "Men will die for peace and freedom but not for the terms of a treaty," MacLeish wrote, "and it was the conviction of my generation in the war of its youth and the war of its middle age that the American government and the governments of the free world had made some progress toward a more effective democracy by the recognition of that fact."

Lippmann erred especially, MacLeish continued, in his conception of freedom. In *The Public Philosophy* he was con-

cerned with "modern men who find a freedom from constraints of the ancestral order an intolerable loss of guidance
and support," who find that "the burden of freedom is too
great an anxiety." True freedom for Lippmann was "founded
on the postulate that there was a universal order on which all
reasonable men were agreed: *within that public agreement . . .*
it was safe to permit . . . dissent." That argument rejected
MacLeish's "basic philosophy of liberalism—the belief in the
liberation of the individual human spirit to find its own way
to . . . truth." Liberal democracy, MacLeish held, rested on
the "proposition that men may shape their own destiny and
are capable of realizing their dreams of the good life." Particular generations, dreading loneliness, might retreat "into the
warmth . . . and protection of conformity as millions in Europe
and Asia have done in our time," but the human journey had
not turned back. So the arts attested: "In all the modern arts
of words, in modern painting, in modern music, a common
impulse is at work . . . almost a compulsion, to penetrate
the undiscovered country of the individual human consciousness, the human self." Safety and security lay not in a ren-
unciation of individual freedom but in the achievement of
individuality, in "the deeper reality of the world within." So
for MacLeish the mission of the arts defined the politics of
freedom. His poetry and his liberalism remained a whole.

MACLEISH'S art and his politics alike expressed his faith in
man, a faith hardened over the years. He acknowledged the
injustice of the times and affirmed the indispensability of love
in *J.B.* (1958), his most beautiful and most successful play
in verse. It was his reworking in modern terms of the Book
of Job. In the prologue, two circus vendors, Nickles and Mr.
Zuss, introduced the themes of the play. Job, Mr. Zuss says,
challenged God, demanded justice of God. That was ridicu-

lous, Nickles replies. God has killed Job's sons and daughters, stolen his livestock, left him "stricken on a dung heap," all for no reason. Nickles sings: "If God is God He is not good, / If God is good he is not God . . ." Millions of mankind have known injustice, he says, millions slaughtered for walking around in "the wrong skin, the wrong-shaped noses, eyelids: / Sleeping the wrong night wrong city—London, Dresden, Hiroshima." The play begins. J.B., at the first a prosperous and grateful man who believes that God is just, proceeds to lose his children in various accidents, to lose his wealth and his wife Sarah who leaves him because he persists in believing that "God is just . . . the fault is mine." His guilt is misplaced, as several comforters show him. Innocence is irrelevant; suffering, random. Sarah returns as J.B. learns, as she had, the futility of guilt, the futility of challenging God or expecting justice. "You wanted justice," Sarah says, "and there is none—only love." J.B. replies that God does not love: "He is." Sarah: "But we do. That's the wonder." And with love, they accept their place in the universe.

"J.B.'s recognition," MacLeish wrote the director of the play, "is a recognition not only of the insignificance of his human place but of the *significance* of that insignificance. He is at least a *man*. It is his 'integrity' as a man (Job's word) that he has been struggling for"—a struggle "to accept life again, which means . . . the struggle to accept love, to risk himself again in love." In *J.B.* MacLeish, as ever, dealt with human nature, and also as ever he saw the social and political implications of his message. "It is part of the essential naivety of the successful American business man," he wrote the editor of the Sunday *New York Times,* "to believe that something in the order of things justifies his having what he has. Rich men in my father's generation were candid about this to the point of embarrassment."

MacLeish had reached the age when the friends he loved

were dying one after another: Mark Van Doren, Ernest Hemingway, Eleanor Roosevelt, Adlai Stevenson—his generation of artists, his generation of liberals. He eulogized Mrs. Roosevelt in 1962: "To most of us, the world . . . has become an abstraction . . . an economic mechanism such as the Marxists still believe they have discovered; the Absurdity which contemporary literary fashion plays with; the hard-headed Reality which only Republicans can ever know; the ultimate Equation which science will someday write. To Mrs. Roosevelt the world was never an abstraction. It was human."

MacLeish of course was also speaking of himself. He reached seventy that year. During the next two decades he carried on much as he had before. He held to his lifelong "Theory of Poetry": "Know the world by heart / Or never know it! / Let the pedant stand apart— / Nothing he can name will show it." He accepted old age with good humor: "Your eyes change. / Your handwriting changes. / You can't read what you once wrote. / Even your own thoughts sound wrong to you, / something some old idiot has misquoted." The Vietnam war appalled him. Three names were not to be spoken, he wrote in "National Security." The first was Cambodia, the second Laos: "The third is Vietnam, / a dried child / mailed to its mother / by B-52s / in a cellophane envelope"—Those names hidden in a secret room refuse concealment. They bleed, and then blood runs "under the secret / door and down / the classified stair / . . . The country is steeped in it."

And corrupted by it, as evidenced alike by Richard Nixon and those of the young who protested with violence against both Nixon and the war. Like explicit sex in literature, MacLeish complained, revolution in politics had become a cause: "What was once a means—often a noble means—to attain an essential human end has become a fad, an intellectual obsession. Act first and find out later why you acted." For the counterculture, even individual freedom had become a "cause" and "turned to irresponsibility." "No society," MacLeish concluded, still the liberal, "can live without intellectual and moral order, and the fact that order decays with time like everything else merely means that order must be recreated with time. But order cannot be recreated by the pursuit of causes however grandiose and whatever they call themselves. . . . Only justice and the love of man can produce an order humanity will accept."

Justice, the love of man, and liberty—these were sacred to MacLeish. His critique of Lippmann and his *J.B.* constituted two of three late statements of his creed. Fittingly he made a third late statement in his essay "The Venetian Grave," a defense of the award of the Bollingen Prize for poetry, the very first award of that prize, to Ezra Pound. Pound was certainly no friend to MacLeish. He had continually criticized MacLeish's poetry and his politics; he had never thanked MacLeish for leading the successful effort to have him released from the insane asylum in which the federal government had confined him for broadcasting support for the enemy during World War II. But Pound had been a great poet. MacLeish agreed that Pound had apparently embraced fascism, but that fascist ranter, he argued, that "fabricated man," was Pound's own creation. Now with the Vietnam war fraud had become a form of government. "Fraud and government may exist together," MacLeish proposed, "but not fraud and art." And Pound "was unarguably a poet." When Pound was tried for treason, his lawyer had chosen not to contest the case on the basis of the First Amendment but instead had entered a plea of guilty by reason of insanity. Though that plea prevailed, MacLeish considered it "wrong in law." Some twenty years later, he noted, Ramsey Clark, a former Attorney General of the United States, while in Hanoi, the capital of an enemy country, had attacked American policy. Yet Clark was not tried or even arrested. "And for the good and sufficient reason," MacLeish went on, "that the right to dissent, the right to criticize, had by then been exercised in time of war by so large a majority of the American people that if wartime criticism was treason, the Republic itself would have had to be indicted."

Pound, MacLeish continued, had admired the fascist government of Italy. He had often been virulently anti-Semitic. But he thought of himself as an oldtime Jeffersonian, "and though his notions . . . would have astonished Mr. Jefferson . . . there is no reason to doubt that he honestly held them." As MacLeish saw him, Pound was guilty only of "that peculiar naivete . . . of intellectuals: that infatuation with ideas at the expense of experience." He was widely read "but his experience of the world was thin." So he totally misread his own times. Yet he was "the principal inventor of modern poetry," a poetry "committed to the human world, to the historical world, the moral world," and also the author of the *Cantos,* "the nearest thing we have, either in prose or verse, to a moral history of our tragic age . . . that descent, not into Dante's hell, but into ours." Pound was deluded but not insane. His "Venetian grave holds neither dilettante nor traitor but . . . a foolish and unhappy man . . . who was a . . . master poet." And so MacLeish stitched together freedom of speech, political dissent, the morality of art and their significance in his own tragic era.

He had had his say with courage, with compassion, with beauty. Even as death approached his liberalism was undaunted, and the metaphors of his best poetry still informed his verse: "Only the old know time . . . It frightens them. / Time to the old is world, is will, / turning world, unswerving will, / interval / until."

12

WALTER LIPPMANN AND THE PROBLEM OF ORDER*

EVEN in his childhood, at the turn of the century, Walter Lippmann led an ordered life. A grade school classmate recalled that "what made Walter special was his extraordinary intellectual capacity and discipline." Six decades later, Lippmann's "reflective and disciplined life" impressed a fellow journalist: "His life is not commanded by events. . . . If you ask him on New Year's Eve what he is going to do the coming year, the chances are that he has a fully detailed plan worked out." By the 1950s Lippmann's days in Washington had come to follow a strict routine: before nine o'clock, breakfast and the morning papers; then two or more hours of concentration in the uninterrupted silence of his soundproof study, where he drafted his columns before dictating them for transcription; then the mail, luncheon with a friend or notable, and an early afternoon of recreation; thereafter a rest, reflection about future columns or books, and dinner, often in the company of men

---

*This essay, with notes not republished here, served as the Introduction to *Public Philosopher: Selected Letters of Walter Lippmann* (New York: Ticknor & Fields, 1985).

and women of station and influence. Appointments with the same kind of people punctuated the days he spent traveling in Europe, days planned in deliberate detail long before his journey. So firm were those plans that Lippmann in 1961 declined a request to change the date of his appointment with Soviet Premier Nikita Khrushchev, who then bent to Lippmann's convenience.

The order that Lippmann imposed on himself and his circle had long seemed to those who knew him to reflect his inner being. Mabel Dodge, the keeper of New York's most celebrated salon, one Lippmann often frequented, found him "in possession of himself. There was no incontinence there, no flowing sensuality." And John Reed, his radical and romantic Harvard classmate, had characterized the young Lippmann's manner in lines of bemused verse, appropriate both when they were written and indefinitely thereafter: "But were there one / Who builds a world, and leaves out all the fun— / Who dreams a fragrant gorgeous infinite, / And then leaves all the color out of it— / Who wants to make the human race, and me, / March to a geometric Q.E.D.— / Who but must laugh, if such a man there be? / Who would not weep, if Walter L. were he?"

Yet the young Lippmann, as Mabel Dodge discerned, had a capacity for deep and spontaneous sympathy for the impoverished and the oppressed. To his intimates, he also revealed a guarded romanticism redolent in expression of the Germanic cultural set of his childhood home. He felt that sentimentality himself in his response to music. "I am," Lippmann wrote, "the perfect example for Santayana's remark about musical appreciation being for most persons 'a drowsy revery interrupted by nervous thrills.' " He romanticized his first courtship. "You're the only girl I ever knew," he wrote Lucile Elsas when he was eighteen, "who loved beauty, not for the sake of languorous dreaminess, but because beauty was a part of existence,—tell me if this attitude towards nature is not the last word in idealism." Lippmann's own dreamy idealizations outran their relationship, for though he apparently never kissed her, much less proposed to her, he resented her decision to marry another man.

He had a second crush on a somewhat older woman, Hazel Albertson, the young wife of his friend Ralph Albertson, who was the father of Lippmann's future bride. Hazel, "a superior flirt," charmed the Harvard undergraduates who lounged about the Albertson farm near Boston during their long discussions about politics and life. She liked Lippmann, so articulate, so carefully distanced from the others, so formally attired even at leisure in the country. On account of his rather chubby appearance and his shy detachment, she called him "Buddha." She also warned him against self-satisfaction while she allowed him to address her by pet names and in his letters to trade affectionate "pinches" with her. For his part, Lippmann overlooked Hazel's endemic disorganization in his gratitude for her fond understanding. He also outgrew her. Her romantic attachment to good causes conflicted with his sense of reality, particularly with his decision, after a brief experience with socialism in practice, to organize his life for other purposes.

The young Lippmann—the Buddha, on the surface serene, already wise—became the older Lippmann, renowned, organized, prophetic. But neither young nor old did Lippmann lack normal human qualities: ambition, sentiment, passion. The last of these he controlled so tightly that it did not much mark his life until his love affair, in his middle years, with Helen Armstrong, who became his second wife. Lippmann always knew that passion was there, and almost always he succeeded in disciplining it. His control satisfied his sense of the fitness of things, not for himself only but for mankind, for he was like other social critics in seeing human nature largely through the lenses of his own experience. From that sense of self, perhaps as much as from the study of politics and philosophy, Lippmann fashioned his public discourses and devised his own humanistic ethic. In the process, he had to come to grips with himself, his past, and his preferred social role.

IN the formulation of his beliefs and the development of his style, Judaism, the religion of Lippmann's youth, had little influence. By the time he was an undergraduate at Harvard, he had turned away from his parents' synagogue, Temple Emanu-El in New York City. There, in his view, the tenets of Reform Judaism wrapped a conventional moral code in an antiseptic creed. That creed he considered to be divorced from the zealous faith of traditional Jewry and adapted to the outlook of a socially mobile middle class acculturated in American secularism. Lippmann, as he wrote Lucile Elsas, would have none of it: "Can we tell them that the Temple Emanu-el exhibition is a piece of blatant hypocrisy? that its mechanical service, its bromidic interpretation, its drawing room atmosphere of gentility, its underlying snobbishness, which makes it an exclusive organization for the wealthy, strangle all the religion that is in us? Can we tell our friends—pillars of the Church, all of them—that . . . a visitor in New York on Yom Kippur, fled from the temple to St. Patrick's Cathedral to find there a religious atmosphere?" Religion, Lippmann continued, had to "make life richer, fuller, more splendid . . . touch life at every point, thus creating a harmony between the soul of man and the stars. . . . The scheduled prayer . . . is no prayer at all. . . . The truly religious man needs only the bright sun . . . and the blue beyond blue of the clear night to make him happy and worshipful." The beauty of friends and art increased devotion, as did "a passion for deed," for progress.

Lippmann felt uncomfortable alike with "the dead hand of the past," which he found in Judaism, and with "that rather Jewish feeling of not belonging." As he wrote Helen Armstrong years later, "I have never been oppressed by it. . . . I have never in my life been able to discover in myself any feeling of being disqualified for anything I cared about, and . . . I can find nothing in myself which responds to the specific Jewish ethos in religion or culture as it appears in the Old Testament. . . . I have understood the classical and Christian heritage and feel it to be mine, and always have."

That was a perceptive statement. As a schoolboy, Lippmann had excelled at Latin and Greek. The heritage he described infused Harvard—especially in the courses Lippmann took, in his informal friendship with William James, who had taught at the university, and in his association with James's celebrated colleague George Santayana, the skeptical philosopher whose acid analyses of conventional religion floated on his own humane convictions. Discontented with Judaism, involved in the larger world of American culture, Lippmann for most of his life was an assimilationist, a Jew who renounced both the sustaining certitudes and the constraining proscriptions of Judaism. He could validly claim a classical Christian heritage, for he absorbed one. Not surprisingly, the wives he chose were one a Protestant, the other a Catholic.

Assimilation did not necessarily imply anti-Semitism, though the two sometimes resembled each other. In Lippmann's case, positions that on occasion appeared anti-Semitic may have had different origins, usually political. For example, he was never a Zionist, because he believed that the presence of an independent Jewish state in the Middle East was bound to create a disequilibrium potentially threatening to American interests. Some of his critics considered his columns culpably silent about the Holocaust, for he chose to write about other matters—those that he believed American policy could affect. The United States could not, in his view, prevent Hitler's "final solution" except by winning the war. Lippmann's indifference, during World War II, to the civil rights and human rights of Jews and Japanese-Americans stemmed not from calculated anti-Semitism or racism but from his preoccupation—like Franklin Roosevelt's and Winston Churchill's—with the strategy of victory and of peace making. As Lippmann saw it, he was a realist; some other men discerned a different reality.

Lippmann's posture suggested at least a callousness, which had earlier assumed an anti-Semitic form in his remarks about Harvard's quota on the admission of Jews. Though he said that he disapproved of quotas, he supported restricting the number of Jews admitted in order to facilitate mutual accommodation among various student groups, a process he considered necessary in undergraduate life. To that end, he proposed an admissions test that would have militated against the admission of Jews. The idea was at best disingenuous.

Lippmann's rejection of Judaism left him, as he had suggested it should, with no faith in any church, or indeed in any supernatural authority, though he remained persuaded of the religious experience available in nature. He consciously substituted secular beliefs for conventional faith. As he had put it to Lucile Elsas, religion for him was "expressed in Socialism, Pragmatism, and poetry," a trinity a bright undergraduate might well have admired; disdainful of "the tinsel of the uppercrust of society with its enormous wealth," Lippmann had "come around to Socialism as a creed." He had rejected not just Judaism but the haute bourgeoisie and, as it worked out, his family as well as their conventions. Privileged though he had been as an only child, Lippmann as an adult revealed little affection for either his mother, "a little too ambitious and worthy," or his father, a successful businessman "without much color or force." Neither provided an attractive model. Lippmann selected instead, though always only briefly, models of his own from among the progressive reformers, the intellectuals, and the avant-garde of his young manhood. Then to them, to their goals—which also became his, temporarily to socialism as well as to pragmatism and poetry—he attributed at times a mystical aura. It was as close as he came to having a religion.

THOUGH Lippmann was loath to talk about his inner self, his understanding of that self and of society rested on a foundation of modern psychology, including Freudian psychology. He could become tiresome about that subject. "I wish Walter Lippmann would forget Freud for a little," Harold Laski, the British political scientist, wrote in 1916, "—just a little." But Lippmann considered Freud a successor in insight and influence to Sir Isaac Newton, whose theories about physics had shaped so much of eighteenth-century political thought, and to Charles Darwin, whose ideas about evolution had similarly affected the nineteenth century. In the twentieth century, an understanding of politics depended on "an objective understanding of what we really are." On that account, Lippmann wrote *A Preface to Morals* (1929), his effort to establish a basis for morality in the absence of traditional faith.

"We can begin to see," Lippmann wrote near the end of *A Preface to Morals,* " . . . that what the sages have prophesied as high religion, what psychologists delineate as matured personality, and the disinterestedness which the Great Society requires for its practical fulfillment, are all of a piece, and are the basic elements of a modern morality." "The Great Society," a phrase Lippmann had borrowed from Graham Wallas, would objectify the social ideas he valued. "A matured personality," in a Freudian sense, would discipline its impulses to social use. Both polity and individual would substitute a humanism rooted in science and reason for now implausible religious belief.

"An understanding of what we really are" occupied Lippmann in *A Preface to Morals,* of which the first quarter continually struck apparently autobiographical notes that disclosed much about the author, perhaps inadvertently on his part. Critics at the time remarked that the book spoke the mind of an unbelieving Jew making a nonreligious case for the Judeo-Christian ethic. The text seemed to start that way: "Among those who no longer believe in the religion of their fathers, some are proudly defiant, and many are indifferent. But there are also a few, perhaps an increasing number, who feel that there is a vacancy in their lives. This inquiry . . . is concerned with those who are perplexed by the consequences of their own irreligion."

Those who were no longer bound by orthodoxy, Lippmann observed, confronted "the greatest difficulties." They missed "the gifts of a vital religion," the conviction that there was "an order in the universe which justified their lives because they were part of it." As he put it, "the acids of modernity have dissolved that order for many of us," but without dissolving the needs religion had satisfied. He sought, therefore, a substitute for religion.

In the past, "the search for moral guidance" independent of "external authority" had invariably ended in the acknowledgment of some new authority. Now modern science made it impossible to "reconstruct an enduring orthodoxy, a God of the ancient faith . . . God the Father, the Lawgiver, the Judge." Modern churchmen no longer believed literally in the God of Genesis, and modern biblical criticism had eroded belief in "an historic drama . . . enacted in Palestine nineteen hundred years ago." Quoting Santayana, Lippmann repeated his point: " 'The idea that religion contains a literal, not a symbolic representation of truth and life is simply an impossible idea.' "

Modern men, nevertheless, did not lack a "sense of mystery, of majesty, of terror, and of wonder." What was missing was "the testimony of faith." As Lippmann characteristically understood it, faith had always related to men's experience with government. Since an Asiatic people naturally imagined a divine government as despotic, Yahweh in the Old Testament was "very evidently an oriental monarch inclined to be somewhat moody and vain." Lippmann had long since disavowed that God. He had never put credence in the feudal lord whom God resembled, as he saw it, in medieval Christianity, or in the God of the Enlightenment, who reigned without ruling. He was equally dissatisfied with that modern God who was deemed to be "the élan vital within the extraordinary person." "With the best will in the world," Lippmann held, modern man (of whom he was one) found himself "not quite believing."

To that point, *A Preface to Morals* had dwelt upon Lippmann's personal predicament, which was by no means his alone. From that point, Lippmann suggested for modern man his own solution, one that postulated an intellectual basis for morals and an intellectual order, a "disinterestedness," essential for moral behavior. Traditional moral commandments, he argued, had worked in "some rough way" as long as people had lived close to the soil. But ways of life had changed; morality could no longer be imposed by faith or by habit. Instead the "difference between good and evil" had to become a difference "which men themselves recognize and understand." Happiness had to be an "intelligible consequence"; virtue, to be "willed out of conviction and desire." That was a Jamesian assertion demanding not belief but testing. "Such a morality," Lippmann wrote, "may properly be called humanism, for it is centered not in superhuman but in human nature." In that formulation, man faced the difficult but unavoidable obligation of making the will conform to "the surest knowledge of the conditions of human happiness." The orderliness, the control so important to Lippmann, imbued the last sentence of his analysis. When men, he wrote, "find that they no longer believe seriously and deeply that they are governed from heaven, there is an anarchy in their souls until by conscious effort they find ways of governing themselves."

Modern man, Lippmann continued in the second half of his study, freed as he was from superstition, had no further cause to be afraid of evil. Evil continued to exist "only because we feel it to be painful," a condition, once understood, that allowed man to dissociate that feeling from evil. That was "a momentous achievement in the inner life of man. To be able to observe our own feelings as if they were objective facts, to detach ourselves from our fears, hates, and lusts, to examine them, identify them, understand their origins, and finally, to judge them, is somehow to rob them of their imperiousness. . . . They no longer dominate the whole field of consciousness . . . no longer . . . command the whole energy of our being."

The psychological mechanism he was describing, Lippmann wrote, had been commended by the philosophers of antiquity and elaborated by the discoveries of Freud. "To become detached from one's passions," he went on, "and to understand them consciously is to render them disinterested. A disinterested mind is harmonious with itself and with reality." The principle of humanism, he concluded, was "detachment, understanding, and disinterestedness in the presence of reality itself."

In the last chapter of *A Preface to Morals*, Lippmann examined the idea of disinterestedness as "implicit and necessary" in "the great phases of human interest, in business, in government, and in sexual relations." On the subject of love, he concluded that "by the happy ordering of their personal affections" (his stress on order again), men and women could "establish the type and the quality and the direction of their desires for all things." In a parallel passage, he had written that "the prime business of government" was not to divert the affairs of the community, but "to harmonize the direction which the community gives to its affairs." To that purpose, the great statesman was "bound to act boldly in advance of his constituents. When he does this, he stakes his judgment as to what the people will in the end find good against what the people happen ardently to desire. This capacity to act upon the hidden realities of a situation . . . is the essence of statesmanship." It was also, for Lippmann, the essence of an individual life.

As a political theorist, as a journalist and columnist, Lippmann strove to realize his ideal of disinterestedness. He recognized a moral responsibility to base his commentaries upon reality divested of the distortions of emotions. Of course he did not always succeed, but his continuing effort made his failures at the worst those of a temporarily lapsed humanist, a secular sinner. Lippmann would never have denied his fallibility or his susceptibility to emotions common to all men. At the simplest level, he found pleasure in graceful entertainments—in the heaven that was "Green Pastures," in the bear who was Winnie-the-Pooh. On a grander scale, the "happy ordering" of his inner self took expression, both before and after he wrote *A Preface to Morals,* in his continual assay in political theory.

EVEN as a young man, only several years out of college, Lippmann revealed the exceptional intelligence and broad learning that marked him always. Those traits, along with his concern for the nonrational, the instinctive, marked *A Preface to Politics* (1913), his first book, published when he was twenty-four. A youthful work, it catalogued, sometimes indiscriminately, the ideas of authors who had aroused his interest, among them William James, George Santayana, the French philosopher Henri Bergson, Sigmund Freud, and especially Graham Wallas, the most influential of Lippmann's teachers. Following Wallas, Lippmann took human nature as the basis for politics and read human nature as illogical. On that premise, he departed, of course, from eighteenth- and much nineteenth-century political theory, with its assumption of rationality in politics and other forms of human behavior. James, Santayana, Bergson, and others familiar to Lippmann had questioned that assumption, while Freud, whose early work much impressed Lippmann, demolished it.

Writing, as Lippmann was, in "an attempt to sketch an attitude toward statecraft," not to define a constitution·or a program, he tested his approach not only in theory but in the context of concrete political experience—his own especially. He had served briefly as an assistant to the newly elected Socialist mayor of Schenectady. His quick disenchantment with the banal practicalities of local politics provided the foundation for his criticism of socialism. His view of the nature of man ("all the passions of men are the motive powers of a fine life") underlay his dismissal not just of a socialism he found dull but, more important, of Marxist doctrine altogether—though he praised Marx's own prophetic genius.

Most often Lippmann cited examples of his contention that "human nature seems to have wants that must be filled. If nobody else supplies them, the devil will." Consequently, he reasoned, taboos were ineffectual. Building on James's concept of a "moral equivalent of war," Lippmann called for a moral equivalent of evil, a device to redirect human impulses that could not be contained. The mayor of Milwaukee, he wrote, had to that end provided public dance halls to compete with the sleazy private dance halls of that city. The Chicago report on vice, to which Lippmann devoted two chapters, showed "that lust has a thousand avenues." The report proposed the suppression of prostitution. That would do no good, Lippmann argued, unless new routes were opened for the release of lust. The report, in his opinion, "studied a human problem but left humanity out." Sex, Lippmann explained, here following Freud, was an instinct "which can be transmuted and turned into one of the values of life." Jane Addams at Hull House had abetted that transformation by providing access to the arts and crafts, "other methods of expression that lust can seek."

That, for Lippmann, was the essence of statecraft. Practical moralist that he then was, he turned Freud's theory of sublimation, as he would later turn it again and again, into a lesson in politics. He recommended to his readers his own self-conscious purpose: to "ventilate society with frankness, and fill life with play and art . . . with passions which hold and suffuse the imagination"—a revolutionary task.

For Lippmann, those who merely followed precedent, "the routineers," the keepers of conventions, could not adapt government to modern conditions. For that task he looked to the "inventors," of whom he saw himself as one. Those inventors, in the manner of William James, regarded "all social organizations as an instrument." They provided the natural leadership society needed, as Theodore Roosevelt had during his presidency. Under the control of inventors, Lippmann wrote, modern corporations, modern labor unions, indeed even the federal government would serve as instruments for social, economic, and political reforms. The inventors—Lippmann himself not the least—were, like Roosevelt, committed opponents of the status quo.

A Preface to Politics commended at once a politics of sublimation and a politics of energy, of dedication. Metaphorically, in his own striving, Lippmann practiced both. "If we have the vigor," he had written while he was at work on the book, "we find joy in effort itself. . . . An odyssey that never ends—it's not an unmixed joy. . . . In a personal way I am very happy—now especially. There is so much to love and do in the world—so much that after all does answer to our needs." A man of emotions was the young Lippmann, but a man of intellect and morality, too, a man of emotions under control.

THE condition of control seemed to Lippmann, as his next book indicated, no less desirable in politics. "Scientific invention and blind social currents," he wrote in his introduction to *Drift and Mastery* (1914), "have made the old authority impossible. . . . The dominant forces in our world are not the sacredness of property, nor the intellectual leadership of the priest; they are not . . . Victorian sentiment, New England respectability, the Republican Party." On the contrary, he asserted, enlisting with youth in its political discontents, *"the rebel program is stated* . . . Our time . . . believes in change." But even youth was "somewhat stunned by the rarified atmosphere" of the day. Consequently the "battle for us . . . lies against the chaos of a new freedom."

That disorder arose because "human beings . . . cling passionately to the emotion of certainty" in their social and political as well as their personal behavior. Bothered by the resulting "unrest," or "drift," Lippmann searched "for the conditions of mastery" that would "contribute to a conscious revolution."

In large measure, *Drift and Mastery* spoke directly to the political issues of the day. It attacked President Woodrow Wilson's program, the New Freedom, which Lippmann considered anachronistic. Conversely he commended Theodore

Roosevelt's program, the New Nationalism, the progressive charter to which he, like the other founders of *The New Republic,* subscribed. As he did as an editor of that journal, so in his new book Lippmann criticized private commercialism. Based on the profit motive, it had inaugurated modern industry but become "antiquated" and "feeble" as a method of realizing the promise of industry. Labor unions and consumer cooperatives expressed the social dissatisfaction with commercialism, as also did the changing structure of industry itself.

"The huge corporation, the integrated industry, production for a world market," Lippmann contended, echoing Graham Wallas, were part of "a general change of social scale." That new scale had produced "a new kind of businessman," for the giant corporation had to have managers of broad interests and abilities—managers able "to preserve intimate contact with physicists and chemists . . . to deal with huge masses of workingmen . . .to think about the kind of training our public schools give . . . to consider . . . the psychology of races . . . the structure of credit."

Managers had also to educate and pacify "thousands of ignorant stockholders," the owners of corporations. Consequently administration was "becoming an applied science, capable of devising executive methods for dealing with tremendous units." Since shareholders lacked the competence to exercise that function, the great corporations had separated ownership from management and concentrated control under the managers. In that sense, "most of the rights of property had already disappeared."

With that conclusion, Lippmann defined a satisfying substitute for the undergraduate socialism he had abandoned. As he often remarked, he had never been a Marxist. His youthful socialism had derived from the beliefs of the English Fabians, Wallas particularly. It envisaged a humane society with public programs to combat poverty, with institutional restraints (such as labor unions) on predatory capitalism, with ample public support and social space for the arts—all under the direction of men and women of exceptional intelligence and generous sympathy. Lippmann both sought and expected a place within that elite. His experience with urban socialism in Schenectady had been disillusioning because he had found himself a petty bureaucrat, not a philosopher prince. In *Drift and Mastery,* he joined the new royalty of industry, the managers who gave direction to the vital institutions of modernity. They had altered the nature of property ownership more to his satisfaction than could conventional socialism.

That alteration took many shapes. "The right to fix rates," Lippmann wrote, "has been absorbed by the state; the right to fix wages is conditioned by very powerful unions." Those changes so threatened traditional prospects for profit that stockholders in railroads might soon be eager "to give up the few vestiges of private property which are left to them, if they can secure instead government bonds." Government ownership in that case would provide a haven for rentiers. What had happened to the railroads, Lippmann predicted, "is merely a demonstration of what is likely to happen to the other great industries. . . . Private property will melt away; its functions will be taken over by . . . salaried men . . . government commissions . . . labor unions."

Obviously then, the "collectivism" of the modern corporation was due, not to the institution of private property but "to the fact that management is autocratic, that administrators are . . . given power adequate to their responsibility. When governments are willing to pursue that course, they can be just as efficient."

But Lippmann recognized a major problem for government. Because of the diffusion of stock ownership, corporate management had escaped a challenge from "decadent stockholders." Governments would be less free of their constituencies. "The real problem of collectivism," Lippmann wrote, "is the difficulty of combining popular control with administrative power." Lippmann had no confidence in the populace. "The existence of great masses of unorganized, perhaps unorganizable workers" imperiled the nation, he believed, for they would foment "street fights . . . beatings . . . sabotage . . . threats to order." Consequently he was convinced of the indispensability of leadership by an administrative elite who would introduce "order and purpose" in business and government alike.

A modern nation, Lippmann continued, could not be built "out of Georgia crackers, poverty-stricken negroes, the homeless and helpless of great cities. They make a governing class essential." That class alone could provide the essential guidance for society: "This is what mastery means: the substitution of conscious intent for unconscious striving." Only those who could govern themselves qualified as members of the governing class: "What civilized men aim at is . . . a frank recognition of desire, disciplined by a knowledge of what is possible, and ordered by the conscious purpose of their lives."

The mastery that Lippmann sought was obviously incompatible with popular democracy, just as the self-discipline he practiced was beyond the reach of most men and women. As one of Lippmann's shrewdest critics put it: "Never was he able to think of himself as a man no more important than other men." And never was he at ease with the emotions of the mass of men.

The depth of those emotions, and the federal government's facility in arousing and exploiting them, characterized American experience both as a neutral and later as a belligerent in World War I. Lippmann was involved in those years both in generating official propaganda and in devising terms for an enduring peace, terms that were lost in the heat of clashing chauvinisms. The experience provided both desolate confirmation of his earlier doubts about the populace and a disturbing contradiction to his earlier confidence in the organized intelligence of a governing class. The problem of order became more exigent in the glare of the furnace of war.

LIKE almost all Americans and many Europeans, Lippmann was not prepared intellectually or emotionally for the outbreak of war in Europe in August 1914. "It all came so incredibly fast," he wrote from England in September. He had been "overcome with a general feeling of futility," he confided to his diary, where he went on to define his own self-constituted role: "My own part in this is to understand world-politics, to be interested in National and Military affairs, and to get away from the old liberalism which concentrates entirely on liberal problems. We cannot lose all that but see now that our really civilized effort is set in a structure of raw necessity."

A year of study led Lippmann to conclude that the great issues of world order resembled those of domestic order. "I've learned a lot," he wrote Graham Wallas on August 5, 1915. "I feel now as if I had never before risen above the problems of a district nurse, a middle western political reformer, and an amiable civic enthusiast. . . . I've come to see that international politics is not essentially different from 'domestic' politics. . . . They are phases and aspects of one another."

As Lippmann also said, he distrusted simplistic analogies. It did not necessarily follow, as so many British and American statesmen seemed to think, that world federation would develop as federalism had among the thirteen original American states. Those states, for one example, had governed property common to them all during the period of the Articles of Confederation. Since the Western nations had no such property, it would be necessary in the postwar settlement to establish a number of "internationalizations." Further, "the dangers of perverted nationalism" would threaten the making of peace and the establishment of order. The breakup of Austria, Lippmann believed, was "a real world tragedy. Perhaps one should say, the conquest of Austria by Hungary." The ethnic aspirations to nationhood of the several peoples of the Hungarian kingdom constituted exactly the kind of nationalism Lippmann feared. Ethnic particularism, he wrote, resembled the traditional profit motive among firms in American industry. That particularism impeded the kind of collectivism subject to intelligent management that he had so praised in *Drift and Mastery.*

Most of all, Lippmann in 1915 began to stress sea power. The use of sea power by the belligerents had come to command diplomacy by provoking American efforts to limit Great Britain's blockade of Germany and to control German submarine warfare. The German definition of freedom of the seas, Lippmann wrote Wallas, meant "freedom in time of war"— by implication freedom to use submarines without restriction. That was a freedom of chaos, Lippmann continued, because Great Britain would struggle to prevent it. "The whole discussion," he added, "is vitiated . . . by the old notion that freedom can be had by competition rather than cooperation." British sea power, he concluded, "is the decisive factor in the future arrangement of the globe but I personally prefer its semi-benevolent autocracy to the anarchy of 'equal.' And I am prepared to have the U.S. join with Britain in the control of the seas, rather than see a race of 'sovereign states' oscillating in insecure 'balance.' " He had come to support an Anglo-American alliance, a position from which he never departed.

Lippmann's reflections about the war during its first year formed the basis of his book *The Stakes of Diplomacy* (1915). The substance of that work followed the contours of his letters, especially about sea power and his concept of interna-

tionalizations. The latter prospect seemed to him the best
basis for postwar world order. "The crux of our problem," he
wrote, "is whether the flag is to follow trade . . . the essence,
the power, the prestige of imperialism depend upon the theory that the flag covers its citizens in backward territory."
The task of internationalism was to destroy that excuse. Further, any postwar organization could "command a world
patriotism," an essential sentiment, only by "providing its
usefulness." To attain the objectives he had described,
Lippmann proposed the establishment of a number of continuing conferences to solve regional problems—as the Algeciras
Conference temporarily had in its decisions about Morocco in
1906.

He also suggested establishing protectorates like that of
the United States in Haiti. "The chief task of diplomacy,"
Lippmann maintained in a characteristic assertion, was the
organization of disorderly areas. Protectorates would create
"efficient authority in weak states." Concurrently, the development of international political agencies, his continuing
commissions, would control "imperialistic competition" and
"reorganize the country under joint supervision." In that role,
the commissions would proceed by "employing experts from
the developed nations" who would be responsible to the
"Diplomatic Body" of the supervised nation. From that experience "would arise the beginnings of a world state."

As Lippmann saw it, that world state would not soon
resemble a "Federation of Mankind." Rather, at the outset,
it would consist of a federation of Western powers. It was
"likely to be unequal, coercive, manipulative, and unsatisfactory." Only after demonstrated usefulness could it become
more inclusive and benign. Yet peace was "to be had as a
result of wise organization" and of a beginning that would
lead, as in the United States under the Constitution, to the
peaceful resolution of differences between nations by means

of elections. "We do by elections," Lippmann said of the forty-eight states, "what sovereign states do by war." Consequently "the supreme task of world politics" was "a satisfactory organization of mankind." Peace would then prevail not because of "the abolition of force" but because of "its sublimation."

With that conclusion, Lippmann, at least by implication, drew concentric Freudian rings. Sublimation would create order for the individual, the state, and the world of nations alike. For all of them, sublimation, as he conceived of it, was a necessary means to protect the civility and rationality essential to their well-being.

As the war drew toward its close, Lippmann's formulations for an enduring peace clashed in several respects with those of Woodrow Wilson, particularly with Wilson's notions about absolute freedom of the seas, with his support for ethnic self-determination, and with his advocacy of a world confederation—his League of Nations. Lippmann had served on Colonel Edward M. House's Inquiry, the semi-official group preparing analyses of international problems for Wilson's use in making peace, but the president did not much consult the resulting studies during his tribulations at the Paris Conference. The treaty negotiated there and signed at Versailles fell short of Lippmann's expectations. In an article in *The New Republic,* later reprinted as *The Political Scene,* Lippmann mounted an attack that was part of a larger charge against the treaty.

The Treaty of Versailles, Lippmann held, would not prevent disorder in Europe. *The Political Scene* exhorted the Western democracies to "devote themselves unreservedly" to making a cooperative peace in the face of "international revolution." With bolshevism gaining in Russia and spreading westward,

Wilson's proposals lacked "the precision and downrightness" of both the revolution and the strenuous resistance to it among European powers. In destroying the German Empire, Lippmann argued, the Allies had torn down "the authority which rules in central and eastern Europe. . . . It was a vile authority, but it was the existing authority in law and fact." Its demise left "chaos . . . wild and dangerous, perhaps infectious." Because the military campaigns of 1918 had become revolutionary in their effect, Wilson's proposals provided an insufficient basis for a stable peace. Both in international and domestic affairs, Wilson's ideas rested on "the Old Manchester"—the mechanistic conceptions that Lippmann had long considered anachronistic.

Like Jan Smuts, the South African statesman, Lippmann viewed Wilson's League as both essential and inadequate. On the broadest scale, the League, Lippmann wrote, would assume the functions he had assigned to his continuing commissions. But along with many, perhaps most, other Americans, Lippmann disliked many of the terms of the Treaty of Versailles, particularly the ethnic particularism it endorsed (though much of that particularism could not have been prevented). He also criticized the Covenant of the League, especially Article X. That article guaranteed the political independence and territorial integrity of members of the League. Wilson believed that guarantee would make the League an instrument for the effective mobilization of the opinion of the world against any aggressive nation. In contrast Lippmann feared the guarantee would make the League an instrument for preserving an unsatisfactory status quo (and by and large, he proved correct). Lippmann also argued that if the United States approved the treaty and the League, Congress would be forced to "abandon power over foreign affairs." He therefore urged the Senate to "insist upon representation of the legislature in the

structure of the League"—a demand Wilson would not contemplate.

As he had in 1915, so again in 1919 Lippmann contended
that Anglo-American sea power would best provide a foundation for a lasting peace. He did not mean to restore the
nineteenth-century balance of power. Rather, as he saw it,
the victory of 1918 had left Great Britain and the United
States as "the two great states with the resources and the
wealth for really modern munitions manufacture." If the two
nations worked out "their common purposes, then such a
preponderance of power is created as to make all notion of a
balance impossible. An Anglo-American entente means the
substitution of a pool for a balance, and in that pool will be
found the ultimate force upon which rests the League of
Nations. The reason for this is that they exercise a form of
force—sea power—which is irresistible in conflict." Sea power,
Lippmann went on, "can be all-powerful without destroying
the liberties of the nation which exercises it, and only free
peoples can be trusted with sea power."

The Covenant of the League provided the procedure "to
insure delay accompanied by publicity" in the event of a dispute between nations. During that delay, a democratic power
uninvolved in the dispute, probably the United States, could
generate the publicity that would convince the members of
the League to use the "pooling of force"—Anglo-American
sea power—to end the emergency. Here Lippmann was link-
ing Wilson's League with an Anglo-American alliance, a
combination designed to establish and maintain world order—
to serve, as it were, as a substitute for the sublimation that
the rival powers of Europe and Asia were still too hostile to
experience.

In his letters, Lippmann had referred to the decisions at
Paris as "an impossible settlement" that would "provoke a

class war." That conviction and a growing bitterness about Wilson, as well as his own ideas, prompted him to cooperate with Senator Hiram Johnson and others in their fierce opposition to the treaty and the League. But Lippmann was never an isolationist. No one concerned about world order could be. Possibly his political behavior detracted from his trenchant analyses, but he was not alone. The passions generated by the war and by the fight over the treaty temporarily cost many men, Lippmann not the least, their normal civility.

DURING the war, Lippmann had been prepared to forgo absolute freedom of speech for the sake of suppressing disloyalty or imposing a tolerant censorship, but he had also warned against official repression of criticism and poisonous official propaganda. "Freedom of thought and speech," he wrote in 1919, "present themselves in a new light and raise new problems because of the discovery that opinion can be manufactured." That discovery, a part of his own experience with the dissemination of propaganda, led him to explore the interaction of public opinion and government in *Liberty and the News* (1920). Because government could control opinion and thereby avoid its negative impact, Lippmann concluded that freedom of expression was no longer enough. It was necessary also for the public to have access to accurate information. His investigations had disclosed that newspapers, even the *New York Times,* had supplied biased accounts of bolshevism in Russia. He made a plea, therefore, for "unaltered data . . . disinterested fact." Apparently satisfied that men would respond rationally to accurate facts, Lippmann, in a typical recommendation, proposed the creation of an independent research organization to build a system for supplying neutral information.

An interpreter rather than a reporter of news, Lippmann in 1922 became the chief of the editorial page of the *New York World,* a Democratic newspaper notable for its sprightly style and social consciousness. His new role reflected his new focus. The bias of the reader, he now observed, would filter even trustworthy news. That insight informed *Public Opinion* (1922), probably his most enduring and most completely original book. There he began by contrasting reality and illusion. Freud's study of dreams, he wrote, had illuminated the process by which a pseudo-environment was put together. "Whatever we believe to be a true picture," Lippmann observed, "we treat as if it were the environment itself." So it had been in recent years: "We can best understand the furies of war and politics by remembering that almost the whole of each party believes absolutely in its picture of the opposition, that it takes as fact, not what is, but what it supposes to be fact."

Symbols, particularly stereotypes, which Lippmann addressed at length, were the carriers of those pictures. The symbols were subject "to check and comparison and argument" in ordinary times, but not in times of stress, especially when the government used the symbols to promote its own objectives. During the war and the postwar period of hysteria, individuals had succumbed to a distorted pattern of behavior: "the casual fact, the creative imagination, the will to believe, and out of these three elements a counterfeit of reality to which there was a violent instinctive response." An analysis of public opinion had to take into account "the triangular relationship between the scene of action, the human picture of that scene, and the human response to that picture." The fictions men substituted for reality, moreover, "determined a very great deal of men's political behavior."

Even after wartime propaganda and censorship had ended,

Lippmann continued, an artificial censorship persisted because of "the limitations of social contact, the comparatively meager time available each day for paying attention to public affairs." Distortions resulted "because events have to be compressed into very short messages," because of "the difficulty of making a small vocabulary express a complicated world," because of "the fear of facing those facts which seem to threaten the established routine of men's lives." Consequently representative government could not work successfully "unless there is an independent, expert organization for making unseen facts intelligible to those who have to make the decisions." Lippmann had altered the diagnosis since his *Liberty and the News* but prescribed the same remedy, one in which he could assume a major role.

He also returned to a theme that he had used before. Popular democracy, he maintained, could not provide the check necessary to separate illusion from reality, a check necessary also for making decisions about important matters of state. "The mass of absolutely illiterate, of feeble-minded, grossly neurotic, undernourished and frustrated individuals," he wrote, "is very considerable, much more considerable . . . than we generally suppose." Since that had been the case even in Thomas Jefferson's time, Jefferson had been deluded in putting his faith in the people. Now it was "no longer possible . . . to believe in the original dogma of democracy: that the knowledge needed for the management of human affairs comes up spontaneously from the human heart."

"The specialized class" to which Lippmann looked instead to "report the realities of public life" would replace the "augurs, priests, elders" of earlier eras (the very group he condemned in *A Preface to Morals*). The new specialized class consisted of "statisticians, accountants, auditors . . . engineers . . . scientific managers . . . research men." They and their equivalents in other callings constituted the only group trained to make the "Great Society intelligible to those who manage it." They served to "prepare the facts for the men of action."

IN *The Phantom Public* (1925), an important sequel to *Public Opinion,* Lippmann rephrased the argument of the earlier book and again denied any "ethical superiority" in majority rule. Repeating a Freudian metaphor he had used earlier, he wrote that an election "based on the principle of majority rule is historically and practically a sublimated and denatured civil war, a paper mobilization without physical violence." Though elections were only a social tranquilizer, public opinion in a time of stress served as a "resolve of force. . . . Public opinion in its highest ideal will defend those who are prepared to act on their reason against the interrupting force of those who merely assert their role." But that kind of result would be neither spontaneous nor continuous: "When power, however absolute and unaccountable, reigns without provoking a crisis, public opinion does not challenge it. Somebody must challenge arbitrary power first. The public can only come to his assistance."

Only with help, then, would public opinion recognize a crisis. It would have reached the "limits of its normal power if it judges . . . rule to be defective, and turns then to identify the agency most likely to remedy it." Ordinarily the public should remain neutral: where events were confused or hard to understand, the probabilities were "very great that the public can produce only muddle if it meddles."

Though the body of experts he had recommended in *Public Opinion* was not revived as a solution in *The Phantom Public,* Lippmann remained skeptical about majoritarian rule. He provided no clear role for representative government as a constraint on the authority of those holding high office. There was no way, he wrote, to educate public opinion for self-government: "This democratic conception is false because it fails to note the radical difference between the experience of the insider and the outsider . . . it asks the outsider to deal as successfully with the substance of a question as the insider. He cannot do it. No scheme of education can equip him." It was a liberal fallacy to believe otherwise. "In the struggle against evil," philosophers had avoided that fallacy—Plato wrote his *Republic* "on the proper education of a ruling class"; and Dante, "seeking order and stability," had "addressed himself not to the conscience of Christendom but to the Imperial Party."

Lippmann, the exemplification of the insider, placed his trust, as he always had and as he wrote in his conclusion to *The Phantom Public,* chiefly in the individuals who initiated, administered, and settled affairs. But he continued to trust only those who held to the kinds of standards he had set in his earliest books. He loathed Mussolini. Though he supported the candidacy of Alfred E. Smith for the presidency, he had grave doubts about Smith's understanding of several major issues. With the coming of the Great Depression and the international crises that accompanied it, Lippmann, now a syndicated columnist for the Republican *New York Herald Tribune,* deplored Herbert Hoover's management of affairs. Dubious as he was about the public and its educability, by 1932–33 Lippmann was equally dubious about the visible ruling class—the lawyers, financiers, and politicians who were failing to make their Republican party a useful instrument of positive government; their counterparts who had done no better as Democrats. He was as eager as other responsible observers for new, informed, energetic leadership. He did not expect that kind of leadership from Franklin D. Roosevelt, but he welcomed it when it came; and he began immediately to weave Roosevelt and the New Deal into the tapestry of his political thought.

LOOKING at the world in the summer of 1933, Lippmann could not avoid feeling that "the regime of liberty is almost everywhere on the defensive." The Japanese had wrested Manchuria from China. Mussolini retained his authoritarian rule in Italy, as did Stalin in the Soviet Union. Both were potentially dangerous states. Hitler and his Nazis, even more threatening, had come into power in Germany. The industrialized nations remained in the depths of the worst depression they had ever experienced. That depression had left some 25 to 30 percent of Americans unemployed, millions of families in or close to poverty, thousands of banks threatened, many of them bankrupt. Franklin Roosevelt's exhilarating first months as president had won Lippmann's applause and lifted the spirits of a frightened people, but that brave and productive beginning had left international problems unaffected. Indeed, the Anglo-American entente that Lippmann believed essential to international order had suffered severe strains at the London Naval Conference of 1930, where the two nations could not reach a peaceful agreement. Agreement again eluded them at the London Economic Conference of 1933, when they failed to work out an acceptable formula for international monetary exchange.

After that failure, Lippmann began to assemble his thoughts about both the international and the domestic developments of the previous several years. He prepared a preliminary statement for the Godkin Lectures at Harvard which he delivered in 1934. Published later that year as *The Method of Freedom,* those lectures linked the renascent militarism of the Fascist and Communist states to the domestic absolutism they had embraced. In the face of that threat, and as in other periods of great disorder, Lippmann wrote, men needed positive convictions to defend freedom, indeed to defend civilization itself. He set out, therefore, to provide "a statement of principles by means of which . . . a nation possessing a highly developed economy and habituated to freedom can make freedom secure amidst the disorders of the modern world."

Lippmann built *The Method of Freedom* on the social psychology of *Public Opinion* and *The Phantom Public,* as well as on the inspiration of celebrated defenders of an orderly and principled freedom—particularly Edmund Burke and Edward Coke. As before, he had no confidence in the mass of the electorate or in "legislative supremacy," though he considered legislative consent to executive initiatives essential to political liberty. More than ever Lippmann rejected what he again defined as the anachronistic ideas of nineteenth-century laissez-faire economics. He was most concerned with the question of the proper role of the state in the crisis of the time.

With the end of the war in 1918, Lippmann argued, "the mass of people . . . wished to recover the peace, the plenty, and the liberties" the war had denied them. But with the depression, the failure to achieve "a restoration of the pre-war economy" brought about a generally revolutionary condition. The disruption of previous customs left men in such confusion that they listened to "unfamiliar ideas." After the financial panic of 1931 and its related developments, the international economy collapsed as "each state seized the control of that part of the cosmopolitan economy which lay within its frontiers or the reach of its army and navy." Managed economies replaced what remained of the "regulating mechanism of the market" and destroyed "the separation of political and economic power" so vital to the old order of "free capitalism and political democracy."

That order, only marginally affected by public supervision before the war, was now gone forever: "Capitalism has become so complicated that private initiative is insufficient to regulate it; the democratization of political power had made collective initiative imperative. . . . The state is now compelled to look upon the economy as a national establishment for which it is responsible." Consequently "the assumptions of laissez-faire have given way to the assumptions of collectivism."

"Collectivism" for Lippmann implied collective responsibility and collective action, not authoritarianism. He cited in that connection the ambiguous case of Herbert Hoover, who while celebrating laissez faire had nevertheless regarded it as the government's duty to spend public funds to protect banks, to try to maintain the price of wheat and cotton, and in other ways also to influence the economy in the first years of the depression. Hoover had acted on a doctrine, collectivism, which he professed to reject. In so doing, he had anticipated many of the major policies that Franklin Roosevelt adopted.

Much of what the New Deal had undertaken was essential, both in the United States and in other democratic countries. In the absence of remedy, debtors facing foreclosure on their homes, workers thrown out of their jobs, depositors threatened by loss of their savings, would "fight back," if necessary "overturn the government and the social order when their own security is destroyed." The state had, therefore, to intervene to prevent unemployment and to protect the standard of living: "Only by making its people economically secure can a modern government have independence, wield influence in the world, preserve law, order, and liberty."

Yet government had also threatened liberty. During the war, in most belligerent countries, national plans were imposed on production and enforced by military law. After the war, "military collectivism" perpetuated itself as communism and fascism. The military pattern abolished freedom. It allowed no room for "argument, persuasion, bargaining and compromise." In an economy "which is directed according to a plan and for definite national objectives," Lippmann warned, "the official must be superior to the citizen. . . . The citizen is conscript." A state of that type had to control public opinion and therefore also education and the press, for it could not permit disloyalty or dissent. That was "the logic of absolute collectivism," which turned naturally to violence "to suppress the contrariness of free men."

Fortunately it was not necessary to choose between laissez faire and military collectivism. There was a third, "a radically different method" to insure both freedom and security. The English-speaking people, the people most experienced in self-government and economic enterprise, had developed that method, "the method of free collectivism." It acknowledged the responsibility of the state for the standard of living and the operation of the economy as a whole, and it also preserved "within very wide limits the liberty of private transaction." Its object was not to direct individual behavior but to "redress the balance of private actions by compensating public actions."

In the compensated economy of free collectivism, the state prevented fraud between buyer and seller, enforced "equitable contracts," equalized "the bargaining power of the consumer and of the employee," regulated public utilities as well as conditions of work in factories, and set minimum wages. The state also broke up monopolies, restricted speculation, and prevented "a too rampant individualism in the use of property." Since the crash of 1929 and the ensuing depression had revealed that "individual decisions were not sufficient to create a lasting prosperity," the state had to provide a "compensating mechanism" to offset and correct private economic judgments. That mechanism would require public management of money and credit, the planning and timing of public works, and the utilization of taxation to encourage or curtail consumption in order to smooth the business cycle by preserving a sufficient "equilibrium between saving and investment."

Lippmann had drawn together the agenda of American progressivism and the developing policies of the New Deal. He had also placed that agglomeration within the broad context of the emerging economics of his friend John Maynard Keynes, who was at work on his momentous *General Theory of Employment, Interest and Money* (1936). Though Lippmann had reservations about some New Deal programs, he believed—as did Roosevelt and Keynes—that financial panic and economic instability created the mood on which fascism fed, that "the existence of plenty is a condition of liberty."

The "special concern" of free collectivism, Lippmann wrote near the end of *The Method of Freedom,* was "to bring as many as possible" to the "middle condition"—a phrase from Aristotle that translated in 1934 as "the middle class." "Free men," Lippmann continued, "with vested rights in their own living: men like these alone, and not employees of the state or the disinherited who today walk the streets . . . can constitute a free society. . . . With them peace and order are most likely to prevail against the violence of faction and the stratagems of adventurers." To be sure, the bourgeois were often dull, but they had hold "of the substance of liberty and they cling to it"; they were stubborn and careful and "of their fate, though it be a small one and private . . . the masters." In the modern world, the authority of the state had to be enlarged. About that enlargement, free men were cautious, "in the knowledge that it is expedient but not glorious, that it is necessary but dangerous, that it is useful but costly." About free collectivism and about the New Deal, Lippmann was cautious himself. Within two years, the dangers that he perceived had come to command his continuing inquiry into the process of governing men.

BY the spring of 1937, when Lippmann completed *The Good Society,* Hitler had reoccupied the Rhineland; Japan had invaded China; in Germany, Italy, and the Soviet Union, totalitarian regimes had turned to systematic brutality in order to hold and enlarge their authority. "The dominant fact in the contemporary world," Lippmann wrote, was "the return of the European and Asiatic great powers to the conception of total war."

The Good Society, a treatise on political economy, was intended to set forth, Lippmann later recalled, the enduring principles on which a postwar reconstruction should be based. In his discussion of those principles, Lippmann criticized some programs of the New Deal, particularly those of the National Recovery Administration and the Agricultural Adjustment Administration, agencies created during the emergency of 1933 and since abandoned or modified. He had come to believe that the president was excessively fond of authority, and he had opposed his re-election in 1936. But *The Good Society* was only incidentally a criticism of the New Deal. It was primarily a condemnation of "the increasing ascendancy of the state"— of fascism, whatever its guise—and a plea for personal freedom under the law. In writing it, Lippmann drew upon the idea he had developed in *Public Opinion* and *A Preface to Morals,* expanded and refined his argument in *The Method of Freedom,* and dispelled the potential confusion of that book's distinction between two kinds of collectivism. Indeed, *The Good Society* departed only toward its end from the main contention of its immediate predecessors.

In *The Good Society,* Lippmann gave up the phrase "free collectivism." He now reserved "collectivism," unmodified, for Fascist and Communist states. He also wrote less about the international than the domestic market, but he wrote with his characteristic criticism of laissez-faire doctrines. As he so often had, he expressed his reservations about majoritarian democracy, though now he was at least equally dubious about governments not subjected to constitutional limitations. Where earlier he had hoped for the sublimation of the passions of the governors, he now looked instead to the rule of law, to a controlling superego, as it were.

The Good Society affirmed the first "and most fundamental" of the principles on which Lippmann was building his case: "that the politics, law and morality of the Western world are an evolution from the religious conviction that all men are persons and that the human person is inviolable." The second principle held that the continuing industrial revolution "posed all the great issues of the epoch" and arose "primarily from the increasing division of labor in ever-widening markets." He intended to reconcile those principles.

Lippmann immediately rejected "the gigantic heresy of an apostate generation," the mistaken belief in the authoritarian principle and the collectivist state as somehow indispensable for controlling modern technology. That apostasy grew out of a confusion about the development of "concentrated corporate capitalism," which Lippmann considered (in a reversal of *Drift and Mastery*) a transitory and correctable distortion of the free market. The functioning of that market, he maintained, had released the energy of men and permitted their inventiveness to lift the bondage of "authority, monopoly, and special privilege." Regrettably, since the war the leaders of the world had lost their way and "abandoned the method of freedom" for intensified national rivalries. They had been able to do so because "the acids of modernity" (a phrase from *A Preface to Morals*) had unsettled prewar routines: "In the disorder, men became . . . bewildered . . . credulous . . . more anxiously compulsive," ready to turn to a government of technicians to restore the order they missed. "To magnify the purposes of the state," they had to "forget the limitations of men." They were deceived because no device of social control could approximate "the mastery" once attributed to "God as the creator and ruler of the universe" (though Lippmann had himself once attributed mastery to talented men, technicians included). Men were incapable, he now argued, to construct a planned society consciously directed.

The movement toward collectivism, Lippmann continued in a familiar vein, had fed on the invocations by "great corporate capitalists" of "the shibboleths of liberalism." Those shibboleths erroneously equated the free market—essential for the release of human energy—with laissez-faire government, a transient and expendable theory. Laissez faire, in that self-serving view, had come to connote freedom for monopolies, which in fact were corrupting the free market. Reformers and labor leaders, for their part, while talking about liberty, had actually tried to obtain control over the monopolies for themselves. "In their belief that popular majorities must be unrestrained," Lippmann went on, "in their persistent demands for the magnification of government, in their fundamental aim to dominate . . . the private collectivism of the corporate system, rather than to break up monopoly and disestablish privilege, they became the adversaries of freedom and the founders of the new authoritarian society."

In support of his case, Lippmann cited the Soviet Union, Germany, and Italy. The absolutism of those countries, he argued, was the outgrowth of "the essential principle of a full-blown collectivist society." Its "ultimate ideal" had been defined by Mussolini; it was the state, "nothing outside the State, nothing against the State." Lippmann then returned to a theme of *The Method of Freedom*. "All collectivism," he wrote, "whether . . . communist or fascist, is military in method, in purpose, in spirit, and can be nothing else." Therein lay "the tragic irony" of the time: "The search for security . . . if it seeks salvation through political authority, ends in the most irrational form of government . . . in the dictatorship of casual oligarchs."

Collectivism, Lippmann argued, had perverted nationalism. In the early nineteenth century, nationalism had originated in "a passion to overcome the particularism of petty states." Later it became a reaction against the free market, an effort, as in high tariffs, to provide exclusive privilege for a particular state and the economic interests within it. Almost simultaneously the perpetuation of special interests had spawned collectivism, which sought further to insulate the state from its neighbors. "Collectivism," Lippmann wrote, "moves toward autarchy, the totalitarian state toward isolation."

In the collectivist state, rulers used instruments of terror to indoctrinate the masses "with the view that their real enemies were not the privileged classes at home but the privileged nations abroad." The proletarian became imperialist. Thus arose the dreadful prospect of "total war . . . fought not for specific objects but for supremacy." In that observation, Lippmann had succeeded, so he wrote a friend, in "relating domestic and foreign policy organically one to the other."

Lippmann went on to warn against the dangers of gradual collectivisms and the related assumption, so often his target, that majorities expressed the will of society. He differentiated gradual collectivism, which inhered in intrusive microeconomic programs such as that of the New Deal's National Recovery Adminstration, from what he now called "liberalism," which many New Deal policies advanced. The liberalism he promoted was not the liberalism of laissez faire but the program of the compensatory state. "The first principle of liberalism," he held, ". . . is that the market must be preserved and protected." To that end, he again advocated the very policies he had praised in *The Method of Freedom,* including the outlawing of monopoly; the provision of equal bargaining power to farmers, workers, and consumers; and the redistribution of income toward "a middle-class standard of life."

The liberal state recognized that the "populace had the power to rule" and "the right to rule." It was necessary also to structure the government so as to enable the populace to rule. That was the purpose of the Founding Fathers, who "conceived of the people as subjecting themselves to a legal system in which their power to rule was carefully organized." The Constitution protected both the masses and American society "from the hypnosis of the moment." The Constitution refined the will of the people.

It did so partly through the role assigned to the judiciary, though the courts were not devised to obstruct the popular will. Rather, the courts were a part of "the oldest, the best established, the most successful" method of social control necessary for a civilized order, the Anglo-American common law. The common law, Lippmann wrote, which the framers of the Constitution had taken for granted, defined "the reciprocal rights and duties of persons" and invited them to enforce the law by proving their case in a court. In contrast to collectivism, liberalism under the law sought to govern "primarily by applying and perfecting reciprocal obligations." Liberalism operated "chiefly through the judicial hearing of individual complaints and the provision of individual remedies." The agencies of the liberal state, unlike the agencies of collectivism, while hospitable to "all manner of concerted action," would function only "as creatures of the law invested with special rights and duties which . . . may be repealed or amended."

Lippmann's emphasis on the rule of law carried him beyond the argument of *The Method of Freedom* and the books that preceded it. The rule of law, as he described it, solved many of the problems that he had contemplated so long. It checked the will of the majority. It guarded against the tyranny of the governor. It permitted established, informed, and accountable public agencies to shape the economy of the state. The liberalism Lippmann advocated continued "the persistent search by the noblest men of our civilization for a higher law which would bind and overcome the arbitrariness of their lords and masters, of mobs at home and barbarians abroad, and the vagrant willfulness of their own spirits." The denial "that men may be arbitrary," Lippmann held, "*is* the higher law," a higher law particularly important in the period in which he wrote, one of the "great periods of disorder."

With that conclusion, Lippmann, involved as ever with the problem of order, reached toward a conception of a secular natural law that emerged fully only after almost two more decades of reflection. In the intervening years, the coming of World War II and the issues arising out of the tenuous settlement of that war—issues of American foreign and military policy—commanded Lippmann's attention and analysis. Those issues took him back to his work during the Wilson years and forward to the exigent questions of national power and national survival.

THE European war that began in 1939, in contrast to the war of 1914, came to Americans as no surprise. At the outset, most of them hoped and expected to avoid involvement in the war. Lippmann, distressed by the concessions that Britain and France had been making to Hitler and saddened by the foreseeable horror of war, nevertheless believed that the time had come to stand up to Germany and its allies, and that the United States could not avoid the predictable challenge to its own interests. American anxieties soared in the spring of 1940 when German divisions overran most of Western Europe. That conquest left Britain alone between the victorious Nazis on the western coast of France and the inadequate and ill-equipped American forces on the eastern coast of the United States. War overspread the Atlantic in 1940–41 as the United States attempted to supply Great Britain in the face of the growing German submarine fleet. In that time, the long coast from Argentina to Labrador remained substantially undefended.

The surprise Japanese attack on Pearl Harbor in December 1941 demonstrated a parallel vulnerability across the Pacific, while it also precipitated the declarations of war that made the United States a belligerent in the global struggle against Germany, Italy, and Japan. For almost another year, however, the United States and its major allies—Great Britain, the Soviet Union, and China—continued to suffer shattering defeats from advancing German and Japanese forces. In that grim time, with the civilization he cherished everywhere in danger of extinction, Lippmann wrote *U.S. Foreign Policy: Shield of the Republic* (1943).

"This is the time of reckoning," he warned. "We are liquidating . . . at our mortal peril, the fact that we made commitments, asserted rights, and proclaimed ideals while we left our frontiers unguarded, our armaments unprepared, and our alliances unformed and unsustained." Consequently, as he wrote the French philosopher Jacques Maritain, Lippmann devoted his book, his "speech of a public man at a critical juncture in public affairs," to the specific purpose of "showing how the people of the United States could unite quickly on a decision which, if it is not taken within the next twelve months, would leave us paralyzed and would render impossible an orderly solution of the war."

Rejecting the views of American isolationists, as he always had, Lippmann located the proper foundations of American foreign policy in the insights of the first national statesmen, Washington and his early successors in the presidency. They had recognized the American stake in a European balance of power that would prevent a potentially hostile nation from controlling the eastern Atlantic. That stake required alliances of convenience to sustain the balance of power and with it the security of the Atlantic Ocean. The Monroe Doctrine, Lippmann wrote, drawing upon the best historical account of its origin, appeared to extend the beneficent protection of the United States over the whole of the Americas. The preservation of the American continents from European encroachments remained an essential purpose of foreign policy. But the Monroe Doctrine during the nineteenth century depended upon the unacknowledged domination of the Atlantic by the British navy.

The failure of Americans to acknowledge and formalize that dependency contributed to the national illusion of superiority. That failure, as Lippmann saw it, was immoral as well as deluding. "Unearned security," he wrote," . . . had the effect upon our national . . . mind which the lazy employment of unearned income so often has on the descendants of a hard-working grandfather. It caused us to forget that man has to earn his security and his liberty. . . . We came to think that our privileged position was a natural right . . . the reward of our moral superiority."

Misled by that belief, convinced of their exceptional virtue, most Americans had "come to argue . . . that a concern with the foundations of national security, with arms, with strategy, and with diplomacy, was beneath our dignity as idealists." That fallacy resembled the "vice of the pacifist ideal": that peace was the "supreme end of foreign policy." A surrender to Germany or Japan, as Lippmann argued, would bring no real peace. Rather, the "true end" of foreign policy was "to provide for the security of the nation in peace *and* in war."

A nation that had security did not have to sacrifice its legitimate interests to avoid war and was able to maintain those interests during war. But during the interbella years, the United States, Great Britain, and France had neglected the essential elements of national security, "armaments, suitable frontiers, and appropriate alliances." In those democratic countries, the pacifist ideal had led to military weakness and the appeasement of aggressor nations, who were thereby encouraged to turn to war. The Wilsonian ideal, for Lippmann a variant of the pacifist ideal, had falsely identified collective security with an antipathy to alliances. In reality the League of Nations could have enforced peace only if it had been led by "a strong combination of powers" (a contention similar to Lippmann's conclusion in *The Political Scene*).

"Americans in particular had ignored the basic principle of foreign relations"—that a foreign policy consists in bringing into balance, "with a comfortable surplus of power in reserve, the nation's commitments and the nation's power." That postulate guided Lippmann's approach to foreign policy through the rest of his life. In 1943 he defined it in terms from which he afterward never deviated. A foreign commitment, he wrote, was "an obligation, outside of the continental limits of the United States, which may in the last analysis have to be met by waging war." Power was "the force . . . necessary to prevent such a war or to win it." "Necessary power" included both American military force and reinforcements from "dependable allies."

A solvent American foreign policy, one that balanced power and commitments, had to be formulated by "responsible statesmen" whose decisions would unite "the common sense of the nation." As he expected them to, so did he identify the vital interests of the United States. The first of those interests, the defense of "the continental homeland . . . against foreign powers," had been extended by the Monroe Doctrine to "the whole of the Western Hemisphere." That region had "to be defended against the invasion, intrusion, and absorption by conspiracy within; and if lost, would have to be liberated." The Americas could not be defended "by waiting to repel an attack . . . by a formidable enemy." Rather, strategic defense reached "across both oceans and to all transoceanic lands from which an attack by sea or by air can be launched." North America had become most accessible from "the British Isles, Western Europe, Russia, and Japan." Consequently relations among Great Britain, Russia, and Japan "as foes, as allies, or as neutrals" regulated "the issues of peace and war for the United States."

As Lippmann saw it, Germany affected the Americas as the enemy or ally of those three powers. In 1917, he wrote, the United States went to war when Germany threatened to conquer Great Britain and "to become our nearest neighbor." In 1940 neutrality had become impossible for the same reason. In those as in all cases, the paramount concern for American foreign policy related to the alignment of the great powers. Foreign policy was solvent only when the combination of powers allied with the United States was stronger than the combination allied against it. In the latter event, American commitments would exceed American means. Consequently the makers of foreign policy had to "organize and regulate the politics of power."

National interest, the Monroe Doctrine, and, so Lippmann argued, the Open Door policy, which guaranteed China's political and territorial integrity, taken together committed the United States to defend half the globe. Standing alone, the nation could not do so. It had, therefore, to turn to dependable friends in the Old World, as Woodrow Wilson and Franklin Roosevelt had by joining alliances already in the field. In the future, in "the postwar order of the great powers," it would be the business of diplomacy to form similar dependable alliances. Victory in the war would destroy the effective power of Japan and Germany. China had little available strength. The postwar order would, therefore, rest in three "great military states," Britain, the Soviet Union, and the United States. Unless their alliance persisted after victory, one of them would seek realignment with Germany or Japan and then rearm that new ally and disrupt the order of power necessary for peace.

Lippmann went on to focus, as he had in *The Political Scene*, on the importance of the alliance between the United States and Great Britain with its dominions. American commitments in Europe and Asia "dictated the need" for that alliance, which was "natural" because the "overthrow of the American position in the world would mean the break-up of the British community of nations," just as the overthrow of the British position would revolutionize the system of American defense. As Lippmann saw it, the Anglo-American connection was the product of "the facts of geography and . . . historic expedience" of a community of interest. Other European nations bordering the Atlantic belonged to the same community, whose security turned upon the Anglo-American alliance. It provided "the nucleus of force . . . of the whole region."

Lippmann also perceived a complementarity of interests between the United States and the Soviet Union. In spite of American dislike of czarist autocracy and Soviet dictatorship, the two nations had, "each in its own interest, supported one another in the crucial moments of their history." Now both nations retained an interest in the European settlement. It would require the willingness of both the Soviet Union and the Atlantic community to neutralize the border region— Poland, Czechoslovakia, and other "remains" of ancient empires. Neutralization would protect the interests of the partners to it, the most powerful states, and provide the basis for general peace.

In 1943 the outcome of the war remained too uncertain

for Lippmann to proceed beyond his "guessing and hoping" about the future. But by 1944, great decisions had been made, and he was ready to add to his analysis another chapter, which built on the major points of *U.S. Foreign Policy* and considered their application in the foreseeable postwar world. That sequel, a brief hortatory book, Lippmann entitled *U.S. War Aims* (1944).

The four-power alliance that was winning the war—the alliance of the United States, Britain, the Soviet Union, and China—was "not an international order" but the "nucleus around which order can be organized." First it would be necessary to define and stabilize "the strategic defenses and the foreign relations of all states within the same strategical system." The Atlantic community constituted one such system. The Soviet Union provided the nucleus for a second that was already grouping; China, for an incipient but still inchoate third.

The Atlantic community, Lippmann held, was the "historic center of the international exchange economy." From that condition there followed "the essential political character which fits our way of life . . . that the state exists for man, and not man for the state; that the state is under the law, not above it." No social program that violated that heritage, Lippmann wrote, citing *The Good Society,* would "long be endured." Among the Atlantic nations, war had to be outlawed, and "any idea of preparation for such a war . . . excluded from all plans." The security of the weaker members of the community would be assured by their participation in a common defensive system and its combined force and combined command. The nations of the community would also, he wrote—with more logic than European nationalisms permitted—have to agree to pursue a "common foreign policy in their relations with the non-Atlantic world." That policy would require " 'organic consultation' . . . something more elastic than a formal treaty of alliance, and . . . much less than political federation."

The alliance faced the immediate task of working out with the Soviet orbit a settlement with Germany—as Lippmann saw it, a neutralization of Germany so that it would not become an object of a dangerous rivalry. As he observed, the Russians, after German invasions in two wars, were bound to consider the region east of Germany as part of their own strategic system. The eastern frontier of the Atlantic community would, therefore, follow a fluctuating line through central Europe. There, as in Asia (where the future remained opaque), the relationship between the Atlantic and the Soviet orbit would "decide the outcome of the war."

The European settlement Lippmann envisaged depended on Soviet as well as American self-restraint, for which in 1944 he had considerable hope—as did many Americans, the president among them. But Lippmann also understood the possibilities of international disorder. "It will disrupt the peace of the world," he wrote, "if the Soviet Union and the Atlantic nations become rivals and potential enemies in respect to China, India, and the Middle East." The Atlantic region, therefore, could permit no nation to act on its own in those areas. "Colonial policy," he warned, "can no longer be the sole prerogative of the imperial state, and will have to be set by consultation and agreement." That was a wise admonition that few nations were then ready to accept.

"Under the regional principle," Lippmann also wrote, ". . . it would be . . . an overt act of aggression for any state to reach beyond its own strategical orbit for an alliance with a state in another orbit." If the Soviet Union, for one example, made an alliance with a Latin American country, the peace would be "troubled," as it would also be if the United States made an alliance with Iran or Romania. Further, ideology could create disorder. Unless "the ideological conflict over the elemental civil rights of man" were resolved, Lippmann predicted, secrecy and repression would prevail in the Soviet Union and breed reciprocal redbaiting within democratic societies afraid of subversion. There would then follow not peace but "only a *modus vivendi,* only compromises, bargains, specific agreements, only a diplomacy of checks and counter-checks."

U.S. War Aims in general prescribed self-contained regionalism as the basis for postwar order. It also related that order to the prevalence of the liberal rule of law Lippmann had earlier advocated. But even before the victories over Germany and Japan, the rivalry between the Atlantic and the Soviet communities made possible only the modus vivendi Lippmann had hoped the settlement would transcend. Once the Cold War began, *U.S. War Aims* perforce became in large part a catalogue of his prescient fears.

The exhaustion of British strength during World War II left the United States and the Soviet Union as the only great military powers in the world. That condition alone might have produced the antagonistic bipolarity of the early Cold War. As it happened, both great powers acted in a manner that bred distrust. In the perceived interest of national security, the United States acquired a ring of air bases from which a new generation of conventional bombers could reach Soviet territory and, theoretically at least, deliver an atom bomb— a weapon then still an American monopoly. For its part, the Soviet Union, while encouraging the Communist revolution in China, also closed its grip on the countries of Eastern Europe, including the Soviet eastern zone in Germany, which was also to become a satellite nation. That European development reflected the traditional Russian concern about the security of the western border, so often crossed by invading armies. Now a resurgence of activity by Communist parties in both Eastern and Western Europe seemed to reach beyond the Soviet needs for security toward subversive threats to established governments in Western nations already disturbed by the immediate postwar economic distress.

In the resulting climate of anxiety and suspicion, of accusation and counteraccusation, President Harry S Truman devised the policies through which the United States pursued its ends in the Cold War. In 1947, with England no longer able to sustain an amicable order in the eastern Mediterranean, Truman pledged the United States to provide immediate assistance in Greece and Turkey, countries with obviously shaky economies and allegedly threatened, non-Communist governments. The Truman Doctrine also promised everywhere "to support free peoples who are resisting attempted subjugation of armed minorities or by outside pressures." That commitment, which far exceeded American means, drew Lippmann's predictable attack; just as the announcement of the Marshall Plan, designed to provide American assistance for the rebuilding by Europeans of their economies, predictably drew Lippmann's praise. The former violated, while the latter advanced, the principles of his wartime reflections about foreign policy.

Characteristically, Lippmann directed his critical analysis of American policy against the theory that provided its rationale. That theory had received its most influential expression in an article published in July 1947 in *Foreign Affairs:* "The Sources of Soviet Conduct," written by one "X." In reality, as most informed readers knew, "X" was George F. Kennan, the director of the policy planning staff of the Department of State. Earlier Kennan, while stationed in Moscow, had put forth similar ideas in a secret "long telegram" that both affirmed and provoked the anti-Soviet feelings of most of Truman's advisers. Addressed to a wider audience, the X article ascribed to Marxism, as Lenin and Stalin had reinterpreted it, an intense, inherent antagonism to the capitalist world that was accentuated by the internal insecurities of the Stalinist regime and armed with religious fervor. Yet Soviet doctrine, Kennan wrote, in its certainty that Marxism would prevail in the end, encouraged accommodation to transient barriers to that ultimate triumph. Consequently Kennan argued that the American policy toward the Soviet Union should be "long-term, patient but firm and vigilant containment of Russian expansive tendencies." By containment he meant "the adroit . . . application of counter-force at a series of constantly shifting geographical and political points, corresponding to the shifts and maneuvers of Soviet policy." Properly applied, that policy would promote "either the break-up or the gradual mellowing of Soviet power."

Though Kennan later asserted that in the X article he had not meant to recommend military counterforce, Truman did give containment a distinctly military cast across a global reach. Both the military and the global aspects of the Truman Doctrine and its implications dismayed Lippmann. He was not deluded about the nature of the Soviet state. As he wrote in *The Cold War* (1947), his criticism of Truman's policy did "not arise from any belief or hope that our conflict with the Soviet government is imaginary or that it can be avoided, or ignored, or easily disposed of. . . . I agree entirely that Soviet power will expand unless it is prevented from expanding because it is confronted with power, primarily American power." But the concept of containment that he ascribed to Kennan struck Lippmann as "unsound," bound to "cause us to squander our substance and our prestige."

After criticizing Kennan's reasoning, Lippmann proceeded with his own case, little modified since 1944. The continual application of a counterforce at shifting points all over the world, he contended, would require unlimited money and military power. Congress, however, could not provide a blank check on the Treasury or a blanket authorization for the use of the armed forces without violating the Constitution. Further, if the United States awaited Soviet initiatives before responding, American forces would always enter the field too late and with too little. "A policy of shifts and maneuvers," he believed, though perhaps suited to the Soviet system, was "not suited to the American system of government. . . . It is even more unsuited," he continued in the spirit of *The Good Society,* "to the American economy which is unregimented and uncontrolled, and therefore cannot be administered according to a plan."

Unsound in its domestic ramifications, containment was also a "strategic monstrosity," for there was "no rational ground for confidence that the United States could muster 'unalterable counterforce' at all . . . sectors." American military power, great though it was, could not cover all of Europe. American reserves of infantry, difficult to transport across the ocean, did not match Soviet reserves. Indeed American power was "peculiarly unsuited" to the policy of containment. It was, instead, "distinguished by its mobility, its speed, its ranges and its offensive striking force," characteristics inappropriate for a strategy "of waiting, countering, blocking, with no more specific objective than the eventual frustration of the opponent." As Lippmann foresaw, Americans "would themselves . . . be frustrated by Mr. X's policy long before the Russians were."

Lippmann also predicted (wisely, as it developed) that, because of the limits of American power, a policy of containment could "be implemented only by recruiting, subsidizing and supporting a heterogeneous array of satellites, clients, dependents and puppets." The resulting coalition would be disorganized, a loose combination of "feeble and disorderly nations, tribes and factions around the perimeter of the Soviet Union." That disorder would require "continual . . . intervention by the United States in the affairs of all the members of the coalition," an impossible task in the face of Soviet resistance. The Russians, Lippmann realized, "can defeat us by disorganizing states that are already disorganized . . . and by inciting discontent which is already very great." The United States would then have to disown its puppets or "support them at incalculable cost."

In 1947, as Lippmann observed, the United States had not yet consolidated "the old and familiar coalition of the Atlantic Community." That task deserved immediate priority. Fortunately the nations of the Atlantic community were not yet occupied by the Soviet army and could not be unless the Kremlin was "prepared to face a full scale world war, atomic bombs and the rest." Though "impoverished and weakened," those Western European countries were "incomparably stronger, richer . . . more democratic and mature than any of the nations of the Russian perimeter." The United States should therefore concentrate, as George Marshall had proposed, on reconstructing the "economic life" of the members of the Atlantic community. It was necessary also for the United States to promote a German settlement on which the Western Europeans could agree—an objective spelled out in *U.S. War Aims*. But now Lippmann gave Western Europe a new role. Reconstructed along the lines he recommended, Western Europe would "hold the balance of power between Russia and America," would become the mediator of their conflict.

Reconstruction, however, was not yet possible. The threat of the Red army, "not the ideology of Karl Marx," gave "the Kremlin and the native communist parties of western Europe an abnormal and intolerable influence in the affairs of the European continent." Consequently the "immediate and decisive problem" of American relations with the Soviet Union was "whether, when, on what conditions the Red Army can be prevailed upon to evacuate Europe." That evacuation would require, too, the removal from Europe of British and American forces. Lippmann recognized the difficulties of accepting a settlement in which the nations of Eastern Europe "lost all independence," but he deplored the entanglement of American and British diplomacy "in all manner of secondary issues . . . in the Russian borderlands." In that preoccupation, Britain and the United States "failed to see . . . that until the Red Army evacuated eastern Europe and withdrew to the frontiers of the Soviet Union, none of these objectives could be achieved."

In 1944, in *U.S. War Aims,* Lippmann had feared that a conflict in ideologies between the Atlantic community and the Soviet orbit would prevent a world settlement. Partly because his fears had materialized, in 1947 in *The Cold War* he was proposing a settlement based upon two worlds, each separate and secure, each willing to allow the developing nations ultimately to form an orbit of their own. At both times, with consistent emphasis, he looked to negotiations, rather than to confrontations, to establish international order; and he stressed the importance of solvency in national foreign policy. Americans, he wrote in *The Cold War,* had "to reduce, not to extend, our commitments in Asia, to give up the attempt to control events which we do not have the power, the influence, the means, and the knowledge to control." If the Soviet Union refused to evacuate Europe, the Atlantic community would be no worse off than it already was, "but our energies will be concentrated, not dispersed all over the globe, and the real issues will be much clearer." The policy of containment, he concluded, had to give way to a policy of settlement.

In those views Lippmann persisted. They accounted for his criticisms of the adventurism of Dean Acheson, for his attacks on John Foster Dulles with his alarming threats and multiple regional pacts, for Lippmann's later dismay about American involvement in Vietnam, for his continual advocacy of a neutralized settlement in Germany. The makers of American foreign policy and their supporters during the two decades and more that followed the end of World War II frequently shared a trinity of illusory beliefs. They believed too often in the exceptional virtue of the American people and, therefore, of American policy. They believed too often in the necessity for opposing communism everywhere, in a universal American commitment. They believed too often in the omnipotence of American power. Lippmann had no such illusions. Predictably, in one administration after another, those who held power in the United States became restless with his continual demands for negotiation. Had they tried more often to negotiate, even if they had failed, the United States, as Lippmann had suggested, would have been no worse off for the effort. In the absence of continual and successful negotiations, the tension between the United States and the Soviet Union persisted, and with it the disorder that Lippmann deplored.

U.S. Foreign Policy, U.S. War Aims, and *The Cold War*—all tracts for their times—advocated a consistent conception of international order that did not materialize during Lippmann's life. Though his ideas were no less cogent on that account, he had to explore an issue other than foreign policy with its somber expedients if he was to complete the task he had long since undertaken—the definition, at once theoretical and practicable, of the foundations of a beneficent political order.

ALMOST immediately after publishing *The Good Society,* Lippmann embarked in 1938 on a study that took various shapes during the next decade and a half. At times he worked on a new manuscript designed to carry his analysis of the state beyond anything he had yet done. At other times, he contemplated revising *The Good Society* or commissioning some younger but sympathetic friend to do so for him. Even while addressing foreign policy, he never abandoned his project. In the end, he finished a new book, his last major work, *Essays in the Public Philosophy* (1955). Deeply rooted in his earlier work, it also ventured onto ground he had not previously staked.

"During the fateful summer of 1938," Lippmann undertook his "effort to come to terms . . . with the mounting disorder in our Western society." "I was filled with foreboding," he recalled, "that the nations of the Atlantic Community would not prove equal to the challenge, and that . . . we should lose our great tradition of civility, the liberties Western man had won for himself after centuries of struggle . . . now threatened by the rising tide of barbarity." The war did not cure the continuing "sickness of the Western liberal democracies." During the postwar years, Lippmann still discerned "a deep disorder in our society which comes not from the machinations of our enemies and from the adversities of the human condition but from within ourselves." As he saw it, "we were . . . not wounded but sick . . . we were failing to bring order and peace to the world, and we were beset by those who believed they have been chosen to succeed us."

In that dour humor, Lippmann turned to eminent philosophical conservatives who had in their own way admonished their contemporaries, to political theorists such as Aristotle, Edmund Burke, and Alexander Hamilton. Consulting also celebrated diagnosticians of the modern condition, he borrowed again from Freud's interpretations of dreams; from Vilfredo Pareto's theory of social equilibrium; and from Emile Durkheim's concept of anomie, particularly as the concept informed Erich Fromm's discourses about modern man's proclivity to "escape from freedom." In one way or another, all of those theorists shared Lippmann's distrust of popular

majorities and his related belief in rule by an elite responsible
to society but uninfluenced by transient opinion.

So armed, Lippmann began *The Public Philosophy* by examining the "decline of the West" as revealed in the incapacity
of the democracies to "cope with reality, to govern their affairs,
to defend their vital interests." As he had before, he dated
that decline from 1917, the devastating year of the First World
War in which "there had occurred . . . an unrecognized revolution within the democratic states." After their cumulative
losses, their "institutional order . . . gave way under the
strain." In the defeated countries—the Hohenzollern, Haps-
burg, Ottoman, and Romanoff empires—revolution toppled
established order. Within the victorious nations—France, Italy,
Great Britain, and the United States—"the constitutional order
was altered subtly and yet radically."

That order had arisen during the antecedent century while
democratic governments were "spared the necessity of dealing
with the hard issues of war and peace, of security and solvency, of constitutional order and revolution." In that time,
liberals had become "habituated to the notion that in a free
and progressive society it is a good thing that the government
should be weak." But in the crisis of 1917, "the old structure
of executive government with the consent of a representative
assembly" could no longer function. The existing governments had "exhausted their imperium"; they could not carry
on the war except by "democratizing" its conduct and "by
pursuing total victory and . . . promising total peace." Then
occurred the subtle revolution as a "cession of power to representative assemblies," which further ceded powers to "the
masses of voters," who in their turn passed them on to "the
party bosses, the agents of pressure groups, the managers of
the new media of mass communication"—all in all the development Lippmann had long deprecated.

Earlier he had ordinarily attributed the collapse of constitutional order primarily to economic changes, to the persistence of nineteenth-century laissez-faire doctrines into the oligopolistic and protected markets of the twentieth century. *The Public Philosophy* emphasized a different but not unfamiliar theme, the "hyperbolic" war as it had emerged in 1917. That condition had caused "the paralysis of government" and the resulting "functional derangement of the relationship between the mass of the people and the government." The "malady of the democratic states" arose when "the executive and judicial departments, with their civil servants and technicians" lost "their power to decide."

For Lippmann the solution to the problem he had again identified lay, as it had before, partly in restoring the executive as "the active power in the state" and using the "representative assembly" only as the consenting power. The health of the constitutional system depended upon that relationship, for "the government must be able to govern and the citizens must be represented in order that they shall not be oppressed." Indeed for Lippmann that relationship was "rooted in the nature of things." That conclusion inhered in his historical argument; but not for the first time, he had used history perhaps better than he had understood it—used it, in spite of the astonishing variety of the past and of its unpredictability, as if history were metaphysics. On that account, his case for a strong executive was less than wholly persuasive, even in the context of representative government.

Yet his conviction carried him on. Citing Edmund Burke, he also warned against the ephemeral demands of the masses, demands threatening to "the connected generation"—the links Burke was "talking about when he invoked the partnership 'not only between those who are living' but also with 'those who are dead, and those who are to be born.' " That community gave "rational meaning to the necessary objectives of government," Lippmann continued. He also bemoaned the lost capacity of democratic peoples to believe in the intangible realities that had once sustained royalty—the "imponderable authority . . . derived from tradition . . . consecration, veneration . . . prestige . : . hierarchy." Here by projection he seemed to cloak his strong executive in trappings that could become ludicrous in American practice, trappings that served as an odd substitute for the obligations, now omitted, that he had once attached to that strong executive and his technicians in the compensatory state.

Still, Burke's community of generations and its traditional venerations had, as Lippmann contended, checked those impulses for chaos which the Jacobin revolution had unleashed. The Jacobins were his targets, and the Founding Fathers still his models, for unlike the revolutionary French in the eighteenth century, "Jefferson and his colleagues . . . were interested in government"—thus the American Constitution. In contrast Jacobin doctrine was nihilistic: "The peculiar essence of the dogma is that the revolution itself is a creative act." So, too, with Karl Marx, who also preached a fallacious doctrine of redemption. The Marxist heresy held that, with revolution, "men who were evil were to be made good"—a delusion of demagogues who thought they were gods. That delusion, an expression of our "uncivilized selves," called for a revolution against "freedom . . . justice . . . the laws . . . the order of the good society . . . as they are contained in the traditions of civility, as they are articulated in the public philosophy."

By extension, then, in the good society the strong executive would venerate the values of the historical community that was the polity. A legislature, involved not with initiatives but with consent, would also protect those values, among them the freedom of the people. For those values, for the preservation of civility—of civilized order—Lippmann used

a name, "the public philosophy," which expounded tradition
and undergirded the good society. "The public philosophy,"
he wrote, "is known as *natural law.* . . . This philosophy is
the premise of the institutions of the Western society, and
. . . unworkable in communities that do not adhere to it."
Here were his two worlds. But here again, his use of history
had become overtly metaphysical; here his logic, so convincing to him, was uncharacteristically reductionist, its conclusions inherent in its premises.

Lippmann's natural law was secular, not supernatural. As
such it violated none of his personal canons, while it also
satisfied his concern for rational order. His conception of natural law closely resembled the constitutional principles he
had earlier derived from a similar logic. Rational man, he
believed, could "produce a common conception of law and
order which possesses a universal validity." Alexander the Great
had done so, as had the Stoics and Cicero, and as had Anglo-
American constitutional theorists who understood "that a large
plural society cannot be governed without recognizing that,
transcending its plural interests, there is a rational order with
a superior common law."

Modern man, Lippmann wrote, had forgotten the natural
law of civility. Indeed nineteenth-century populist democracy had been hostile to that law and its rhetoric. Nevertheless, until the devastation of 1917, "the loneliness and anxiety
of modern man had been private, without public and overt
political effect." It remained private so long as "public order
provided external security." But the breakdown of public order
intensified private anxieties. "The inner disorder provoked
the impulse to escape" from freedom to authoritarianism.
Patently the metaphor of sublimation could no longer serve
for Lippmann in the condition he described, a condition of
"anomic man," lawless states, and by extension a lawless world.
The solution to those related disasters could not spring up

from within but had to be summoned from without, from a revivified past.

It followed, as he went on, that only a renewal of the public philosophy, of secular natural law, would restore public security. That renewal could not be accomplished by force. It was necessary, rather, to "demonstrate the practical relevance . . . of the public philosophy." Its practicality, Lippmann argued,. not some supernatural faith, would establish its validity. Here he seemed to be applying a Jamesian test for a singularly un-Jamesian ideal. He had always felt that Santayana had saved him from a total conversion to James, but now he appeared implicitly to have tried to merge them. He took one test, as he often had, in the case of property. Since the rights of property, he wrote, were "a creation of the laws of the state," no man had "an absolute title." Rather, owners of property, beholden to the state, were obligated to promote, in Blackstone's phrase, "the grand ends of a civil society." "Private property," Lippmann continued, "is . . . a system of legal rights and duties. Under changing conditions the system must be kept in accord with the grand ends of civil society." That conclusion, he wrote, would be self-evident to a lucid and rational man. In that sense, it was a natural law, a "principle of right behavior in the good society, governed by the Western tradition of civility." In his test, Lippmann had come full circle.

He moved on to familiar territory. He did not expect, he wrote, that many individuals would master the public philosophy: "Most people . . . may have heard almost nothing about it." No matter, for "if among the people of light and leading the public philosophy has, as the Chinese say, the Mandate of Heaven, the beliefs and habits which cause men to collaborate will remain whole." As ever, Lippmann put his faith in an elite of intelligence and character; as ever, he wrote for them and counted himself among them.

As ever, too, Lippmann anchored his argument in his view of human nature. A good citizen in a good society, a man fit to rule, was himself ruled by "his second and civilized nature," not by his instincts. He was "the noble master of his own weaker and meaner passions," as he always had been in Lippmann's chain of being. That mastery was "the aristocratic code," which was not inherent in prerogative and birth "but functional to the capacity to rule."

But Lippmann did not expect a new Jerusalem. "The ideals of the good life and of the good society," he warned, would fall short of perfection. They were "worldly ideas concerned with the best that is possible among mortal . . . men." Words such as "liberty, equality, fraternity, justice" had various meanings "which reflect the variability of the flux of things." That was a phrase from William James, whom Lippmann continued to quote: " 'The essence of life is its continually changing character . . . our concepts are all discontinuous and fixed.' " That was the human condition, in its nature imprecise and inconclusive. That admission of fluidity made *The Public Philosophy* not Lippmann's final statement of a universal truth but his latest statement in a long series of intellectual ventures. As his letters and his newspaper columns continued to reveal, he had not lost in a monistic natural law his lifelong hopes for a liberal state.

He had not lost his old preoccupation: "The principles of the good society call for a concern with an order of being," an order, like the order he had continually sought, where "the human being is inviolable . . . reason shall regulate the will . . . truth shall prevail." That order, which had to rest upon a constitutional system, also had to be earned: "The public philosophy is addressed to the government of our appetites. . . . The regime it imposes is hard."

As some of his friends had warned him before the publication of *The Public Philosophy,* the book was vulnerable in several respects. Even his admirers found it so—Arthur Schlesinger, Jr., for its monism and its too simplistic confidence in a strong executive; Reinhold Niebuhr on those grounds as well as because of the book's presupposition of "a classical ontology, which equates history with nature and does not allow for the endless contingencies of history." Lippmann felt that they and other critics had "not wholly understood or sympathized with" *The Public Philosophy;* but he agreed with Schlesinger's description of his quest, of "a long search and much turmoil," that had begun even before the publication of *A Preface to Politics.*

THOUGH Lippmann published no major book after *The Public Philosophy,* his search, his Jamesian testing, had brought him to conclusions inherent in his earliest formulations about individual and social morality, about civility, order and their relationship—conclusions now more prudent and less unconventional than had been his youthful views. Essentially he had always been a conservative, for he had never trusted the mass of people or had much confidence in their elected representatives. He had always had a shaping faith in the basic values of Western civilization, though not always in their contemporary focus or expression. Never a Jeffersonian, he had believed consistently in a strong federal government, particularly a strong executive, in an active but not intrusive government directed by alert and intelligent managers resolved to promote efficient and equitable social and economic policies. To be sure, he had described the compensatory functions of government as characteristics of a liberal state, but he was a liberal only in that special meaning of the word, and only if government operated within the constitutional restraints that he commended. Those related principles drew strength from his interpretations of the continual crises in American foreign policy. In every context, his observations about the fallability of governors (as well as the fallability of those they governed) moved him increasingly to stress the necessity of protecting human freedom by constitutional means, and consequently of holding government to that higher law. As he wrote, Lippmann had embraced the conservatism of Edmund Burke, and like Burke, he cherished the continuity between generations. "The question you are asking yourselves," he wrote to a group of student rebels of the 1960s, "is whether 'revolution' is not the only way of achieving the good life. I had asked myself that question when I . . . was a student in college. . . . In the advanced nations of the modern age, the old conception of revolution—the overthrow and the replacement of an established governing class—is . . . antiquated. . . . I believe that society can be improved and reformed but not transformed by disruption." So he had long believed. And he had long since concluded, though his argument changed with his times, that reform and improvement were essential for preserving order, without which man could not lead a good life.

THE POLITICS OF
THE WARREN COURT*

BETWEEN 1961 and 1968, the time of the New Frontier and
the Great Society, the federal government compiled a stun-
ning record of social and economic reform. Two activist presidents and their responsive congresses advanced and expanded
the democratic agenda, stalled for the previous quarter century. Yet their accomplishments did not surpass the compatible record of the Supreme Court. In the fifteen years
beginning in 1954 that Court rendered momentous decisions
in behalf of social justice and individual rights.

Those were the years in which Earl Warren presided as
chief justice of the United States—the years of the Warren
Court, in the nomenclature of judicial history. President
Eisenhower had appointed Warren chief justice to pay off an
obligation incurred in 1952. At the Republican National
Convention that year Warren had allowed the California del-
egation to move into Ike's column at a propitious time. A

*Adapted from *Years of Discord: American Politics and Society, 1961–1974* (New York: W. W. Norton, 1991), pp. 187–217.

favorite son candidate, Warren was then governor of California and had been the GOP nominee for vice president in 1948. Like most other Republicans, Eisenhower considered him a moderate. Warren was a fiscal moderate, but he possessed other qualities that Eisenhower failed to take into account: a determined independence of mind and a commitment, as one of his biographers put it, to "ethical imperatives."

"Warren," that biographer wrote, "held a set of values that he believed represented moral truths about decent, civilized life. It was inconceivable to Warren that these values should not be embodied in constitutional principles. . . . Indeed Warren felt bound, as a judge, to consider ethical imperatives in his adjudication." Warren's pursuit of moral ends often guided his perceptions about legal principles. Contrary to Ike's expectations, Warren proved to be rather more a liberal politician with a program than a master of constitutional law. That characteristic made him something of a maverick in the opinion of adverse academic experts.

Though the membership of the Warren Court changed gradually as one associate justice or another left the bench, the years in which Warren presided were characterized by a continuity of decisions. Both admirers and critics of the Warren Court remarked on that continuity, as well as exceptions to it, in their analyses of the jurisprudence in the Court's opinions. While Warren himself wrote only a few of the court's majority opinions, his leadership encouraged his brethren to reach conclusions notable for their judicial activism.

1. Preferred Freedoms

THE thinking of the Warren Court reflected the influence of the doctrine of preferred freedoms. That doctrine was first formulated in 1938 by Harlan F. Stone, whom Franklin Roosevelt had appointed chief justice. In a footnote to his decision in an otherwise unexceptional case, *United States v. Carolene Products Co.* (1938), Stone suggested that the judiciary had a special responsibility in reviewing legislation that might impair civil rights or civil liberties. Stone had long subscribed to the principle of judicial restraint in instances of economic regulation by the states or federal government. In other words, he was disposed in such cases to permit the will of legislatures to prevail. That had been the strong preference, too, of Associate Justices Oliver Wendell Holmes, Jr., and Louis D. Brandeis, giants of American jurisprudence in Stone's youth. He remained within their spirit when he wrote the *Carolene* footnote. "The presumption of constitutionality," he observed, might have "narrower scope for operation . . . when legislation appears on its face to be within a specific prohibition of the Constitution, such as those of the first ten amendments, which are deemed equally specific when held to be embraced within the Fourteenth."

In its last clause that sentence raised a constitutional issue of major significance then and later. One of Stone's colleagues, Associate Justice Hugo Black, in 1938 had articulated the principle of incorporation—the principle, in other words, that the Fourteenth Amendment to the Constitution applies to the states the restrictions on the authority of the federal government which are set forth in the Bill of Rights. Black, also a Roosevelt appointee, had wisely made the principle of incorporation a major objective of his judicial argumentation. After 1954 Black seemed to have prevailed; the principle of incorporation was clearly established in the jurisprudence of the Supreme Court.

Stone in his footnote called for "more exacting judicial scrutiny" in particular of those substantive rights he wanted the courts to protect alike from federal and from state incursions. Close judicial oversight was also necessary, in his view, of statutes "directed at particular religions . . . or national . . . or racial minorities." The Court had to ascertain whether prejudice against those minorities curtailed the operation of "those political processes which can ordinarily be expected to bring about repeal of undesirable legislation." Keeping democratic processes open under all circumstances required judicial vigilance, he believed, as in time did the Warren Court.

Stone's observations did not persuade his brethren quickly to modify their continuing practice of judicial restraint, even in the sensitive circumstances he identified. The Supreme Court from 1938 to 1954 moved only partially and tentatively toward the determinations Stone's language implied. But after the appointment of Earl Warren the doctrine of preferred freedoms became appropriately a major pillar of the Court's evolving jurisprudence.

It probably would have done so in any event, but Warren hastened the development. He did so because so many of the issues of his time raised major moral questions that he wanted answered according to his own decent criteria. "Is it *right?*" he was prone to ask lawyers arguing a case before the court. "Is it good?" He was prepared, as one of his severest critics wrote, to "cut through legal technicalities," to pierce "through procedure to substance." Stone's footnote lent itself to that approach. Warren's moralism, and his leadership of the Court in that direction, did produce decisions of outstanding democratic values. But those decisions often stirred political controversy, and they skirted legal technicalities, which, so his conservative critic also wrote, were "the stuff of law." Consequently, the decisions of the Warren Court, however noble, were sometimes vulnerable—susceptible to dissents that portended eventual judicial correction. But in the time in which they were handed down, those decisions carried weighty social and political significance.

2. *From* Brown *to* Green

EARL WARREN assumed his seat on the Court in time to preside over the rehearing and decision in *Brown v. Board of Education* (1954) and four related cases. He also wrote the momentous decision of the unanimous Court, which held that separate schools for black children were inherently unequal and, as such, violations of the equal protection clause of the Fourteenth Amendment. That ruling overturned the Court's earlier decision in *Plessy v. Ferguson* (1896), which had permitted segregated facilities so long as those for blacks were presumably equal to those for whites, an institutional fiction throughout the South. Warren's opinion in *Brown* incorporated much of the argument of the NAACP lawyers who had pleaded the case. With them, he cited some unnecessary sociological evidence. But also with them, he rested his opinion on the commanding, commonsensical meaning of "equal protection of the laws" and its significance for public education.

"Education," the chief justice wrote, "is perhaps the most important function of state and local governments. . . . It is required in the performance of our most basic public responsibilities. . . . It is a right which must be made available to all on equal terms." He asked then if "the segregation of children in public schools solely on the basis of race . . . deprives the children of equal educational opportunities," and he answered: "We believe it does." Segregation, he continued, connoted inferiority, which in turn "had retarded educational and mental development of Negro children." Accordingly, in the field of public education, "the doctrine of 'separate but equal' has no place."

Though the Court had been moving toward that conclusion for a decade, the decision in *Brown* stunned the South.

As white southerners realized at once, it threatened the whole legal apparatus of apartheid that had kept the races socially segregated for more than half a century. Almost immediately, condemnations of Earl Warren became standard fare in southern political oratory, along with angry reassertions in new dress of the antebellum doctrine of nullification and states' rights. As one corollary to that assertion, southern politicians urged their willing constituents to defy the Court. The Southern Manifesto of 1956, signed by 101 members of Congress, expressed the outrage of the region. It declared the *Brown* decision "a clear abuse of judicial power," a substitution of "personal judicial and social ideas for the established law of the land." But that contention, with its accompanying demands for the impeachment of Earl Warren, expressed a futile commitment to a doomed way of life.

Those reactions neglected aspects of the *Brown* decision that made it less coercive than at first it seemed. The Court had condemned segregation in education, but it had not defined an acceptable standard for desegregated schooling, nor had it established a timetable for that eventuality. On the contrary, the Court invited the litigants in *Brown* to reappear to speak to the question of implementing the decision. After hearing their arguments, the Court in *Brown* II (1955), again unanimously and again speaking through the chief justice, set no date for the desegregation of public schools. It ruled instead that the admission of black children on a nondiscriminatory basis should begin "with all deliberate speed." Desegregation, *Brown* II explained, had to await local solutions of "problems related to administration," including the condition of school buildings, the transportation of pupils, and the revision of boundaries for school districts.

Obviously, "all deliberate speed" gave the South time to adjust to *Brown* I. The justices had intended to do just that in order to mitigate racial tensions in the region. They served the same end by assigning to federal district judges the supervision of desegregation. As informed southerners realized, almost all those local federal judges were southerners themselves and sympathetic to educational conditions as they existed. Warren's opinion in *Brown* II said that "the vitality of . . . constitutional principles cannot be allowed to yield simply because of disagreement with them." Yet the decision permitted massive resistance to develop. As one southern newspaper observed, the decision was "pretty much what the Southern attorneys general had asked for." The measure of their victory appeared in the slow pace of change. As late as 1964, a decade after *Brown* I, only 2.3 percent of southern black children attended desegregated schools.

In a sense, the Court waited for ten years for the other branches of the federal government to catch up to its forward egalitarian position. The election of John F. Kennedy abetted that movement. Though Kennedy appointed many segregationist judges to federal courts in the South, the Civil Rights Division of his Justice Department gave important assistance to activists testing southern resistance to desegregation. The gradual conversion of the Kennedys and of Lyndon Johnson to strong support for civil rights brought the executive departments into step with the Court. And Kennedy and Johnson spurred Congress to join the march with the civil rights legislation of 1964 and 1965.

Meanwhile, the Supreme Court had continued to point the way. By overriding the separate but equal doctrine in *Brown* I, it had begun dismantling the legal basis for segregation. From the late 1950s forward the Court advanced in counterpoint with the civil rights movement. Civil rights demonstrators invited arrest by violating local statutes or ordinances prohibiting blacks from using segregated public facilities. With those arrests, NAACP lawyers appealed the question of the constitutionality of those laws from state jurisdictions to the federal courts. Continuing that process, civil rights lawyers carried adverse rulings from federal district courts to United States courts of appeal and, when necessary, on to the Supreme Court. Before 1960 the Supreme Court struck down laws segregating municipal parks, swimming pools, golf courses, transportation lines and terminals, and other such facilities.

Southern diehards tried to use local ordinances and state laws against disturbances of the peace as barriers to civil rights protests. In response, the Supreme Court expanded its reading of the Fourteenth Amendment to protect the right to demonstrate peacefully. In *Garner v. Louisiana* (1961), another unanimous decision, Warren held that blacks sitting quietly at a luncheon counter could not be charged with "violent, boisterous, or disruptive acts" or with behaving in a manner "as to unreasonably disturb or alarm the public." There was no evidence to support those convictions, and that violated the due process clause of the Fourteenth Amendment.

In *Edwards v. South Carolina* (1963), the Court ruled with only one dissent in a case involving the arrest of student demonstrators who, disregarding a police order to disperse, remained on the grounds of the statehouse where they sang patriotic and religious songs and listened to a sermon. The South Carolina statute under review defined as a criminal offense speech that "stirred people to anger, invited public dispute, or brought about a condition of unrest." Associate Justice Potter Stewart, an Eisenhower appointee and often one of the more conservative members of the Court, wrote the opinion. "In arresting, convicting, and punishing" the demonstrators, Stewart held, "South Carolina infringed the . . . constitutionally protected rights of free speech, free assembly, and freedom to petition for redress of . . . grievances." The Fourteenth Amendment, he continued later in his opinion, "does not permit a State to make criminal the peaceful expression of unpopular views." That strong conclusion did not in itself compel integration, but it did call into question southern recourse to disturbance of the peace laws as a device to prevent civil rights protests.

Southern businesses had persisted in apartheid behind the protection of local ordinances requiring segregation of such private facilities as restaurants, hotels, and department stores. The demonstration against those practices in Birmingham in 1963, of course, soon involved the Kennedy administration. In *Shuttlesworth v. Birmingham* (1963), one of five similar cases, the Supreme Court held that laws requiring segregation could not be enforced. Neither could local statutes referring to trespassing, disorderly conduct, or disturbances of the peace when they were used to prevent integration of facilities serving the general public. Such state action violated the equal protection clause of the Fourteenth Amendment.

The Court carried the application of that clause further the next year. In *McLaughlin v. Florida* (1964), it declared invalid a statute on "Adultery and Fornication" that forbade cohabitation between blacks and whites. That decision cut to the core of southern racism. In his concurrence Justice Stewart again spoke eloquently to the central issue: "I cannot conceive of a valid legislative purpose under our Constitution for a state law which makes the color of a person's skin the test of whether his conduct is a criminal offense." That was very much the spirit of the Civil Rights Act of 1964. A week after the *McLaughlin* opinion, the Supreme Court unanimously validated that act as an appropriate exercise of federal authority over interstate commerce.

The Court continued on its egalitarian track in *United States v. Mississippi* (1965). Following the logic of the able solicitor general of the United States Archibald Cox, Justice Black for the Court found unconstitutional the "long-standing, carefully prepared, and faithfully observed plan to bar Negroes from voting." As Black put it, "The Fifteenth Amendment protects the right to vote regardless of race against any denial or abridgement." Later that year the Voting Rights Act of 1965 assured federal enforcement of that straightforward interpretation of the language of the Constitution.

By that time the Court had evinced a revived concern for the desegregation of southern schools. While the civil rights bill of 1964 was still being debated, the Court ruled in a case of particular interest to the Kennedy and Johnson administrations. It related to Prince Edward County, a rural Virginia county that in 1959 had been ordered to desegregate its schools immediately. Instead, in one of the maneuvers by which southern countries evaded *Brown* II, Prince Edward closed its public school system. White children thereafter attended private schools, which were supported by contributions from individuals and accredited by the county. The county also provided a tax credit for the contributions. Black children by and large received no education at all. Prince Edward was just the kind of affront that Warren had said in *Brown* II the Court could not allow. But until 1963 the Supreme Court with few exceptions had ducked cases on the implementation of *Brown* II until the temper of the executive branch and of the public made it more propitious to get tough.

The issue came to a head in *Griffin v. Prince Edward County* (1964), in which Justice Black ruled for the majority that black children in the county had been denied due process of law. Virginia, he held, could not permit public schools to close in one county while they remained open elsewhere in the state, nor could private schools be maintained by public funds when public schools were closed. The opinion empowered the federal district court to enjoin tuition grants and tax credits to those supporting private schools. It also authorized the district court to order Prince Edward officials to reopen and fund racially desegregated public schools.

Those were broad rulings. Obviously "all deliberate speed" did not mean indefinite delay. That message acquired immediate force because of the role assigned the district court. Two associate justices considered that role excessive, as did many members of the bar in the South. The decision gave to the district court the kind of authority normally vested in a local school board, an institution elected by local people or appointed by their local representatives. Southern resistance to desegregation of public schools had left the Supreme Court little choice. It had to discipline Prince Edward County or surrender its own egalitarian principle and constitutional role. In that dilemma the Warren Court, always an activist court, made the lower federal courts powerfully intrusive. Through the district courts it extended federal authority into local affairs, as *Brown* II had portended. To those affected, that authority, once exercised, seemed alien. Since a district court was not answerable to local preferences, its decisions seemed arbitrary to the communities affected. The decision in *Griffin,* long deferred and arguably necessary, was pungent in the vectors it drew.

The Civil Rights Act of 1964 gave added impact to that decision. Besides forbidding discrimination in public accommodations, that act authorized the Justice Department to bring suit "for the orderly achievement of desegregation in public education." Since NAACP lawyers had already begun to challenge segregation in public schools in southern cities, government lawyers focused on rural areas, where resistance to desegregation was strongest. As one observer commented, those initiatives of the Justice Department "tended to deepen and solidify the Executive's commitment to equality." In keeping with the Civil Rights Act, the Department of Health, Education and Welfare (HEW) issued guidelines for desegregation. Relatively mild at first, those standards became exacting by 1966. Southern school districts that failed to meet them faced the prospect of a cutoff of federal educational aid, which in 1965 had reached a considerable amount. Further, the courts began to incorporate HEW standards in desegregation decrees. The United States Court of Appeals for the Fifth Circuit—Alabama, Florida, Georgia, Louisiana, Mississippi, and Texas—explicitly recommended that "courts in this circuit should give great weight to . . . HEW guidelines." Enjoined to do so by those courts, resistant southern school officials faced contempt of court charges that could result in large fines or imprisonment. The resulting process brought the number of black children in the South who were attending desegregated schools from 2.3 percent in 1964 to 12.5 percent in 1966.

The figure still remained appallingly low, especially at a time when black self-consciousness and militancy were rising all over the nation. In the absence of a federal statute mandating the integration of public schools, the continuing southern evasion of the Supreme Court's intentions still depended largely on the permissiveness of the judiciary. But the judges on the Court of Appeals for the Fifth Circuit, in particular Judges Elbert Tuttle and John Minor Wisdom, rendered decisions in 1965 and 1966 that sped desegregation throughout the South. School authorities, they believed, had an "affirmative constitutional duty to furnish equal educational opportunities to all public school children." As Judge Wisdom put it in one of his decisions, "The only adequate redress for a previously overt system-wide policy of segregation . . . is a system-wide policy of integration." Wisdom and his fellow judges on the Fifth Circuit measured integration by results and ordered it on a comprehensive basis. Their decrees affected the assignment to schools of both students and teachers. Those decrees also ordered bus transportation necessary for their goals. With that sweep, judicial intervention in local education assured the ultimate elimination of segregation in the South.

The Supreme Court followed the Fifth Circuit. A case involving New Kent, a rural Virginia county, tested "freedom of choice," a common means by which southern school districts evaded *Brown* II. In theory the system did not discriminate against blacks, for in theory they could choose to attend the school they preferred. But in practice whites never chose black schools, and most blacks were too intimidated to choose white schools. In New Kent, as elsewhere in the South, segregation persisted in counties where the system obtained, with 85 percent of black children remaining in black schools. In *Green v. School Board of New Kent County* (1968), the Supreme Court at last rejected not just the theory but the results of freedom of choice. "The burden," the Court ruled, "is on a school board to provide a plan that promises realistically to work *now*. . . . A dual system is intolerable." The district court was to "assess the effectiveness" of a plan and to retain jurisdiction "until it is clear that . . . segregation has been completely removed."

That requirement spelled the imminent end to southern evasive tactics. Never had it been clearer than *Green* made it that law was policy. The decision left the district courts with little room for maneuver. Now they would have to demand results or expect to be overruled by a United States court of appeals or eventually by the Supreme Court itself. In 1954 *Brown* I had warned the South that segregation faced a serious challenge from the federal judiciary. By 1964, with the *Griffin* case and the Civil Rights Act, the whole federal government had mobilized to end apartheid in the region. In 1968, with *Green*, the Court closed the last loophole. *Green* portended still more: the recourse to forced busing of children to achieve racial balance within a school system. Further, by examining results—the actual racial statistics for schools within a system—*Green* opened the way for the judiciary to attack de facto school segregation in the North and to do so with the same vigor and intensiveness that had offended so many voters in the South. *Green* made palpable the intent implicit in *Griffin.*

Each stage in these developments echoed in national politics. The Goldwater campaign in 1964 rejected the reasoning of the Warren Court in *Brown* I and its successor cases. Goldwater also condemned the Democrats for their complicity in the attack on segregation in the South. As he expected to, he ran best in that section. In 1968 the Republicans again made an issue of the Court. By that time, indeed even by 1964, the Warren Court had made enemies North and South by its interpretations of the Constitution on issues unrelated to segregation. Not surprisingly, hostile responses to those interpretations occurred most viscerally among those Americans who were most inimical to *Brown* I and II, *Griffin,* and *Green.*

3. Respecting an Establishment of Religion

THE First Amendment to the Constitution forbids Congress to make laws prohibiting the "free exercise" of belief or "respecting an establishment of religion." Those preferred freedoms, in Chief Justice Stone's formula, made it necessary for the Supreme Court to scrutinize with special care the rights of religious as well as racial minorities. Before Earl Warren became chief, the Court struck down state laws that restricted the unusual and often annoying practices of Jehovah's Witnesses. Those decisions protected the sect's freedom of belief. The question of the establishment of a religion was less clear, for the Court had allowed the use of public money to pay the fares of parochial school pupils.

The question of establishment reached the Warren Court in *Engel v. Vitale* (1962). Acting under state law, the board of education of New Hyde Park, New York, had directed the recitation of a nondenominational prayer composed by the State Board of Regents. The prayer was to be said daily by each class in the presence of a teacher. Pupils who so desired were to be excused from the exercise. Nevertheless, the parents of ten pupils objected, contending that the official prayer violated the religious beliefs or practices of them and their children. New York, they maintained, was establishing a religion. In arguments before the Supreme Court, attorneys for several Jewish groups supported the parents, while attorneys for twenty-two states supported New York. Speaking for the Court, Justice Hugo Black ruled that "the constitutional prohibition against laws respecting an establishment of religion must at least mean that . . . it is no part of the business of government to compose official prayers for any group of Americans to recite as a part of a religious program carried on by government." Black's opinion reviewed part of the history of the establishment issue in England and in the American colonies, as well as in the drafting of the First Amendment. States could not require the recitation of official prayers, he concluded, "even if the prayer is denominationally neutral and pupils . . . may remain silent or be excused."

Only Associate Justice Potter Stewart dissented. "I cannot see," he wrote, "how an 'official religion' is established by letting those who want to say a prayer say it." He questioned the relevance of the history Black had reviewed. The history of American religious traditions, Stewart proposed, militated to a contrary conclusion. Both the Supreme Court and the houses of Congress opened their sessions with prayers. The president on assuming his office invoked the protection of

God, whose name was also used in the Pledge of Allegiance and on American coins. Only ten years earlier an opinion of the Supreme Court had said: "We are a religious people whose institutions presuppose a Supreme Being." Consequently, Stewart could not agree that New York had established a religion. As he put it, the state had recognized and followed "the deeply entrenched and highly cherished spiritual traditions of our Nation."

Whatever the strength of Stewart's reasoning, conservative religious leaders, particularly in the South, attacked Black's opinion on other grounds. The Supreme Court, they asserted, was promoting atheism, agnosticism, and secularism. The House of Representatives held hearings on a proposed amendment to the Constitution to permit prayer in public schools. A relay of clergymen testified in its support, as did Governor George Wallace of Alabama. Predictably, southern bigots like Wallace associated the Warren Court, a liberal court that was furthering desegregation, with atheistic communism. "They put the Negroes in the schools," said Representative George W. Andrews of Alabama. "Now they have driven God out." It came as no surprise to men like Wallace and Andrews that President Kennedy called on Americans to support the Court's decisions, "even though we may not agree with them." In the *Engel* case, the president added, Americans had "a very easy remedy. And that is, to pray themselves."

The storm over *Engel* broke out briefly again after the Supreme Court decided *School District of Abington Township v. Schempp* (1963) and a companion case. Again only Stewart dissented from the opinion, which built upon the precedent of *Engel*. No state, the Court ruled, could require the recitation of passages from the Bible or of the Lord's Prayer even if individual students could be excused. Most lawyers accepted the Court's position, as did most authorities on the Constitution and most religious leaders. But that was not the political issue. By innuendo at least, Goldwater in 1964 wooed the votes of fundamentalist Protestants, advocates of both prayer and Bible readings in public schools. Along with various evangelical sects, fundamentalists continued thereafter to urge their cause, to condemn the Supreme Court for irreligion, and to organize for political influence. Representing the view of only a minority of Americans, they nevertheless held their opinions devoutly. In ruffling fundamentalist feelings, the Court, though inadvertently, had given its political enemies inexhaustible ammunition.

So, too, though not immediately, did the Court's decision about birth control. That decision also provoked broad disagreement among the justices themselves about constitutional theory. A Connecticut statute forbade the dissemination of information about birth control and the prescription of contraceptive devices. Enacted in the nineteenth century to mollify Roman Catholic opinion in the state, the law, though constantly violated, was rarely enforced. Advocates of family planning and of free speech were nevertheless eager to challenge it and similar statutes in other states. Opportunity for a challenge came following the arrest and conviction of the executive director of the Planned Parenthood League of Connecticut and the league's medical director, who had prescribed a contraceptive pessary for a married woman.

Associate Justice William O. Douglas, noted for his latitudinarian reading of the Constitution, wrote the majority opinion in *Griswold v. Connecticut* (1965), which found the controversial law unconstitutional. Citing earlier cases, Douglas argued that a state could not "consistently with the spirit of the First Amendment, constrict the spectrum of available knowledge." The right of freedom of speech included "freedom of inquiry, freedom of thought, and freedom to teach." That conclusion would have been enough.

But Douglas went on. "In other words," he held, the First Amendment has "a penumbra where privacy is protected from government intrusion." Citing further cases, he suggested "that specific guarantees in the Bill of Rights have penumbras formed by emanations from those guarantees that help give them life and substance." Various of those guarantees created "zones of privacy." Here he referred to the First, Fourth, Fifth, and Ninth amendments before concluding that the "right of privacy" was a "legitimate one" that the Connecticut birth control statute violated. A man much divorced, Douglas ended with unintentional irony: "We deal with a right of privacy older than the Bill of Rights. . . . Marriage is a coming together for better or for worse . . . and intimate to the degree of being sacred. It is an association that promotes a way of life . . . a harmony of living."

By 1965 the time was ripe for recognition of a right of privacy, as many law professors were saying. The late Justice Louis D. Brandeis had long since argued that the Fourth Amendment protected privacy. Certainly, too, marriage was a private institution. Further, Douglas followed precedent in endowing the Bill of Rights with a penumbra. But the phrase "penumbras formed by emanations" confounded exegesis. It suggested at the least some considerable multiplication of rights guaranteed by the Constitution, a prospect about which many proponents of judicial restraint were uneasy. Associate Justice Arthur J. Goldberg, an appointee of President Kennedy, went even further than Douglas. In a concurring opinion in which Chief Justice Earl Warren and Associate Justice William Brennan joined, Goldberg called explicitly "for the creation of a whole body of extra-constitutional rights." Those rights, he contended, would conform with the spirit of the Ninth Amendment and the due process clause of the Fourteenth. With those rights affirmed, Goldberg continued, the Court would be able to strike down all legislation violating "fundamental principles of liberty and justice" rooted in the "tradition and conscience of our people." That was the kind of mandate that exactly suited the moralism of Earl Warren.

Douglas and Goldberg went beyond the limits of interpretation acceptable to four of their colleagues. Justices John M. Harlan and Byron R. White concurred in the conclusion that the Connecticut birth control statute was unconstitutional, but each did so in his own way, simply by finding it in conflict with the due process clause of the Fourteenth Amendment. Justice Hugo Black and Justice Potter Stewart dissented. Stewart observed that Douglas had cited six amendments to the Constitution without saying "which of these Amendments . . . is infringed" by the Connecticut law. Though "an uncommonly silly law," the statute was not on that account unconstitutional. For his part, Goldberg, as Stewart saw it, had turned "somersaults with history." It was not the function of the Supreme Court, Stewart wrote, "to decide cases on the basis of community standards." He reminded his brethren of an earlier decision holding "that courts do not substitute their social and economic beliefs for the judgment of legislative bodies, who we elected to pass laws."

While agreeing with Stewart, Hugo Black delivered an attack of his own on the reasoning of Douglas and Goldberg. The Constitution, he noted, mentioned no "right of privacy." Privacy was a "broad, abstract and ambiguous concept" that could "easily be interpreted as a constitutional ban" against practices not specified in either the First or Fourth Amendment. "I get nowhere in this case," Black wrote, "by talk about a constitutional 'right of privacy,' as an emanation from one or more constitutional provisions. I like my privacy as well as the next one, but I am nevertheless compelled to admit that government has a right to invade it unless prohibited by some specific constitutional provision." Even Harlan and White, Black continued, reached too far. As he saw it, like Goldberg, they claimed "for this Court and the federal judiciary power to invalidate any legislative act which the judges find irrational, unreasonable or offensive." They supposed, Black argued, a "natural justice" or a "natural law . . . philosophy." That concept allowed judges to decide what was or was not constitutional "on the basis of their own appraisal of what laws are wise"—a question properly for legislative bodies. "Subjecting federal and state laws," Black held, "to such an unrestrained and unrestrainable judicial control . . . would . . . jeopardize the separation of governmental powers that the framers set up and at the same time threaten to take away much of the power of States to govern themselves which the Constitution plainly intended them to have."

Both *Griswold*'s result and the content of the opinions delivered about it raised political as well as constitutional issues. Though most Americans practiced birth control and believed in family planning, there were others, some Catholics, some evangelicals, who considered sexual intercourse sinful for any purpose other than procreation. To them, *Griswold* seemed as obnoxious as did *Engel*. It was to seem more so a decade later, after the Court, expanding the doctrine of privacy, banned state laws forbidding abortion. The opinions of Douglas and Goldberg, pointing in that direction, shared a view of the Court's authority that carried beyond the range of *Engel* or *Brown*. It was a view that permeated other decisions of 1964 and 1965 about the rights of individuals accused of crimes and about the representative nature of state senates. For Americans vexed by those and related decisions, *Griswold* portended judicial intercession into all aspects of daily life. They might not have understood the jurisprudence of the justices, but voters offended by *Brown, Griffin, Engel,* or *Griswold* knew what kind of society they liked, and believed that the Court was denying it to them, and they were eager to retaliate through political action.

Many conservative commentators on constitutional law were also disturbed. The Douglas and Goldberg opinions in *Griswold* met severe criticism from legal scholars like Alexander Bickel, who believed that principled decisions required close legal reasoning comprehending a knowledge of the Constitution, judicial precedent, and history relevant to both. Those critics believed that *Griswold* asserted a judicial authority that exceeded the implications of Stone's assignments for "exacting judicial scrutiny." Indeed, the question of the Court's appropriate authority was becoming as controversial, and concurrently as politicized, as the results of the Court's decisions.

4. "One Person, One Vote"

THE activism and assertiveness of the Warren Court accompanied and encompassed its commitment to majoritarian democracy. In *Gomillion v. Lightfoot* (1960), the Court ruled on an Alabama statute of 1957 that had drawn the boundary lines of the city of Tuskegee so as to alter its shape from a square to an "uncouth twenty-eight-sided figure." That shape excluded from the franchise almost all of the city's two hundred black voters. In the spirit of Stone's footnote, the justices unanimously struck down the statute. Legislative acts, they held, "generally lawful may become unlawful when done to accomplish an unlawful end." The gerrymander in Alabama had deprived the affected black voters of participation in the political process. Without denying that result, the state of Alabama had questioned the Court's jurisdiction, but the Court had acted under the Fifteenth Amendment. Associate Justice Charles E. Whittaker in a concurring opinion held that the issue also fell within the meaning of the equal protection clause of the Fourteenth Amendment.

Whittaker's view had a bearing on the apportionment of electoral districts, historically a prerogative of the states. In most states rural areas were overrepresented. For a century and more, rural population had been falling and urban population rising, but characteristically the geographic definitions of electoral districts placed many more voters in the average urban district than in the average rural. Consequently, rural areas, especially but not exclusively in the South, dominated state legislatures, whose members, eager to retain the offices they held, persistently and successfully resisted efforts at redistricting. Yet as late as 1946 the Supreme Court, though not without dissent, had ruled that reapportionment was a political question outside the range of adjudication.

A reexamination of that question lay at the center of the Court's decision in *Baker v. Carr* (1962). The state of Tennessee, required by its constitution to reapportion legislative districts every ten years, had not done so since 1901. As decennial census figures indicated, only redistricting could correct the increasing imbalance of population among the state's counties. A suit to force that action had the support of the United States Department of Justice. Speaking for the Court, Justice William J. Brennan held that the constitutionality of the Tennessee districting related to judicial standards familiar under the equal protection clause of the Fourteenth Amendment. On that basis he remanded—that is, returned the case for decision—to the federal district court in Tennessee. Brennan's opinion, in other words, made reapportionment an appropriate matter for adjudication. In a concurring opinion Justice Tom Clark said he "would not consider intervention by this Court into so delicate a field if there were any other relief available to the people of Tennessee." Justice Stewart, in a separate concurrence, held that the Supreme Court was deciding only that the district court had jurisdiction over the "subject matter" and that the "appellants have standing"—that is, the right to have their case heard.

Even those narrow grounds provoked the dissenting opinion of Justice Felix Frankfurter, whom Justice Harlan joined. In Frankfurter's view, the Court was casting aside an impressive body of precedent. "Disregard of inherent limits in the effective exercise of the Court's 'judicial power,' " Frankfurter warned, ". . . presages the futility of judicial intervention in the essentially political conflict of forces by which the relation between population and representation has time out of mind been and now is determined." The Court's authority, he argued, ultimately rested on "sustained public confidence in its moral sanction." That confidence depended upon the "Court's complete detachment . . . from political entanglements." It was not for the judiciary but for the electorate to remedy malapportionment: "In a democratic society like ours, relief must come through an aroused popular conscience that sears the conscience of the people's representatives." The issue, he concluded, was beyond the reach of the federal judiciary.

Among legal scholars who shared Frankfurter's conviction, the decision in *Baker v. Carr* raised a lasting storm. Yet the Supreme Court had disposed of issues no less political in *Brown* I, in which Frankfurter had been influential in forging unanimity, and in other cases bearing on segregation. By 1962, of course, those cases were under political attack, as *Engel* was about to be. Further, *Brown* II had provided no clear guidelines to the district courts, a failing that *Baker* repeated, as Frankfurter indirectly observed. The judiciary was clearly enmeshed in conflicts of political forces. Perhaps especially on that account, Frankfurter was so intense in opposing another political foray.

But Frankfurter, whose failing health soon forced him to resign, had not influenced other justices on the matter of apportionment. The decision in *Baker* opened the way for citizens in thirty-nine states to seek judicial remedy for various instances of malapportionment. Their cases quickly reached the Supreme Court on appeal. In *Gray v. Sanders* (1963) the Court ruled against Georgia's notoriously imbalanced county unit system of voting as it affected primaries for the nomination of both United States senators and statewide officers. In the majority opinion Douglas offended his critics by his typically loose use of history. "The conception of political equality," he wrote, "from the Declaration of Independence, to Lincoln's Gettysburg Address, to the Fifteenth, Seventeenth, and Nineteenth Amendments can mean only one thing, one person, one vote." An informed schoolboy would have known better, but the simplism in Douglas's reading of the past did not alter the facts of the case. The Georgia system had a rural bias worse even than Tennessee's.

The ruling in *Gray* built toward the Court's decision in *Reynolds v. Sims* (1964), in which Chief Justice Warren, speaking for the majority, made "one person, one vote" the general rule for apportioning all state representative bodies, including upper houses in state legislatures. In a companion case Warren made it clear that the Court would reject plans that did not conform to that rule. In his opinion in *Reynolds* the chief justice observed that "the right to vote freely for the candidate of one's choice is the essence of a democratic society . . . the bedrock of our political system." Overweighting the votes of those residing in rural districts diluted that right and therefore violated the due process clause of the Fourteenth Amendment.

That reasoning did not convince Justice Harlan, who stood alone in dissenting. The Fourteenth Amendment, as he understood its history and meaning, did not apply at all to the right to vote. The majority decision gave federal district courts "blanket authority . . . to supervise apportionment of State legislatures." It was difficult, Harlan wrote, "to imagine a more intolerable and inappropriate interference by the judiciary with the independent legislatures of the States." But so it had been with school districts since *Brown* II. Harlan, of course, realized as much. As he put it, he opposed the "current mistaken view of the Constitution. . . . This view, in a nutshell, is that every social ill in this country can find its cure in some constitutional 'principle,' and that this Court should 'take the lead' in promoting reform when other branches of government fail to act." The Constitution, he continued, was "not a panacea for every blot upon the public welfare." The Court did not "serve its high purpose when it exceeds its authority, even to satisfy justified impatience with the slow workings of the political process."

Harlan's admonition, like Frankfurter's earlier caution, deserved reflection. The Constitution, as both justices noted, provided a form of representation that gave weight to geography, among other considerations. It explicitly guaranteed a "republican," not a "democratic," form of government. Indeed, some members of Congress proposed a constitutional amendment to permit the election of upper houses of state legislatures on a basis other than population. After all, the United States Senate represented such a case.

But in asserting its authority over apportionment, the Court imposed a more democratic order. Taken together, its decisions forced the states toward a majoritarian system of government. As several constitutional authorities later observed, those decisions proved to be a major success story for the Warren Court. Harlan and Frankfurter believed the Court incurred grave political risks in assuming the lead in reform. But to Warren and his supporters, the results of the rulings made those risks necessary. That was true, as they saw it, for

desegregation, for reapportionment, for privacy, and for the
rights of the accused, which the Court's decisions were vigorously expanding.

5. *From* Mallory *to* Miranda

IN 1957 the Supreme Court reviewed the conviction of Andrew
Mallory, a mentally retarded black man who had raped a
white woman in Washington, D.C. He had confessed to that
crime after the police held him without arraignment for some
seven and a half hours, during which they used intimidating
techniques. In *Mallory v. United States* (1957), the Court,
speaking through Justice Frankfurter, invalidated the conviction because the police had violated the federal criminal code,
which called for "arraignment without delay." The District
police and their champions in Congress, many of them from
the South, at once objected to the decision for complicating
law enforcement.

That angry response was to recur with each succeeding
decision in which the Court enlarged its definition of the
rights of the accused under the Fourth through the Eighth
amendments, all of which applied to aspects of criminal or
civil prosecutions. The Kennedy administration was urging
improvement and standardization of criminal justice
throughout the country, an objective also of the Johnson Justice Department. Doubtless the Court would have moved as
it did anyway, but as the judiciary and the executive moved
together, both became targets of self-proclaimed defenders of
law and order, police forces not the least. Those critics had a
receptive audience among Americans, of whom many found
urban life increasingly vulnerable to crime in the streets, to
muggings, rapes, and murders that no city could wholly prevent. Prevention was becoming especially difficult in a time

of growing drug use, teenage violence, and racial tensions. The resulting public awareness of crime exposed the Supreme Court to charges of coddling criminals; in fact, it was protecting the rights of all Americans from violation by ignorant or overzealous police. In so doing, the Court was ruling against the kind of dangerous police procedures that characterized totalitarian governments, fascist and Communist alike.

So it was in *Mapp v. Ohio* (1961), a case involving a search and arrest without a warrant. Police in Cleveland, Ohio, forcibly entered the home of Dollree Mapp over her protest. They were looking for policy paraphernalia—evidence of illegal gambling—but found none. Instead, they came upon some obscene material, and for possessing it, Mapp was arrested and convicted. In a six to three decision, the Supreme Court threw out the conviction because it violated the Fourth Amendment. That amendment, Justice Clark ruled for the majority, meant that "conviction by means of unlawful seizure and enforced confessions . . . should find no sanction in the jurisdiction of the courts." Half the states had already excluded from trials evidence illegally seized. Now local police forces in all states would have to obtain warrants from judges before undertaking searches. "Nothing can destroy a government more quickly," Clark wrote, "than its failure to observe its own laws, or worse, its disregard for the charter of its own existence."

The Sixth Amendment to that charter stipulated that in all criminal prosecutions "the accused shall . . . have the Assistance of Counsel for his defence." In a dissent in 1942 Justice Black had invoked that guarantee in arguing that no one charged with a crime should be deprived of counsel because of poverty. The court reconsidered that issue in *Gideon v. Wainwright* (1965), a case that received wide publicity. Clarence E. Gideon, an indigent, stood convicted of breaking and entering a poolroom in Florida and of stealing some wine, cigarettes, and petty cash. He had asked for a lawyer, but the trial judge had denied him one. After conviction, Gideon composed his own petition to the Supreme Court for review, as many other prisoners had. In accepting Gideon's eloquent petition, the Court assigned to him an experienced and accomplished attorney, Abe Fortas, who undertook the task without a fee—as was customary under the circumstances.

In his plea Fortas urged the justices to keep in mind "what happens to . . . poor, miserable, indigent people when they are arrested and . . . brought into the jail and . . . questioned and . . . brought in . . . strange and awesome circumstances before a magistrate" and then forced to defend themselves. Fortas argued in a vein designed to please Justices Black and Harlan, both opposed to intervention by federal courts in state criminal proceedings. In Gideon's case, Fortas contended, the Supreme Court should intervene, for the Sixth Amendment was obviously involved. In a unanimous decision the Court agreed. Justice Black wrote the opinion. Guarantee of counsel, he ruled, was a fundamental right, essential to a fair trial, spelled out in the Bill of Rights, and made "obligatory upon the States by the Fourteenth Amendment." Gideon's conviction was therefore reversed.

In arguing against that reversal, the attorney for the state of Florida had warned that it would open the prison gates to criminals who had been tried without counsel. In states that had not provided counsel, the decision had that effect. During the next three years, in Florida alone, more than six thousand of the state's eight thousand inmates filed for reconsideration of their cases. Some twenty-five hundred received new trials, and some thirteen hundred were released. But thirty-seven states had made provision for counsel for the indigent before *Gideon*. The decision, as one constitutional historian said, conformed to the American sense of fair play. In 1964 Congress passed the Criminal Justice Act, which provided defense attorneys for poor defendants in federal jurisdictions and at government expense.

The law and order issued revived, however, over the Court's decision in *Escobedo v. Illinois* (1964). Danny Escobedo, a young Chicago laborer of Mexican descent, had been arrested for shooting and killing his brother-in-law. Under interrogation at the police station, he asked to see his lawyer, who was in the building. Declining that request, the police proceeded to harass Escobedo until they extracted a confession. After Escobedo's conviction, his lawyer appealed his case, ultimately to the Supreme Court. By a margin of only five to four, the Court invalidated the conviction. Joined by Chief Justice Warren and Justices Black, Brennan, and Douglas, Justice Goldberg wrote the opinion. The police, he held, had employed "a process of interrogation that lends itself to eliciting incriminating statements." In violation of the Sixth Amendment they had denied Escobedo "an opportunity to consult with his lawyer" and had not "effectively warned him of his absolute . . . right to remain silent." Then Goldberg went on: "A system of law enforcement which comes to depend on the confession, will in the long run be less reliable than a system which depends on extrinsic evidence . . . secured through skillful investigation. If the exercise of constitutional rights will thwart the effectiveness of a system of law enforcement, then there is something wrong with the system."

Those sentences, indeed the opinion in general, met with three acid dissents. Justice Harlan believed the decision "unjustifiably fetters perfectly legitimate methods of law enforcement." Justice Stewart argued that the majority had moved the beginning of judicial proceedings from the trial to the arrest stage. In so doing, it had converted "a routine police investigation of an unsolved murder into a distorted analogue of a judicial trial." It had thereby frustrated "the

vital interests of society in preserving . . . functions of honest
. . . police investigations." Justice White, joined by Justice
Clark, claimed that the majority was inventing a new constitutional right. Soon, he predicted, the Court would exclude
all confessions from evidence.

Police officers applauded those dissents. They complained
that the Court had removed their most effective means of
obtaining confessions. The Court, so one of them said, was
"hampering the administration of criminal justice, while
'vicious beasts' were loose in the streets." That belief, widely
held, intensified adverse public reactions to decisions about
racial and religious issues. It helped foster proposals to limit
the Court's jurisdiction or at least the effect of its decisions.
The American Bar Association, the National Association of
Attorneys General, and the International Association of Chiefs
of Police published statements criticizing the Court's expansion of its authority. That view was common among members of the bar and of the bench, including Judge Learned
Hand of the United States Court of Appeals for the Second
Circuit, a jurist of immense reputation.

Escobedo raised the storm against the Court to gale force.
Congress increased the salaries of all federal judges except for
those on the Supreme Court. At the 1964 Republican National
Convention former President Eisenhower, still a national hero,
urged the delegates "not to be guilty of maudlin sympathy
for the criminal who, roaming the street with switchblade
knife and illegal firearms seeking a prey . . . counts upon the
compassion of our society and the . . . weakness of too many
courts to forgive his offense." Barry Goldwater used that theme
in his campaign. The Court, he contended, was fostering a
breakdown of law and order. "No wonder," Goldwater said,
"that our law enforcement officers have been demoralized and
rendered ineffective in their jobs." Striking a note the

Republicans continued to play, he expressed his worry about "who is the President for the next four . . . years thinking of . . . the make-up of the Supreme Court."

Undeterred, the Court continued along the line of decisions begun with *Mallory* and *Mapp*. Justice Stewart, so often a dissenter, wrote the majority opinion in *Stanford v. Texas* (1965), which denied to the states the use of a general search warrant. Also in 1965, the Court, invoking the Sixth Amendment, reaffirmed the right of a witness to confront and cross-examine his accusers. Those rulings rested on strong historical and constitutional precedents that the states were violating. In the absence of corrective legislation, the burden of upholding the Constitution lay on the Court. On that account the American Law Institute devised a Model Code of Pre-Arraignment Procedures. It was less restrictive on the police than Justice White had predicted the Court would become, and it won the endorsement of an impressive number of legal scholars and judges, several of whom had spoken out against any expansion of the *Escobedo* ruling.

That decision had produced confusions about criminal procedure that needed clarification. With both the states and the Congress delaying in that task, Chief Justice Warren assumed it in the opinion he wrote for the majority in *Miranda v. Arizona* (1966). Ernesto Miranda, a poor Mexican laborer with a record of burglary and sexual offenses, was arrested and convicted of rape. The conviction depended upon evidence that included a confession obtained after a police interrogation in an isolated room and in the absence of an attorney. Miranda had no apparent knowledge of his constitutional rights. In his and four companion cases, the Supreme Court, again by a majority of only five to four, reversed the decision of the states' trial courts. The majority ruled that the prosecution could not use any statement "stemming from custodial interrogation of the defendant unless it demonstrates the use of procedural safeguards effective to secure the privilege against self-incrimination."

Warren's lengthy opinion then spelled out those safeguards. Prior to any questioning, Warren wrote in a sentence that was to become famous, an accused "person must be warned that he has a right to remain silent, that any statement he does make may be used in evidence against him, and that he has a right to the presence of an attorney, either retained or appointed." A defendant might "voluntarily, knowingly, and intelligently" waive these rights, but at any stage in the process he could reassert them. Warren cited historical precedents for the Court's ruling, one of them from a thirteenth-century commentary on the Old Testament Book of Judges, ordinarily not a source for American jurisprudence. "There is no doubt," he asserted, "that the Fifth Amendment privilege is available . . . to protect persons in all settings . . . from being compelled to incriminate themselves."

The opinion was typical of the chief justice. To specify police procedure as he did, he had extended the reach of the Court beyond precedent. His argument for doing so rested more on the strength of his convictions than on judicial craftsmanship. His purpose was clear. As he said in an oral aside, when the police neglected fairness, they became "a menace to society." Those who then most often suffered were the uneducated, the poor, the black and Hispanic who did not know their rights or how to find out about them. They needed protection from the police, which Warren felt morally as well as legally obliged to provide. In that sense, *Miranda,* like *Escobedo* and *Gideon,* was distinctly egalitarian.

The chief's opinion occasioned three strong dissents, in two of which Justice Stewart joined. Unpersuaded by Warren's excursion into history, Justice White called the majority ruling "a departure from a long line of precedents." He went on; "The obvious under-pinning of the Court's decision is a deep-seated distrust of all confessions." The decision was making "new law" and "new public policy" that would "impede the conviction of murderers and rapists." Justice Clark, upset by Warren's criticism of the police, condemned the chief's "strict constitutional specific" as a hindrance to law enforcement. Justice Harlan objected that the decision hastily imposed new rules at a time when serious considerations of "long-range and lasting reforms" were under way by the American Bar Association, the American Law Institute, and the President's Commission on Law Enforcement. The *Miranda* rules, Harlan argued, would "impair, if they will not eventually serve wholly to frustrate, an instrument of law enforcement that has long and quite reasonably been thought worth the price paid for it. . . . The Court is taking a real risk with society's welfare in imposing its new regime on the country."

Amplified by those dissents, the uproar that followed the *Miranda* decision refreshed the hostility to the Warren Court. Democratic Senator John L. McClellan of Arkansas, a fervid enemy of the Court since *Brown* I, attacked *Miranda*. "This 5–4 decision," he said, "is of such adverse significance to law enforcement that it . . . demands . . . legislation . . . to alleviate the damage it will do to society." Senator Samuel J. Ervin of North Carolina, also a conservative Democrat but a respectable legal scholar, called for a constitutional amendment to allow any confession as evidence so long as it was voluntary. "Enough has been done," he said, "for those who murder and rape and riot! It is time to do something for those who do not wish to be murdered or raped or robbed."

Protests against *Miranda* mounted in spite of evidence that the decision was far less crippling than its detractors claimed. In a separate case the Supreme Court held that *Miranda* did not apply retroactively. In a second trial Ernesto Miranda was again convicted, now without recourse to a confession. United

States Attorney General Ramsey Clark, the son of Justice Clark, from the first defended the decision so disturbing to his father. Several studies concluded that *Miranda* did not significantly damage law enforcement even though the rate of confessions dropped. And for its part, the Supreme Court became somewhat less restrictive about police procedures. Over Warren's dissent, it allowed the use of undercover agents to obtain narcotics convictions. It also permitted informers to provide evidence from self-incriminating statements that the accused had made to them. And it allowed bugging where police had prior judicial approval. Police, the Court held, could enter a home without a warrant "in hot pursuit" of a suspect. Those rulings notwithstanding, by 1968, an election year, the controversial decisions from *Mallory* through *Miranda* had entangled the Court in a political thicket from which it could not escape.

6. Law and Order

EARLY in Earl Warren's term as chief justice, soon after the most vicious congressional witch-hunts for alleged subversives, the Supreme Court handed down several decisions that limited the conditions under which the state and federal governments could discharge or penalize "leftists." Those decisions accorded with the continuing efforts of the Warren Court to protect the freedoms of belief and of expression guaranteed by the First Amendment. But those decisions upset President Eisenhower. They protected "Commies," he said. The appointment of Warren, Eisenhower believed, was "the biggest damn fool mistake I made." The innocence of Ike's understanding of the Constitution was not uncommon. By 1968 many Americans were eager to get rid of the chief justice.

Under any circumstances the Court's decisions about police procedures would have contributed to that mood. As it was, by 1968 the issue of law enforcement had taken on meaning far beyond the rights of accused persons. Several developments had brought unusual discord and unusual violence to American society. From 1964 onward, opposition to the Vietnam War and social and racial unrest in the cities had continually disrupted the surface serenity normal in American life. The unrest and the violence, moreover, commonly involved angry confrontations about values and behavior between the youth of the country and their parents' generation. The Supreme Court was responsible for none of those developments, nor did the Court speak directly to the central questions they raised. What little of relevance the Court did say was on the whole ambiguous. Yet that little said enough to permit the Court's opponents, as they had for more than a decade, to link the issue of law and order to the disruptions caused by other questions agitating and dividing the American people, particularly race, poverty, and war.

The Court took care to avoid having to rule on the legality of the war in Vietnam, a war Congress never declared. Citing the First Amendment, it did rule that a state legislature had to seat a properly elected representative despite his opposition to the war and the draft. But it also held that the public burning of draft cards was not an act of "symbolic speech." It required protesters to abide by regular judicial processes in seeking permits to hold parades. Nevertheless, conservative critics of *Escobedo* and *Miranda* looked upon demonstrations against the war in Vietnam as just another kind of violation of law and order. And they held the Warren Court responsible.

So, too, with the race riots that swept American cities in the late 1960s. The Court never condoned them. But it had provided crucial support for the civil rights movement.

Opponents of that movement, especially white racists north and south, saw the Court as a friend to blacks and an enemy of the police. Americans of that temperament associated disorder in general with the Court's decisions and associated it, too, with the youth movements of the 1960s. Some leaders of those protest movements boasted of their radical and disruptive goals. Those goals, as conservatives interpreted them, were inseparable from the drug culture and promiscuous sex of outré young rebels. Here, too, complicity visited the Warren Court because of its newly permissive decisions about the definition of obscene literature and film and about restrictions on their circulation. Courtbashers liked to think of obscenity as a characteristic primarily of lewd and sinful radicals.

Exaggerated and distorted in the climate of 1968, the Court's reputation for coddling criminals made it particularly vulnerable. Members of Congress returning to Washington that January reported that among their constituents "anger over riots and crimes overshadowed all other domestic issues." That punitive mood contrasted directly with the report of the President's Commission on Law Enforcement. The commission's majority had pointed out that the criminal justice system was not "designed to eliminate the conditions in which crime breeds." Its report concluded: "Warring on poverty . . . is warring on crime. A civil rights law is a law against crime. . . . A community's most enduring protection against crime is to right the wrongs . . . that tempt men to harm their neighbors." That had been a premise of the Great Society, and that was Earl Warren's belief. But many, probably most Americans disagreed. By 1968 they had come to reject explanations of the relationship between poverty and crime. They dismissed the commission's report as a permissive liberal litany. Their responsive representatives on the Hill passed the Omnibus Crime Control Act. Title II of the statute attempted to modify the *Miranda* decision by making confessions admissible in evidence if they were voluntary. It also allowed police to hold a suspect six hours before arraignment. President Johnson reluctantly signed the measure. He would otherwise have risked the political consequences of a veto.

It was, as it turned out, too late for Johnson or for the Court to avoid further political retaliation. In June 1968 Earl Warren, feeling his age, resigned as chief justice, effective at the pleasure of the president. Johnson nominated his close adviser Associate Justice Abe Fortas to succeed as chief, and for the place Fortas would vacate as associate justice, he named an old friend from Texas, Judge Homer Thornberry. Fortas, a lifelong defender of civil liberties and an advocate of judicial activism, had pleaded the *Gideon* case and joined the majority in *Miranda*. His nomination at once ran into a roadblock constructed by the Republicans with some help from antiadministration Democrats. "With the Court in adjournment," one Republican senator said, "and the American people about to pick a new administration which may considerably re-orient the philosophy of our national government, it would be a major mistake to presume to fill such an important role."

That was emphatically the opinion of Senator Strom Thurmond, the political leader of the Dixiecrat South. Still unreconciled to *Brown* I, Thurmond was outraged by the potential effects of the *Green* decision. The Republicans had to have his support if they were to carry the white southern votes that Governor Wallace was courting in his third-party campaign against desegregation and for law and order. Richard Nixon secured Thurmond's support by promising to appoint federal judges satisfactory to the senator. Such judges would not be judicial activists. Further, Nixon and the GOP made the issue of law and order, with its racial overtones, a centerpiece of their campaign. Meanwhile, the Senate held up the nominations of Fortas and Thornberry. The era of the Warren Court had just about reached its end.

7. Coda

As the Supreme Court had been through most of its history, the Warren Court was of its time. Both the spirit and the results of its decisions resonated in harmony with the New Frontier and the Great Society. It was an activist court in a period of activist government. It was activist in order to effect egalitarian and democratic ends, as that government endeavored to effect similar ends. Even more than that government, the Warren Court was committed to the protection of the rights of individuals, especially to freedom of belief and expression. Like all law, the law handed down by the Warren Court was policy, policy that complemented the programs of the Great Society. And the majority opinions of the Warren Court framed a political theory consonant with those democratic goals.

As the Great Society was flawed, so was the Warren Court. Qualities of haste in drafting legislation and of sloppiness in administration damaged the functioning of the Great Society. Similar qualities characterized the majority opinions of the Warren Court. Those opinions lacked the judicial craftsmanship to protect them from future modification, as the dissents from them suggested. That vulnerability played into the hands of conservatives determined to see the decisions overturned. And that political threat endangered the democratic results of the Warren Court's rulings.

A leading advocate of judicial restraint, Alexander Bickel, later complained about the "powerful strain of populism in the rhetoric by which the Court supported its one-man, one-vote doctrine." That rhetoric and doctrine emerged ironically from a court which in most of its other major decisions exercised its large authority for purposes not in the least majoritarian. "The whole *point* of an independent judiciary," as

Laurence Tribe later put it, in the liberal spirit of Earl Warren, "is to be 'antidemocratic,' to preserve from transient
majorities those human rights and other principles to which
our legal and political system is committed." But in using
its power that way, in giving vitality to the preferred freedoms, the Warren Court invited retribution. Majoritarian
doctrine then became a weapon of the Court's political enemies.

INDEX

DATE DUE

JAN 11 1995			
JUN 14 1996			
MAR 28 1995			
NOV 1996			
MAR 21 1997			
DEC 04 1997			
FEB 28 1998			
MAY 1998			
JAN 09 2002			
NOV 2007			
			Printed in USA